BEING THE GROWNUP

BEING THE GROWNUP

Love, Limits,
and the
Natural Authority of Parenthood

ADELIA MOORE

HOLLOW HILL BOOKS

ISBN: 978-0-9848560-6-0 (Paperback)
ISBN: 978-0-9848560-7-7 (Hardcover)

Cover design by Oliver Munday
Book design by Valerie Sauers

Printed by IngramSpark in the United States of America.

First printing edition 2019.

Hollow Hill Books
530 Canaan Road
Canaan, N.Y. 12029

www.Adeliamoore.com

For Tommy
— for our sons, Finn, Carrick, Amias, and Rowan,
and for their families, present and future —
with all my love

The natural authority of adults—and the needs of children—
are the great reservoir of the organic structuring that comes
into being when arbitrary rules of order are dispensed with.

The child is always finding himself, moving toward himself, as
it were, in the near distance. The adult is his ally, his model—
and his obstacle (for there are natural conflicts, too, and they
must be given their due).

— George Dennison, *The Lives of Children*

Babies may be swaddled or wear diapers. They may be draped
with amulets, dusted with talcum, basted with palm oil, or
ceremoniously finger-painted with protective symbols. But
regardless of language or custom, the message conveyed by
such ministrations is equivalent: You are cared for and will
continue to be. Love (and that is a perfectly good word for what
we are talking about here) is a message babies are all too eager
to receive, and small wonder...

— Sarah Hrdy, *Mothers and Others*

Contents

Foreword

In *Being the Grownup: Love, Limits, and the Natural Authority of Parenthood,* Adelia Moore has composed a forceful, engaging account of the authority implicit in parenthood. Instead of addressing the angst and challenges Western parents find in being the "boss" in the family, Moore starts with a simple premise: Authority comes with the territory of parenthood. In other words, it just is. Situating this premise within both developmental psychology and anthropology, Moore's book revolves around the relationship underpinning parental authority and the way it emerges, interaction by interaction, between parent and child. She illustrates the push-pull between parents being in charge and parents being facilitators of a child's autonomy and emotional development.

Being the Grownup is both a unique and groundbreaking book written from the perspective of an author who has gotten her finger on the pulse of parental authority as a clinical psychologist, as a parent and grandparent, and as a member of the community in which she lives. From these multiple perspectives, Moore draws on the fields of child development, relational psychology, and neuroscience, in companionship with historical, sociological, anthropological, and literary sources. The book follows the trope of books written at the turn of the 20th to 21st century exploring Western parents' dilemmas and anxieties about authority, such as *Spoiling Childhood: How Well-Meaning Parents Are Giving Children Too Much—But Not What They Need (1997), The Price of Privilege: How Parental Pressure and Material Advantage Are Creating a Generation of Disconnected and Unhappy Kids (2009),* and more recently, *The Game Theorist's Guide to Parenting: How the Science of Strategic Thinking Can Help You Deal with the Toughest Negotiators You Know—Your Kids (2016).* At the same time, *Being the Grownup* is a welcome contrast to more recent 21st century books about parenthood with a singular focus on the responsibilities of parents to bring their children to the highest realms of success, like *Battle*

Hymn of the Tiger Mother (2011), *How to Raise Successful Children: Unleashing Their Hidden Potentials* (2018), and *Positive Pushing: How to Raise a Successful and Happy Child (2002)*. As we move toward the third decade of the 21st century, we continue to witness authority on one side and success on the other, as the prevailing themes in contemporary books for and about parents.

Over a quarter of a century ago, I set out to write *Spoiling Childhood*. My goal was to capture what I had experienced as a clinician working with parents: Mothers and fathers were delivering conflicting messages to their children. On the one hand, they had high expectations for their children's autonomy; on the other, they hovered and doted and hesitated to take on the mantle of authority, intent instead on being friends with their children. As I wrote then: "To be an authority figure to our children is to instill in them a respect for our wisdom and trust in our ability to shepherd them through childhood with their best interests in mind. When fused with love, it allows the child to feel both cared for and protected, while at the same time setting up a 'benign opposition' in which a child can test his or her muster by challenging authority, but only with certain limits...." Moore's book functions as the perfect sequel, carrying the torch of my expressed concern about parents' struggles to align authority with affection as they shepherd their sons and daughters through childhood. The beauty of *Being the Grownup* is that it challenges the question, "To be or not to be an authority figure?" Moore asserts that there is no way out: just by the act of becoming a parent, you *are* an authority, like it or not. What she offers the reader is an understanding of why this is, how it unfolds, and what you can do to operate as an authority figure in the healthiest way—for your child, for yourself, for the relationship, and indeed, for the child's success.

Being the Grownup will be a treasured resource for parents and professionals alike—and grandparents too, indeed for anyone who is responsible for children, whatever their gender or their biological or non-biological ties to the child. As Moore writes: "Being a parent is not something you do to a child but something you are with a child. Parental authority is not simply a matter of discipline with time-outs and consequences, or even skilled negotiation and conflict resolution. Parent and child are two human beings whose bodies and voices, experiences, perspectives and emotions shape their interactions with each other." Rather than telling parents what to do, Moore offers a lens to parents through which they can see more clearly the many influences that shape their relationships with their children, and at the same time embrace their authority free of fear of negative or untoward consequences. She shows, most convincingly, that the ideal of the authoritative parenting style is within reach of every parent: Love and limits go hand in hand.

As a developmental and clinical psychologist, I found Moore's rich narratives about her clinical work with parents tremendously thought-provoking and applicable to my own therapeutic work with parents. Before *Being the Grownup* has even come to print, I find myself using her ideas and techniques while I sit with parents in the consultation room. As a fellow writer in this field, I have been both impressed and inspired by the breadth of her scholarship. Few authors are able to distill and integrate ideas generated by investigation of the scientific literature about families to birth a remarkably clear, forthright and accessible text for all of us to learn from, be we parents, professionals, or just interested parties. We learn not only about the universality of parenting across the span of their children's growing years, but also the variations on the theme created by different cultures and different ethnic groups. For everyone about to enter the pages of *Being the Grownup*, you now have in your hands a remarkable GPS for navigating the thicket of decisions, large and small, that shape our children's lives from infancy to adulthood.

— Diane Ehrensaft, PhD
Associate Professor of Pediatrics, UCSF
Author of *Spoiling Childhood* and
The Gender Creative Child
March 2019

Before We Begin

I stood in the sun at an outdoor festival watching two of my grandchildren play in a group of other kids with giant plastic blocks. As I watched, a woman in her 60s made the slightest flick of her finger toward the group, not even pausing in her conversation with a friend. A lively-looking boy of 5 or 6 who had just grabbed a block from another child made a slight scowl and gave the block back. "Where did you learn to do that?" I asked. "I was a kindergarten teacher for 35 years," she answered. Being a teacher must have given her practice—being in charge of 22 5-year-olds gives you little choice—but the child wasn't her student, and they were not in a classroom.

This young boy, presumably her grandson, responded readily to her gesture because he knew exactly what the gesture meant. She was in charge, and she disapproved of what he had done. She didn't have to say a word: They already had a history and an understanding. They came to the town fair to have fun, but if he didn't behave, perhaps they would leave early, or he wouldn't get a promised cotton candy. She might tell his mother or father or give him a time out or other consequence when they got home. How did she know that the flick of her finger would be enough? What exactly did it tell him? Why did he respond so quickly?

When I saw this exchange, I had already begun to write this book, and I found myself coming back repeatedly to a fundamental problem. Being a parent means setting limits and making demands, on what can seem like a constant basis. But it may also mean seeing them met with a stamp of the foot, a scowl, an outburst, or an interaction that escalates into shouting or a slammed door. To the mothers and fathers I knew, the hardest part of being a parent was not mastering techniques but sticking with them when their children protested or pushed back.

I wondered what it was that made some parents more able to feel and express their authority than others. Parents know perfectly well, at least cognitively, that they are responsible for their children, but they often hesitate to put their proverbial foot down because they don't like the idea of being the authority. Others feel ineffective, frustrated, and discouraged with their children because they think they *are* putting their foot down, but their children do not comply. For many parents, the difficulty with authority comes from the ideal of a more democratic, child-centered family life that's become so common in middle-class America over the last 25 years. Other authors have already explored the many causes of this shift.[1] Their work, and my 35 years of clinical experience, form a backdrop for this discussion. My purpose in this book is to help parents feel more confident in their authority, and to help them use it in a way that feels consistent with the love and caring that undergirds every aspect of parenthood.

In the hectic overscheduled rush of many families, this democratic ideal of parenthood translates into more accommodation *of* and fewer demands *on* children. Parents plead and cajole, and many (perhaps most) inevitably and regretfully find themselves yelling—to little effect. Others give up asking in order to avoid the yelling, and do more and more for their children themselves. Parents negotiate with their children about even such basics as clearing a dish or coming to the table in the first place, and some hasten to add, like one mother in a recent blog post, "I don't want to impose rules, just guidelines." Parents who "try everything" and still feel ineffective and overwhelmed, and parents who believe in negotiation but find themselves feeling powerless, might both need a different way of thinking about being a parent.

The grandmother in the park put her foot down, as it were, with a mere flick of a finger. With that gesture she communicated the certainty she felt in the legitimacy of her authority, the clarity she had about the need to intervene, and her confidence that her small intervention would not threaten her loving relationship with her grandson. He understood all of this implicitly and quickly amended his mistake. In the same situation, you might not want *your* child to heed the flick of a finger; you might prefer to pull her out of the group and talk to her about cooperation. But whatever your style, I am sure you would want her to change her behavior. To be effective with either approach, you need confidence that this is what it means to be the grownup, and to communicate that confidence to your child.

Since some parents worry about coming on too strong, and others feel they can't convey authority even when they try, I realized that my task in this book would be to help parents understand two big ideas. The first idea is that the natural authority of parenthood comes from the basic fact of parents' responsibility for their children. Parents use their authority all the time in ways they may not think of as such. It is parents who choose where to live, decide on basic household routines and everyday needs; their children need and expect it from them. They are the grownups. The second big idea is that the natural authority of parenthood does not depend on parenting strategies; it is communicated in, and through, parents' relationships with their children. They make consistent demands and they set firm limits. They do it with a confidence that translates into a feeling of connection, security and safety that children can feel. Love and limits.

As a college junior tutoring elementary school children in one of the first bilingual classrooms in the nation, I was forced to consider my own ability to be an authority. Along with the teacher in that classroom (then my boyfriend, later my husband), I was very taken with a book called *The Lives of Children*, by George Dennison. He had founded a small progressive school in New

York City in the 1960s. Going back to his book recently, I was surprised and pleased to discover this passage with the term *natural authority* described in just the sense I explore it in this book.

> [Children's]...own self-interest will lead them into positive relations with the natural authority of adults, and this is much to be desired, for natural authority is a far cry from authority that is merely arbitrary. Its attributes are obvious: adults are *larger, are experienced*, possess more words, and *have entered into prior agreements among themselves*. When all this takes on a positive instead of a merely negative character, the children see the adults as *protectors and as sources of certitude, approval, novelty, skills*. In the fact that adults have entered into prior agreements, children intuit a seriousness and *a web of relations in the life that surrounds them*. If it is a bit mysterious, it is also impressive and somewhat attractive; they see it quite correctly as *the way of the world*, and they are not indifferent to its benefits and demands. [Italics mine.]

It is more than 50 years since these words were written, but the essence of the relationship between adults and children has not changed. Natural authority is not a matter of simple discipline. It means assuring children of your care and protection in a mostly grownup world. This care encompasses every single thing, big and small, that parents need or want children to do.

Almost 25 years after reading George Dennison, and already the mother of four sons, I met Yolanda. She was a great example of someone who thought she was asserting authority but whose 4-year-old continued to oppose her. She was 20 years old, a Puerto Rican mother of four in my parents' group at a homeless shelter in Hartford. One day she threw up her hands about the persistent defiance of her 4-year-old: "I have tried everything," she said. "He won't do anything he is supposed to do." I asked her what I and many professionals who work with parents ask: "What would you do if he ran ahead of you to the corner?" "Run after him," she said. "Does he wear clothes when he goes to the store with you?" I continued. "Of course!" Everyone in the group, including Yolanda herself, laughed. "What do you think, I'm crazy?" "Well," I answered, "someone had to make sure he got dressed."

In other words, there were ways she was in fact effectively using her natural authority, ways which she didn't recognize. But there was more to it: She had grown up in a family in which physical force was commonplace. "My mother used a belt on us, but I can't do that—even my 7-year-old says he will call DCF if I do," Yolanda said, referring to the Department of Children and Families, the state child services agency. Parents in my private practice (usually from more privileged backgrounds) can sound equally frustrated. They do not consider a belt a desirable alternative, but they remain at wits' end about how to be effective —even if they have a shelf full of parenting books. How could I help parents translate the certainty they felt when their child's safety was at stake to the more ordinary situations they encountered every day around meals, bedtimes, and homework? How could I reassure them that setting limits was consistent with love?

In a Google alert for the phrase "natural authority," virtually all of the uses refer to athletes and coaches. They are usually described as moving with authority or demonstrating calmness and common sense. It is notable that the reference is to their bodies, not their words. Natural authority is akin to what public speakers sometimes call "command presence," or for actors, "stage presence." It emerges from the confidence you feel in your parenthood; the trust you build with your children; your understanding of their perspective and experience; and your capable collaboration with others who care for them.

But it's complicated. Imagine a teenage boy and his parents in my office. The boy makes a rude remark to his father after being chastised for not taking out the trash: "Oh, screw you, Dad, you're just lazy." The father bristles visibly but says nothing. The mother makes a snide comment about the father being a pushover. There is no one disciplinary strategy that will help this family work out this conflict or prevent the next one. From one brief exchange comes at least an hour of conversation about the many factors at play, from family attitudes to rudeness to the history of the relationships involved.

I begin with the question, "What just happened?" The adolescent was rude, as adolescents often are—that's development. But the parent he was rude to was unwilling to call him on it, and the other parent joined in the child's put-down of his father. What past experiences in their relationships and other family relationships would help explain that? And what feelings did the brief exchange evoke for each of them? The boy sits with his arms folded firmly across his chest; his father looks down at the floor. The mother fumes.

As we get into the discussion, both parents say it is easier to do the chores themselves than to deal with their son's resistance. The boy, who seems more anxious than aggressive, adds that he has no time for chores: his schoolwork is too demanding. The mother's widowed father is in the hospital and she is an only child, so she is carrying that burden too. The solution to this family's loaded interaction and chore dilemma is not simply for the father to repeat the demand and hope for the best but rather for both parents to take the time to work on their shared responsibility and to clarify the expectations (and consequences) related to chores. Recognizing the stress on the mother because of her responsibility as a daughter and addressing the sources of their son's anxiety about school would be part of the discussion.

Any moment in family life can be deconstructed in this way to better understand how you express your authority, both implicitly and explicitly, from the organization of the household to the unspoken rules of family relationships. I will take you through an extended discussion about the role of authority in the parent-child relationship, full of ordinary examples from all kinds of households. I will look at everyday moments from varying angles. In some chapters, the focus will be on the people in the interaction and the relationship between them, including the verbal and nonverbal elements that shape it. In others, the emphasis will be on the family and household context in which it is taking place. We will look at child development, not from the point of view of milestones and what to expect at certain ages, but through the experience of children and parents and their relationships—that is, development as it is encountered in real life. It is not about what a 4- or a 14-year-old *does*, but about the forces affecting him and his sense of being someone in the world. In the very particular world of your family and household, it is about how he learns about you, what you care about, and what it is like to be with you.

What I hope to help you do in this book is to worry less about whether you are a good parent and completely consistent in every instance. I want you to think more about the fact that you are the grownup. This conviction is key to the feeling of authority. You communicate your confidence or doubts about your authority throughout the day, all the time, not only in instances of discipline but in *every* interaction. You communicate it moment by moment through body language, tone of voice, and facial expression; in moments of attention and responsiveness throughout the mundane routines of everyday life; in moments of direction, reprimand, or prohibition.

This is not a book of "how-to's," except perhaps how to think about parenthood. My goal in these chapters is the same one I have with parents in my office—that is, to help them find the confidence and clarity they need to use the parenting style or approach that feels right to them. This includes understanding what matters most to them, who they are, who their child is, and the relationship between them. In that sense, this is probably different from other books you may have read or consulted. It is not so much about parenting as parenthood. For the most part, parenting books assume your authority without examining it closely, as we will in this book. We will focus on the meaning of your fundamental responsibility to be the grownup in the relationship with your child. There is not one way to be the authority; you can choose your style. It doesn't have to be harsh nor does it have to mean a loss of the child's autonomy—although it may mean that in certain instances, for example, when you take away a mobile device or ground them. In the throes of the moment, when facing a child's resistance, parents can easily lose sight of the reasons they asserted authority in the first place and back down.

Although parents' individual backgrounds can affect their expectations of their children in a variety of ways, it has been my experience that feelings of powerlessness in the face of children's resistance cross lines of class, education, and profession. I have worked with homeless parents and parents with enormous challenges in the form of unemployment, a child's disability, or a history of abuse and foster care. I have worked with parents holding jobs as various as high school secretary, waitress, school psychologist, bureaucrat, security guard, Wall Street trader, website designer, and architect. Most had some exposure to parenting books but found them confusing; some felt they had done fine with little kids but were finding themselves intimidated by teenagers; still others found toddler bedtimes impossible and couldn't wait until their child was older. Many needed help because they had differences with a co-parent, whether living together or not, but hadn't recognized the effect of those disagreements on their authority. Although I am primarily drawing on theory and research done with American middle-class populations, which are more child-centered than many other societies across the globe, I use examples drawn from sources in cultural anthropology to illustrate cultural differences and parallels.[2]

I felt well-prepared when I became a parent, now nearly 45 years ago. As the third of nine children, I had taken to responsibility for my younger siblings like a fish to water. I credit much of my sense of how a household works to my parents' combination of love, humor, rules, routines, and a good dose of the benign neglect inevitable in such a large family. Although being a big sister included changing diapers and babysitting, I probably spent more time with my younger siblings doing puppet shows, playing tag, and baking cookies. My real education about authority began at 24 with the birth of my first son and continued through the departure of my fourth for college 29 years later. In countless moments with my four sons, some of which I share in this book, I learned just how hard being the authority could be. I have also watched as others—friends, neighbors, siblings, in-laws, my own grown children, nieces, nephews, and, not least, my clients—have confronted this central challenge of parenthood with varying degrees of distress and comfort.

My fascination with the conversations and interactions of my first two little boys led me to enroll in a master's program in child development where I followed my curiosity to linguistics, ethology, and anthropology, abiding interests that have shaped my thinking about development, my work with families, and this book. By the time I had my third son, my curiosity about how families work led me to a year's study of family systems theory, the idea that the family is a web of interdependent relationships. My master's thesis was built on a year's observation and analysis of the three boys' interactions. Having become increasingly interested in doing clinical work with parents and families, I started my doctorate in clinical psychology after my fourth son was born.

Psychology has many subdisciplines: clinical and developmental, social and evolutionary, even a hybrid known as psycholinguistics, all of which have contributed to this book. Much of what I have written here is based on classics in child development that influenced me and a generation of therapists who work with families, including John Bowlby on attachment theory, Diana Baumrind on parental authority, Beatrice Whiting on cross-cultural psychology, Jerome Kagan on temperament, Daniel Stern on the relationship between mother and infant, and family systems pioneers Murray Bowen and Salvador Minuchin. But psychology alone is not enough to help understand what is going on between parent and child.

The early shaping of this book coincided with my stumbling on the Brainscience Podcast (brainsciencepodcast.com) with Dr. Ginger Campbell, which introduced me to the ever-widening world of research on the brain and related fields like neurophilosophy. I have also been influenced by the expanding work on attachment and affect regulation by Daniel Siegel, Alan Schore, Louis Cozolino, and others in the new field of interpersonal neurobiology. Other sources came from primatology and anthropology, especially the work of Marjorie Harness Goodwin, Elinor Ochs and Tamar Kremer-Sadlik, and others at the Center for the Everyday Life of Families at UCLA.

Although I studied child development, I learned more about it from raising kids and working with families. Those were the times my own brain was involved, my own feelings, my own body, and my own emotional and physiological regulation. Being responsible dramatically changed my experience of the dynamics of the interaction. I have tried to evoke your involvement, as a reader, in a wide range of interactions that might resonate with your own experience. When you are the responsible grownup, then it is you who must initiate, manage, and maneuver your way through interactions with a risk of conflict or tension, and therefore at least some stress.

A caveat: I have tried to include a variety of ages and situations in my discussions, but you may not find that your particular situation is represented here. What I hope you do find is resonance with the kinds of issues you find difficult in the ideas and concepts I present. If you have a special needs child, or a child with severe behavioral issues, you may need professional help to find your voice of authority. But the principle is the same: You are the grownup, so finding help, too, is your responsibility. I hope that this exploration of being the grownup—what it means to be a parent—will be useful to all parents of children from birth to adulthood.

Although I won't often use the word love, the elements of what we mean when we say we love our children—security, trust, safety, connection, and well-being—are as much at the core of this book as is authority. Even in the most trivial moments, expressions of both love and limits will give you the chance to be the grownup your child needs and expects. Natural authority is at the core of the parent-child relationship: I am the grownup; I love you, and I will take care of you.

Chapter One

Love and Limits:
What Is Natural Authority?

I t was time to leave the playground. I was 26, pregnant, and the stay-at-home mother of a 2-year-old. My husband and I had just moved to a city that was hundreds of miles away from any family or friends. I knew no one else with a young child. My son was happily swinging, but it was time for lunch, and soon after that, the battleground of nap time. When I told him that it was time to leave, he said, "No, I don't want to go; I want to swing, I want to swing." After at least two more failed efforts at verbal persuasion, I lifted him off the swing. He cried and squirmed out of my arms and finally threw himself on the ground. He kicked and screamed in a full-fledged tantrum. I wanted to cry myself. As I write, through the window I can see a little girl and her mother walking a Chihuahua. He stops several times and refuses to walk, and finally she picks him up—just as I did with my son. What were her alternatives? What were mine?

It was an ordinary moment, but a stressful one. It was one moment among countless others during my years raising children in which I felt the painful paradox of being the grownup. I had to set limits that someone I loved was not going to like. A few years later, in Pittsburgh, we had a friendly and outspoken neighbor whose backyard was in earshot of ours. He didn't yet have kids, but he had opinions. If he overheard my husband or me scolding one of our boys, he might call out, "Love and limits, love and limits, that's what it takes." Authority is both the way a parent responds and the kind of demands he makes. The parent's response and those demands are particular to the nature of their relationship and experience with each other, and to the context of this relationship, family, and household. Some version of a scenario in which a child pushes the limits of or violates family rules until a parent intervenes is acted out over and over again in family life, whatever the age of the child. The nature of the issue and the nature of the communication vary widely, depending on the age of the child, that child's needs, and the existing relationship between her and the parent. (I will use examples from different periods of development throughout this book).

Despite my experience with children as a big sister of six younger siblings, I was new to this relationship of parental authority that day at the playground. Not knowing what else to do, I carried my son, arms and legs flailing, the blessedly short half-block home. I was grateful that the playground was empty. How could it be that hard to get a 2-year-old home? I had obviously stayed at the playground too long and now this tired and hungry little boy was incapable of pulling himself together. As much as I loved him, it was clear that in that moment, I didn't know how to help him. Still, I made a decision for his well-being and my young family's routine. I carried it out because I had a feeling of authority. I knew he needed lunch and a nap. And so did I. This was the moment in my own development that I understood what being a parent meant, even more than struggles over sleep when he was an infant. No number of hugs or kisses would make him feel better. He was more of a person now; he could push back at my authority with words, but in this instance he was beyond words. Stressed and upset and alone as I felt, I knew that I had to be the grownup in our relationship. I had to show him my love with firmness. We had to go home.

If you are long past the days of wrangling 2-year-olds, daily instances in which you are forced to be the grownup who sets limits are more likely to do with technology, meaning all that happens on screens, big and small. What if you discover that your daughter has participated in bullying on Snapchat, for example? What do you do? It is not as simple as picking up a toddler, as stressful as that can be for a new parent. You must deal with your own mixed feelings of empathy for her dilemma and shame that she has been accused of such a thing. Then, you must find your way to show both your love and authority while guiding her to a mature resolution of the situation.

Technology presents one of the hardest parts of being a parent in the 21st century; it is the boon and scourge of family life, affecting every parent and child in some way. Nevertheless, while dilemmas related to technology may be difficult, in the end, they are not that different from almost any other moment of parenthood. Why? Because as a parent, you are responsible for your child, and that responsibility gives you authority. If you are like most parents, you become desperate for the right strategy, the right technique. But what if it turns out that it's not strategies that make the difference as much as *something else*? This book is about that something else. I call it the natural authority of parents, that is, the simple fact that you are the grownup in an always changing and long-lasting relationship of loving responsibility and trusting dependence.

A Relationship of Natural Authority

A combination of frustration, powerlessness, and unease with authority most often leads parents to seek help. They are not quite sure they are in fact in charge. And their children know it. The need for a feeling of authority, with confidence your children feel and trust, is missing from much of the advice parents get from experts and, I suspect, from the conversations parents have with each other. I believe that this is in large part because over the last 50 years, we have slipped into a focus on techniques and strategies of "parenting," forgetting that parenthood is a condition of life defined by one or more relationships with other people. It is constant; it is who you have become, something you *are*, every day. And being a parent means that you are a parent *in relation to someone* who, like you, is a person, another human being with her own experience of the world. She turns to you for safety, responsiveness, and connection. You respond with love and protection—and sometimes limits. You are two people in a relationship with each other, each with a body, a temperament, a perspective, and emotional experience that shapes a pattern of responses to each other, even in infancy.

Like ducks and sheep and chimps, children need adults to survive. Parental authority is both natural and essential to them. You are the big animal to your child's smaller, dependent, and more vulnerable animal, even as he or she gets bigger and bigger and can do more and more without you. Being the responsible grownup in your child's life gives you authority in its broadest sense: in charge, with power, control, influence, knowledge, expertise, and confidence in providing necessary and appropriate care to your dependent children. You build your authority on the natural foundation of shelter, nourishment, and safety. Your child looks to you for answers to the most basic questions of survival: What is there to eat? Where and when do I sleep? Will I be safe? In short, who will take care of me?

But your authority is more than the answers to these questions; it is also the interactions that accumulate to become who you each are with each other in those moments of working things out—whether regarding technology, meal and bedtime routines, or sibling conflict. If you have more than one child, you know how different it can feel to get one dressed and out the door as opposed to the other: Not only each of you, but each relationship has, in effect, its own personality. Your confidence that you can indeed be the grownup that this child needs in this moment builds the trust and predictability that make children feel secure.[3]

In the dynamic unfolding process that is your relationship, you change, your child changes, and your relationship changes. The toddler who won't even voluntarily eat one vegetable becomes a vegetarian. She grows ever more competent and autonomous, and you have to respond. You become more experienced as a parent, and you get to know this child. Some parents find it easier to have infants and young children, while others find their stride when kids can talk. Although you are most likely to notice change at developmental milestones and transitions, in fact change is a constant. What is not safe and therefore not permissible for a 3-year-old is fine for a 5-year-old; what a 16-year-old is capable of and confident about doing is different from what a 12-year-old can do. And the two of you can—and do—talk about it differently. Your child may argue with you: at 3 with a stamp of the foot or a full-blown tantrum, at 6 or 9 perhaps by whining and complaining, at 12 and 14 with sullenness or even a tantrum again, at 16 with logic and persuasion. How you respond of course changes as well, as your child's degree of autonomy, and therefore your relationship, changes. But your job description doesn't change. You are in charge.

The Power of Parenthood

A variety of people can raise a child and have relationships with him. A child whose parents have divorced often has two sets of parents. There are countless combinations of biology and adoption and remarriage, and every version of a parent-child relationship has its own particularities. But there remains between that primary caretaker and the child the core fact that it is the grownups—usually but not always the parents—who have the authority to make decisions, large and small, that will shape the child's development and the child and caretaker's relationship with each other.*

Note that we are talking about authority, not discipline. Discipline refers to rules and a code of behavior, as well as training to obey the code and punishments for disobedience.[4] Discipline of children requires strategies, techniques, and consequences when the rules have been broken. Authority is having the power to enforce the family rules. Because you are responsible for a dependent child, you have power and, as he gets older, influence over even the smallest and most intimate aspects of her life. Just having the power and influence is not enough; reliability is key. Your child won't believe you if *you* don't feel that your power is legitimate and appropriate, something you communicate through your behavior, both verbal and nonverbal. She knows you love her, but she won't trust you unless your authority is accompanied by a concurrent recognition of and responsiveness to her needs and perspective. To further complicate the picture, neither you nor a co-parent will be effective if either of you undermines the other.

Navigating the shoals of dinner with picky eaters takes authority. Making sure homework gets done takes authority. In order to keep Instagram and Snapchat at bay, for example, you might try the technique of an evening study hall. But what if you discover that your daughter has used the bathroom or stepped outside for a breath of fresh air—"It's healthy, Dad!"—to sneak in some social media time? She has violated a rule or an agreement that you made with her, and she knows that there is a consequence. It takes authority to enforce it when she is

---

* To simplify my prose, I vary in my references to the possibility of more than one primary caretaker or a co-parent. But whether or not I make it explicit in the pages that follow, I recognize the existence and influence of a co-parent, even if one parent is doing the lion's share or even all of the daily parenting work, even if the parents do not live in the same house, even if the child has little or no relationship with another parent. I do not make special reference to step-parents, multiple caretakers, relatives, or paid babysitters, except to note that any adult responsible for a child has at least borrowed natural authority.

pleading with you to understand. If your 13-year-old son begins swearing at you, at first when he's angry and then more and more as part of normal conversation, it takes authority to decide whether or not you care and then discipline with authority to get him to stop. Chances are you won't wash his mouth out with soap, as parents often did in days gone by. But you might have a conversation about civility and respect, and about whether or not he swears at adults at school, or you might start a system of fines for bad language or rewards for dinnertimes completed without swearing. Your authority requires both the decision to act, the choice of which action you will take, and the consistent implementation of the action. In other words, whether it's homework routines or swearing rules, you must have authority to succeed at discipline.

As a parent, you are bigger and stronger (at least for a while), older and more experienced than your child; you are not only the provider but the source of security and the focus of attachment. Although they might feel at odds with each other, it is the love you communicate that fuels your authority. The child's nervous system is tied into yours, connecting you in a way that helps him develop the capacity for emotional regulation and continues to mean that both of you can be easily triggered by the other.[5] The asymmetry of these kinds of power—with dependence on one side and responsibility on the other—helps explain the broad scope of authority.

The Complications of Human Connection

If it is natural, why doesn't authority come more easily? Authority, like almost any other natural process—appetite, sleep, sex, and language—is subject in humans to many forces that can interfere with its healthy expression, whether psychological, developmental, socioeconomic, historical, or cultural. But above all, authority is vulnerable to the complications of human connection. And it is those complications that require us to slow down and explore the moments that accumulate to create the relationship between parents and children. Being the grownup takes more than bullet points and rules: It takes time and attention and thoughtfulness about your own situation, your own family, and your own relationship.

Even the most mundane instances of parenthood can be a challenge, so intimately are you involved with your child's life, awake or asleep or halfway in between. When a 4-year-old tries to postpone bedtime with another glass of water, allowing her that small gesture of power can be a slippery slope: You know it is best to stick to the routine and say no if you really want to get bedtime under control, but that look! So irresistible, so exasperating. It is so hard to say no. Most of the time, parents know that it is their job to make the big and small decisions required of daily life, to say those multiple no's or to have clear routines and expectations for their children. They are the parents. But the nature of family life and child-rearing is such that new instances arise daily, making it easy to lose clarity.

With young children at home, I used to feel as if all I did was say no. No, you can't have a snack now; no, I can't drive you to your friend's house now; no, you can't have those jeans; no, you can't play with Legos here; no, I'm not mad at you—I'm just busy; no, I can't talk to you—I'm on the phone. No, no, no, no, NO! No wonder many parents worry that their children will feel rejected and opt instead for negotiation. In many such instances children are testing the limits that they know quite well: And it truly is okay to say no if the request goes against a routine or a limit you've already set once. We will see more in later chapters how important it is, in fact, for children of any age, to know what they can expect from you, even if they don't like it.

In my conversations with parents struggling with problems of daily family life, we look at how natural authority unfolds in *their* family relationships. We work together to identify the forces and patterns of interaction that shape and influence it in *their* household. We zoom in close to deconstruct moments around bedtime, curfew, Internet, or whatever the instance of difficulty was this week, and then we step back together to consider what seems to make them feel ineffective as an authority. We might talk about past instances of conflict, about how things go in the moment, how they feel physically, what they are afraid might happen if they assert authority. Every conversation includes bringing their attention to the responsibility and authority they have just by being the grownups. Rather than tell them what to do, I try to explain what this means in a way that will strengthen their efforts to be the grownup their children need and want them to be—even when children seem to be doing everything to tell their parents they want to be in charge.

Primate Parents

Although it is tempting to think that only human parents need to assert authority, a look at the habits of primate parents may help, since these close evolutionary relatives harbor fewer doubts than we do. For all primates, humans included, there are three areas of care in early childhood with key transitions determined by parents: feeding, getting children from place to place, and sleeping arrangements. Each of these transitions has to do with some kind of separation: weaning from the breast (or bottle), the end of riding on a parent or being carried, and the end of sleeping in the parents' nest—or bed. And the young chimps don't like the change.[6]

In nonhuman primates, these three transitions usually take place more or less in relation to the birth of a sibling. When another infant arrives, the toddler is off the breast, off the back, and out of the nest—sometimes rather precipitously. There are even primate tantrums. Evolutionary anthropologists call this "parent-offspring conflict" to communicate an evolutionary difference of interest between mother and child, i.e., the child is interested in his own nutritional and general well-being, and the mother has shifted her primary interest to the new offspring.

These decisions are often abrupt. Not having language with which to prepare the child or soften the blow, chimps and other primates simply make their decisions clear physically.

The getting-place-to-place issue came up not long ago in my own life as a grownup temporarily in charge of grandchildren. My 6-year-old granddaughter lay on the floor in stocking feet moaning, "I don't want to walk." Her brother, 4, already had his coat, hat, and shoes on. The issue: He was going to ride in a stroller for the six-block walk, and she would walk. After a couple of attempts at reason, and at least one outburst of exasperation, I drew on my son's authority and his use of a three-strikes method: "If Papa were here, I think he would say, 'That's one.'" She gave a tiny Mona Lisa smile, clearly a bit surprised at my strategy, and jumped up. She put on her coat and shoes, but as we closed the door behind us, she started complaining again, saying, "I don't want to walk." Emboldened, I said, "That's two." She looked at me as if to see if I really meant it, or indeed if I even knew what "that's two" implied. I must have looked stern because she walked—although halfway through the walk I let her switch places with her brother, who at that point wanted to walk himself.

Even if we humans have more options than chimps or baboons, the human parent too essentially has to say, implicitly or even explicitly, things like, "There will be times when I have to make choices that you may not like, but which, as the parent, I can't avoid." "I can't nurse you and your new sibling." "There isn't room in the bed for all of us." Or "I can't carry both of you." A mother chimp doesn't explain to her 3-year-old that the newborn needs to nurse and be carried and sleep with her; that's just how it is. This is natural authority. And baby chimps don't like it any more than human children. Many of the decisions you make as a parent are, however, not in fact unavoidable; but you will have made them for reasons about which you have some clarity. And once you have made them, whatever your chosen strategy or approach, it is crucial to the development of your voice of authority that you act as if they are unavoidable. When you communicate doubt, your child hears it; she wonders if you really mean it and may decide to test you, bringing you both to a new level of conflict. You can talk more about it later, you can change your strategy next time, but be the grownup and stick to your guns.

Authority in Developmental Psychology

Some parents point to the dangers of being too authoritarian in their hesitation to assert authority. And if you are never willing to take your child's perspective into account, this is indeed a danger. But you can err too far in the other direction too, and many parents do. I like to think of your authority as elastic: You can stay in charge even as you take your child's feelings and perspective into consideration. I think of a moment that impressed me when I was a new mother: A friend was trying to get his 3-year-old son out of the car for an outing to the playground. For no obvious reason, he said no, he didn't want to get out. The father paused and then asked him if he wanted to go home instead. No response beyond a pout and a whined "Noooo!" My friend paused again and then began very slowly counting to three. As if in sync with his father, the toddler started to very, very slowly move out of his car seat, as if to say, "Okay, Daddy, I know I have to do this, but I am going to do it my way." Once out, his mood changed and off they went to the swings. In my friend's choice to present one alternative to the pouting child—going home—he remained in charge without negotiating other alternatives. Giving the child other options, like staying in the car, having a snack, or talking to his mother, who was at home working, could have led to too much negotiation and a relinquishing of authority. Instead, he allowed his authority to stretch enough to provide another option, which respected the child's mood and need for control.

In 1966, a young psychologist named Diana Baumrind published what became the seminal study of parental authority, with a focus on the effect of parents' behavior on the behavior of children. Five decades of positive outcomes for children in research with parents and children from preschool through adolescence strongly support Baumrind's proposition that each of three parenting styles reflects different ratios between two fundamental dimensions of the parent-child relationship, responsiveness and demandingness. Neither negates the other.[7]

Three Scenarios of Authority

An 11-year-old girl is up past her bedtime, doing homework. Her father demands that she go to bed and doesn't listen when she tries to explain what she's working on and why it's taking so long. "I don't care what you're working on, it's time for bed. Now go!" His voice would be raised; his face and body language would express anger and impatience. He might even throw in a sarcastic comment about how much time she wasted on Facebook before getting to her homework. "No wonder you're not finished yet!"

In an alternative, the father listens at length and says, in a sympathetic, slightly pleading voice and perhaps with a little squeeze, "Oh honey, go ahead—stay up if you need to, but don't get too tired, okay?" Or he offers to finish the homework, so the child can go to bed, or to write a note to the teacher. His take on the texting he knows she was doing till 8:30 is, "Maybe you should start your homework a little earlier tomorrow, okay? I'm not so sure you can mix texting with homework."

And in a third version, the father is both less rigid in his demands than in the first scenario and less permissive than in the second, looking for a response that considers the child's predicament (having procrastinated and now being anxious about getting the work done) without relinquishing his authority as a parent in relation to schoolwork. He might also reiterate the homework, technology, and bedtime rules of the household and make it clear that if he gives her a break, it is an exception, perhaps referring to some mitigating circumstance like a hard day at school or having been sick. He might propose a solution: "I want you to get your homework finished, but it's getting awfully late. I'm going to give you 15 more minutes, and if you want, I'll get you up early in the morning." His tone would be firm but warm; his nonverbal message is "I'm taking care of you."

These three scenarios roughly represent the three parenting styles of Baumrind's classic view of parental authority as functioning in two dimensions she called responsiveness and demandingness – not dissimilar to the more colloquial love and limits. The authoritarian parent *demands a lot* from the child's behavior but *responds little* to the child's needs, while the permissive parent *makes few demands* of the child but is *highly*—even overly—*responsive* to him. Finally, the authoritative parent is *highly demanding*, asserting his responsibility, experience, and power. But he is also *highly responsive*: firm without being rigid and responsive without being indulgent. He tailors his responses (mostly without thinking) to the child's temperament and development and, I would add, to their relationship with each other, to what they both understand to be acceptable behavior in the family and to what they remember about past interactions. Baumrind believed firmly in the parent's obligation to care for children and in the resulting legitimacy of parental authority. Her research demonstrated that adult control could coexist with the child's increasing autonomy without ill effects, a finding that modern parents would do well to remember.

If parents worry too much about how their children feel or whether their children will be angry at them, it makes it that much harder to get through the day, which is your main task: how to get your children to school, dressed and with homework in hand, how to get them to after-school activities or daycare and home again, homework done, dinner eaten, baths taken, lights out, without undue stress, conflict, shouting, or crying. If a parent decides that practicing the piano or taking a bath is important, or if he needs his children's help with household tasks, the children are not to blame if whatever is in question doesn't get done. He is the grownup.

The Authority of the Family

Another influential view in developmental psychology takes relationships and the family context more into account. For William Damon, the family is a social order, with parents and siblings functioning as the teachers and enforcers of both the family's and society's rules. Damon emphasizes affect in communications between parent and child. What he says is consistent with contemporary research on neurobiology about nonverbal communication. "By the second year of life," he writes, "children actively monitor their parents' faces and voices for emotional signals…[C]hildren generally ignore their parents' commands unless the commands are vigorously pressed with a strong emotional overtone."[8]

Does this mean that a parent's every response should communicate authority? In a sense, yes—because the child depends on it. That's what being the grownup means. It could be argued that even "I love you" should communicate authority, so that the child can rely on it. Love is a given between parents and children in the form of security and attachment. In the next chapter we will explore its biological foundations. But authority is also at the core of parenthood: authority to decide, to reassure, to protect, and to communicate that you are confident and competent to do so. The relationship you have with your child is inherently unequal and asymmetrical. As the parent, you are saying with your behavior and often with words as well: I am the parent; I love you; it is my job to take care of you and keep you safe; I know more than you; I make my decisions about your safety based on our family's values and my life experience; I care about what you think and what you want or need, but finally, I have the power; I am the boss.

Chapter Two

You Are the Big Object:
Relationship, Security, and Connection

My father was very tall and used to tell us this story: Riding on a New York subway car, he noticed a little boy staring at him. My father smiled down at him, and the boy screwed up his courage to ask, "Are you a giant?" It is easy to forget that any adult is indeed a giant to a child, especially when the child refuses to come to dinner or talks back when you remind her to put her dishes in the dishwasher. You are a giant just by being the grownup. It is, in essence, what this book is about. It is why your authority is natural.

Setting Limits, from Mealtime to Curfew

It's 5:30 p.m. You have been doing household chores and looking for jobs online all day. You are a single parent. Michael, 5, is immersed in a video game. "Fifteen minutes, then it's time for dinner," you call from the kitchen, feeling slightly optimistic because of a job listing you saw online, and looking forward to sitting down as a twosome. "Okay," he calls back, glad to have some more time for his play. It is a little later than your usual routine because the weather is nice, and Michael was reluctant to leave the playground. "I'm playing tag with my friends! I want to stay," he had pleaded. In a moment of generous—perhaps foolhardy—compromise, you had said, "If you come now, you and I can play tag later."

Now it is "later." You have told him that 15 minutes is up and it's time to wash hands for dinner, but he suddenly remembers that you "promised" to race with him. He can't yet tell time, but he knows what later means. You purposely did not *promise*, and in your mind, later was any time but that moment, and certainly not now, when it is time for dinner. *You* are counting the minutes until you can get him into the tub, read him two stories, and put him to bed, while *he* is thinking about how he can keep playing and stay up later. The battle lines are drawn—not only between his video warriors but between you and him. Who is going to win the next battle? You get testy, he whines, and before you know it, you raise your voice: "Put that away now, or else!" And he says, "You're yelling at me! You are *always* mean to me!" Although his words express anger, his body and voice suggest hurt and betrayal. And you know that such a mood is often followed by a tantrum, especially right before dinner.

Or imagine a text exchange between you and your middle school daughter, Samantha, who doesn't want to come home the morning after a sleepover because you had said that *maybe* she could stay longer than usual this time. She didn't hear, or at least didn't register, the "maybe," and you probably didn't mean it but slid it in to be nice because you'd had a cozy chat before she left yesterday. She too is angry: "You never stick to what you say!" But you know that her anger comes from disappointment and that there will be slammed doors and glares when she gets home. You will have to coax her into talking about how she feels—or maybe you will be so annoyed that you'll glare, even if inside you feel a twinge of guilt.

When you try to get Michael to come to dinner or repeatedly text Samantha to remind her of her curfew, you represent, along with your co-parent or other significant caretaker, your child's most essential security and one of your child's most fundamental models of a relationship, a relationship with a growing history of moments beginning at your first meeting, whether at birth, adoption, or the blending of families. It is natural, then, that you are the authority.

Being a Parent Means Being in a Relationship

As young parents, my husband and I and another couple were discussing our infant sons, only a few months old. Inevitably, the conversation turned to sleep: how little we were getting and what to do about a wakeful infant. "Well," the other father said, with a voice of social science authority, "we have read that it is important for babies to learn to use their own resources." My husband and I joked after they left that maybe our 4-month-old son could count sheep. By being parents, we had entered a world of warring ideas about getting babies to sleep. In the intervening decades, discussions about sleeping and crying have not gotten any easier, and camps supporting "crying it out," sleep training, and co-sleeping can be intense. But what we didn't talk about, and what many parents don't think about, was that each of us was beginning a relationship with someone else and that these interactions around bedtime were among the first ways we and our infants were getting to know each other.

A few years later, in the late '70s, child development researchers began to focus more on the family and community context for development and its fundamentally relational nature than on the qualities of the individual child. It mattered if a baby were sensitive or hard to soothe, but how parents and babies interacted mattered too. Every human being develops in relationship to other human beings and to the nested environments in which their lives take place: the family, the community, the wider culture, and now, social media. The child is not the sum of her traits, but rather, over time, she makes connections, perceives patterns, and constructs meaning through her experience with people and with the world, including whether she will be expected to go to sleep on her own or with your help. Research over the intervening decades shows us the child is born social and therefore born ready to interact and build a relationship with you and others.[9]

These views are now fundamental to theories of child development, but most of us, when confronted with other human beings who won't do what we want them to do, wonder what is wrong with *them* and how we can get *them* to change. We're certainly not thinking in those moments of how much we love them! As a new parent, you are much more likely to think about choosing the right strategies for feeding and sleeping than about the fact that with the birth of a child you will begin a new relationship. And most books for parents are all about an activity called parenting, as if it were akin to learning to ski or play the violin. Even at their best, books can't possibly address the particular relationship you have with each child. And neither can I. But I can help you understand more about that relationship and understand more about how the authority that comes with being a parent is communicated through this relationship. It is a relationship characterized by an essential asymmetry: by the great tenderness of having someone depend on you and the great challenge of being responsible for her.

A Different Kind of Relationship

You surely were amazed when you first held the little body swaddled up with a tiny clenched hand up by her face. As one of my sons said to me as he held his firstborn, "The longest time I ever held a baby before was five minutes—and now look at me!" But what you may not realize is this: Even before this first moment, you have already begun to exercise your natural authority by your choices about where to have your baby, whether she will be breast- or bottle-fed, whether one parent will stay home with her, and if not, who will take care of her. Your choices are limited by your own experience and the human and cultural context in which you live. Still, once you decide to have a baby, you must make these and other choices or choose to let others make them for you, even if you feel there aren't many options for your family.

Unlike the long-legged colt who stumbles to her feet in the first minutes after birth, your child is born essentially helpless—except in the crucial matter of being able to get your attention so that you will take care of her. Just as you are wired to be the boss, your child, dependent as she is on you, is wired to pay close attention to you, to imitate you, to interact with you, and even, in effect, *to do what you say*. Not because you are her mother or father, per se, but because you are a caregiving adult and she is helpless. Your natural authority is inextricably embedded in your relationship and experiences together. You may not be able to see it; you may not always feel it. But like yeast in bread, it is a core ingredient, a catalyst for the other ingredients to work together.

Evolution has given you both the tools to recognize each other because the relationship with an adult caretaker is, for young animals, a matter of survival. Your baby needs to feed, needs to be held and touched and kept warm, needs to pee and poop, needs to sleep, and could not possibly protect herself from danger, except by crying for you or the nearest competent care-taker: the other parent, a sibling, a grandmother, or a babysit-ter. Your baby's brain will not develop normally without other humans to interact with, touch, and imitate. You know all of this, but it bears repeating. You might need to remember that when you feel at a loss with your infant: You have to figure it out, with help if necessary, because her life literally depends on you.[10]

This balance of responsibility and dependence makes this a different kind of relationship from any other that you have—except, of course, the relationship with your own parents. When I was a brand-new mother pacing the floor with a fussy infant, it was reassuring to me to chant, "I am a chimpanzee." Why? Not because I knew anything about evolutionary theory but because I was making an intuitive reach to some way to understand and accept the demands of my first early days of motherhood. Saying that reminded me that it was natural for babies to cry and for parents to soothe them by patting and pacing. It reminded me that it was, indeed, the responsibility of any primary caretaker to do so. It helped me cope with my baby's demands when I was feeling exhausted and my affection for this small creature was in short supply. And most important, it helped me to believe that if primates could do it, I could too, whatever momentary doubts I might have and whatever human realities might get in the way.[11]

Everyday Moments

When you are first at home with an infant, responsibility shouts from every diaper, every cry in the night, every time you have to rock her back to sleep. This may be the first time you have felt yourself so in thrall to biology, and so at sea. I'm bottle-feeding, but which formula is best? I want to breastfeed, but I'm finding it hard. When is it okay for a primary caretaker to go back to work? What does a newborn need? How can I manage my worry so it doesn't affect my baby? What if I am single? What if my baby is disabled? Being the parent doesn't mean you have to *know* all of these answers; it does mean that you have the responsibility to come up with answers and resources.

One decision that you will almost certainly make is to recruit what anthropologists call alloparents to help you, whether that is relatives, hired babysitters, or daycare. Given our long period of dependence, we would not have been able to evolve so successfully without such help.[12] Even so, those who help do so under the umbrella of responsibility shared by you and your co-parent, even if you are divorced or never married. The Internet makes this both easier and harder: You can Google anything, but sorting through the answers and determining how they fit with your values and your family require the judgment of natural authority. *(See Chapter Four.)*

Like the hypothetical scenarios involving Michael and Samantha, many everyday moments require you to communicate your authority. What happens next—not only whether you insist that Samantha come home or that Michael come to supper but how you insist and how the child in question responds to you—emerges in the relationship you have created together and contributes to your relationship going forward.

However hard you try, you will encounter instances when you are at a loss for what to do: Is it okay to bring forgotten homework to school? How old should a child be before he goes on a sleepover? Should you push your child to do something she is scared to do? These are the kinds of questions we will explore in the chapters that follow.

Goslings, Ducklings, and Babies: Attachment Theory

Every so often a field is profoundly affected by a theory, sometimes decades after it is first introduced. There is an "aha" moment: Things that didn't make sense now make sense. Something like this has happened with attachment theory in the fields of developmental and clinical psychology in the last 50 years. John Bowlby was deeply affected by written and filmed accounts of the intense reactions shown by young children experiencing separation from their parents during extended stays in hospitals and residential nurseries in the late 1940s. For what we now consider absolutely routine, that it is protective and optimal for a child to have a parent or other trusted consistent caretaker with her in the hospital, we have Bowlby and those who recorded these children's experiences to thank. But it was Bowlby who conceptualized the new theory he called attachment, first in a 1951 report to the World Health Organization and comprehensively in his 1969 book, *Attachment.*[13]

Attachment theory proposes that human infants, like all other organisms, have evolved to adapt to their environments. For humans, the primary adaptation is to caretakers, with whom they are motivated to maintain proximity and communication − both verbal and nonverbal −for their very survival. Researchers since Bowlby have emphasized the developmental benefit of such contact, i.e. the development of the brain through social interaction. Caretakers too have evolved to be sensitive and responsive to both the need for proximity and for soothing and safety. Who can resist outstretched arms? It is in these interactions, fueled by oxytocin, that both partners feel what we are accustomed to calling love: a sense of well-being in the other's company, the grownup's urge to protect and the child's feeling of being cared for.[14]

Bowlby was influenced by Konrad Lorenz, one of the founders of ethology. He replaced a mother mallard duck with himself at the moment a clutch of her eggs hatched and demonstrated what he called "imprinting." Because Lorenz was there at the moment of their birth, the ducklings behaved toward him as they would have behaved toward their mother, the essence of which was that they followed him.[15] As ethologists came to understand in later experiments with both ducklings and goslings, the brains of the young hatchlings had evolved to follow the first big object they saw—in the usual scenario, the mother duck or goose. Because they can walk from the time of birth but are still dependent on the mother for nourishment and protection, imprinting is the mechanism by which goslings and ducklings will stick with her and get fed and stay safe from predators and other dangers. Imprinting was clearly a powerful enough force to overcome the significant differences in appearance between a man and a duck. That is, the ducklings' reliance on the big object that was usually their mother was so great that in her absence, they followed a man with a gray beard.[16] Like all young creatures, they were adapting to their environment in order to survive.

For humans, the adaptation takes the form of what Bowlby called attachment schema. He proposed that the myriad experiences an infant has with his caretakers create a collection of predictions of others' behaviors that he can use to shape his own behavior. With his actions—whether crying or reaching out or turning to see if you are there—the infant can get you to help him stay not only safe but emotionally regulated. Research in the intervening decades now sees these schema as implicit or unconscious memories that are stored in the brain's networks, ready to be triggered in social interaction and influential in the quality of later relationships.[17]

Attachment Takes Many Forms

Attachment theory helps us understand the powerful connection children and parents have with each other in biological terms, a connection in evidence every time you see a parent and child walk down the street holding hands, or a child tearfully hanging on to a parent at the door of her preschool class, even the clinging of a child to a mother who mistreats her.[18] And by extension, the phenomenon of attachment also helps explain your natural authority. You are the *big object* in the life of your child, the one he looks to, the one who will show him where the food is, where the water is, and how to hide or escape from danger. A duck may operate from instinct without benefit of much intelligence or thought, but she is driven, above all, to keep her ducklings safe. So are you. Because your children are dependent on you, you are in charge, even in those moments when circumstances of everyday life or the behavior of your child make it a great challenge.

Children need and are able to develop a hierarchy of attachment figures. If I am reading a story to a grandchild of 1 or 2 and my son or daughter-in-law walks in, the child will almost certainly squirm off my lap, whine, and reach out to the more familiar adult. This should be reassuring to divorced parents, always my most difficult cases, whose split custody arrangements and court battles are extremely painful. It is so important to babies to have trusted caregivers, and it turns out that because babies are so good at making attachments, they can make several. What makes custody cases so difficult is the acute distress of everyone involved, and the feeling that it will be nearly impossible to find a solution that will relieve that distress, which is due, at least in part, to the strong feelings of attachment both *parents* have to their children.[19]

Conditions of human life vary greatly, even from household to household, requiring different practices by parents and different adaptive behaviors by children. Where there is high infant mortality, for example, the idea that a baby is a person may come much later in development, once it is certain that he will survive. Although he emphasized the infant's adaptability, Bowlby didn't address explicitly the enormous cultural variation in caregiving settings, in many of which the infant must trust in a caregiving *environment* rather than in particular individuals with different styles of interaction, different voices and smells. Recent books by American parents living in France and Germany have noted surprising differences in parenting practices and expectations.[20]

What Makes Humans Different?

In humans, it takes at least six to nine months, and sometimes longer, before human babies are mobile enough to move around independently, and a year or more before they can walk. Humans are the only primates who require adults to provide food for them after they have been weaned. As a result, we have longer to develop a bond that, although analogous to the imprinting of Lorenz's goslings, is more complicated and longer-lasting. Neither Lorenz nor the mother goose needed to "get" the goslings to follow—they just did it.

Although humans too are clearly programmed to respond in minute and constant ways to each other, human beings also have a sense of self with a will and, of course, language—both emerging, like attachment, around the time infants begin to be mobile. This trifecta creates something that often seems quite the opposite of Lorenz and his ducks, that is, someone who kicks and screams or runs away and years later won't answer his cell phone one minute and the next wants a hug.[21]

Bowlby recognized that even the infant was an active participant in how much contact with the attachment figure he maintained. In some species, such as birds, rabbits, and mice, the young are cared for in a nest in which the mother can leave them safely hidden until she returns from seeking food. Then, once they are mobile, they are pretty much on their own.[22] A human child remains connected to the caregiving parent for an extended period of time and must develop ways of keeping that care coming. Later, their interacting behavior works to keep them connected, through biological signals including smell, language, mobility, and nonverbal behavior, ensuring not only nourishment and shelter, but emotional regulation. *(See also Chapter Nine.)* Although the connection begins to develop immediately, the attachment behavior emerges when it is most needed, when the child becomes mobile.

The infant, Bowlby thought, would consider the situation and change behavior accordingly: Uh-oh, Dad just went to the kitchen, that doesn't feel so great, I'll just follow him and get a little closer. A baby might be very comfortable with morning transfers from her parents to a caregiver, but come the weekend, she wants to be held most of the time by one or another of her parents as if to catch up on her connection to them. Parents too have their own cues for danger and come to know what is likely to trigger the attachment system in their own children.[23]

Pre-attachment: Sounds, Smells, and Brain Chemistry

For some parents, the expectation of immediate love for a newborn falls short: "I thought I was supposed to fall in love with him the moment I saw him, and all I feel is exhaustion." It can be a terrible feeling. Still, most parents respond adequately to their babies' needs.* And they do so because there are biological signals that attract caretakers enough to infants to give up sleep, to give up time, and to give up freedom. In this period of "pre-attachment" in your relationship, there are two human beings interacting with each other, using nonverbal signals from

---

* If you consistently feel unable to respond to your infant, or if those around you worry about your responses, don't hesitate to speak to your doctor, who can either assess you herself or refer you to a professional.

both parties to draw them together. How you respond to each other begins to shape your relationships because you learn what to expect from each other. When in sync, this connection is also known in the vocabulary of clinical neuroscience as attunement, giving you a feeling of well-being as well as a shared emotional regulation.

Although newborns are relatively indiscriminate about who can soothe or feed them, surely to their evolutionary advantage, various invisible, unconscious chemical and sensory signals help this tiny, helpless creature and her primary caretaker become a couple and help activate adults to care for her. *(See also Chapter Nine.)* Evolution has provided us with oxytocin (the same hormone, interestingly enough, that influences sexuality and romantic attachment) and has provided the baby with soft skin, big eyes, and other features that make her lovable—most of the time.[24]

Newborns have preferences for human faces and are sensitive even to facial characteristics, including race and gender, surprisingly early. They have been shown to demonstrate preferences for their own mother's milk and smell, for human voices, and even for stories they have heard in utero. Some research suggests that having become familiar with the mother's voice in utero, they are able to use that information to build recognition of the mother's face (if she continues to be a primary caretaker). They begin to recognize their caretakers as early as two months. Young infants are also sensitive to spatial location and moving objects, although not like goslings.[25] All of these sensory and chemical mechanisms are part of a neurological system that prepares both the infant and those who care for her for the environment in which she will develop: Both your responsiveness and your willingness to set limits that enhance her safety become part of what she expects from the world.

Maternal responsiveness to the baby's needs is also stimulated by prolactin (also involved in breastfeeding) and the collection of naturally occurring compounds known as opioids or endorphins. Because of the baby's dependence on you, these chemicals, like your gaze, your touch, your voice, and your mood, are a link between "nature," or the genes she was born with, and "nurture," or the way those genes are expressed in interaction with the environment. In other words, the human context in which the baby finds herself matters—not whether she is cared for by a single parent, multiple caretakers, a family, a village, or a daycare center, but that other humans attend to and respond to her.[26] There are cultural, class, and above all, individual differences, of course, in the ways adults respond to infants, which we will touch on throughout the book.[27]

The Timing of Attachment

Why do we attach when we do? The need for proximity between parent and child makes perfect sense when babies are tiny and helpless, a need that is expressed primarily by crying and fussing and satisfied by soothing words and nonverbal behavior, including touch. But why would the infant attach to a specific person or persons after she can eat table food and hold a bottle or a sippy cup by herself? Wouldn't any adult do at that point? But consider. You expect even a preschooler or kindergartner to be somewhat wary on meeting a stranger; when they're not, you make note of it: "Wow, she's a friendly kid." Or it makes you uneasy: "She seems almost too friendly to a stranger." From the evolutionary point of view, if you think about the small bands of humans from whom we are descended, without schools or churches or other institutions beyond informal family and tribal groups, a stranger would almost certainly signify possible danger, and more so once a toddler could wander off alone. Children were more likely to survive, in other words, if their instinct was to stay close to their parents.[28]

Your relationship with your child begins at your first meeting (whether through birth or adoption) and your familiarity with each other grows with each day, but it is the period from about six months to the end of the second year, but often longer, that is the active attachment phase. What for many animals is easy and immediate for humans is a complex and months-long process, coinciding with the beginning of mobility for most children—whether cruising or crawling or walking. Infants of this age from a variety of cultures experience what is often called "stranger danger" and separation anxiety, and for the first time they will look for a ball that has rolled out of sight. This is known as "object permanence," which means they look for the ball because even though they can't see it, they now know it still exists somewhere.[29]

Once he is mobile, your baby can and does move rapidly away from you. My second, third, and fourth sons commonly crawled to where one or more brothers was playing with something attractive at a little distance away, risking separation from me or their father because of the lure of the play of other, secondary attachment figures. But with mobility, a child also begins to be aware that he has strayed, and if he becomes anxious, needs to figure out how to get back to a source of food and warmth and safety. In this process, parent and child adapt to each other. If an infant doesn't crawl until she's a year old, her relationship with her caregiver will inevitably be different from that between a parent and an infant who walks at nine months. By the same token, the relationship between an infant and a parent who is fairly businesslike, although still attentive, will have a different quality than that between an infant and a highly demonstrative, very physically expressive parent. Each adapts their behaviors to ensure connection, the purpose of which is ultimately safety and survival.

Luckily, a mobile infant doesn't always have to depend on physical contact to borrow your mature brain. The baby tracks your whereabouts, maybe looking back over his shoulder, as he experiments with increasing the distance between you while he literally "keeps an eye on you"—and you on him. This was aptly called the "practicing phase" by the developmental theorist

Margaret Mahler.[30] You might consider this a practicing phase for your natural authority as well: If a child toddles away, he wants to see you or some caregiver when he looks back. This kind of checking back is another reason to moderate the amount of time you spend on your phone when you are with young children. He doesn't just want to know you are there—he wants to know *you* know where *he* is. He wants the signal, a major source of natural authority: "You're okay, I'm still here."

In cultures in which children are carried much of the time, there is less mobility and therefore may be less need for such reassurance.[31] But infants feel the stress of separation in more ways than sight. Research with rats suggests a system of hidden regulators in maternal behavior toward rat pups that functions to maintain their homeostasis, implying that for infant mammals, including humans, separation is stressful because of the corollary loss of regulation. It is research like this that has fueled the attachment parenting movement, which prescribes a parenting style with a high level of proximity, including co-sleeping, longer term breastfeeding, and baby slings, implying that the development of attachment will be at risk without these practices. Babies and young children do need frequent contact, responsiveness, and reassurance. But humans are adaptable enough that attachment occurs in most cases and can be maintained without herculean or unusual effort.[32]

When your toddler cries when a new babysitter arrives, or your kindergartener freezes at the sight of a class full of strangers on the first day of school, it is less a cognitive process of "Oh, this is strange" than the activation of at least a mild level of anxiety at the loss of a predictable source of security. Because there is great variability in children's level of arousal and because every relationship has a different history and different patterns of interaction, so may the level of distress. *(See Chapter Seven.)*[33] Many parents worry too much about doing the right thing at any given moment, but it is less that a *particular* moment makes the difference than that the accumulation of moments creates a set of expectations for each of you, a pattern of expectations that gradually creates a relationship with its own personality.

Attachment Is More Than Protection

During the most active attachment period, the primary caregiver goes from being primarily a nurturer to being a socializer as well. Not only are you keeping track of a newly mobile crawler or toddler, but you also now have to start saying "no." And this responsibility doesn't really change significantly until your child leaves home. The keeping track takes different forms as your child matures, and saying no is often harder because it leads to arguments and sometimes the need for limits and consequences, which in turn feel like threats to your connection. Each being in a different body and at a different point in development is likely to want or need something different from a given moment of authority. If your 10-year-old calls you from camp because she's homesick, you can respond to her need for connection without hopping in the car to bring her home, while a screaming newborn needs prompt attention.

Samantha's text is really just a 21st-century way of turning around to see if you're still there and to find out what's okay for her to do. Because you have developed an intimate relationship over time, built on the foundation of attachment, her dependence on you for regulation makes her sensitive to the way you respond to her. Developmental transitions can be so stressful because your child's increasing autonomy and competence as she develops necessarily change how you interact with each other. Ongoing physical, emotional, and social development requires you to stretch and adjust the nature of your natural parental authority and the way you express it.

When Michael says, "you are always so mean," of course you are not, and of course he doesn't really think so. But that's what he feels, right then, and he wants you to know it. Such an accusation can trigger your sensitivity about whether or not you have "done the right thing." If you fight back with a verbal snarl or scolding, the stress of the moment may accumulate for both of you. But being "mean" for a 5-year-old, or a 13-year-old, can simply mean you are in fact doing your job, being the grownup, keeping family life moving from meal to meal, chore to chore. The particular issues change over time, but the essential relationship and the challenges it presents are steady: Whatever the age of your child, whatever the dilemma of the moment, you still ask yourself questions such as, "What does she think and feel? What do I think and feel? Is this normal? What does she need from me? What is my responsibility in this situation? How involved should I be?"

Even parents of grown children surprise themselves with the lasting feelings of responsibility they have, long after their children are adults. Many a conflict between older children and their parents emerges from some well-meaning but inappropriate effort by parents to take care of the "children" or to tell them what to do. Habits of involvement die hard—for both parties. And economic realities often affect how independent young adults can be, even in a culture like ours that values autonomy. Many contemporary parents find themselves with an adult offspring living at home, or with an adult son or daughter more financially dependent on them than either would wish, which invites authority when it otherwise might not be appropriate.[34]

Although I cannot tell you exactly what to do with Michael or Samantha, a sleepless infant or a late-sleeping adolescent, one way of thinking about authority is to put yourself in your child's shoes: However sassy and know-it-all she may seem to be, however resistant to your rules and requirements, she almost certainly still feels very dependent on you and on your care—including the limits you set. One 15-year-old said to her mother in my office, "You're my mother! *Of course* I have to do what you say," notwithstanding her apparent efforts to do everything but. She almost begged her mother to be more confident in her authority.

Emotional Regulation and Attachment Style

Although the most visible and intuitive function of the attachment system is to keep the young child safe, attachment theorists argue that attachment has other crucial relational functions.[35] With increased attention to the attachment system in parenting literature, you may worry about whether you are fostering attachment with your child. Like most of what is important to the parent-child relationship, it is the *patterns* of responsiveness and its ongoing quality more than any one incident that shapes what Bowlby called the child's "internal working model" of her relationship with her attachment figure. In other words, she learns how much she can rely on the primary caregiving adult's responsiveness or "availability," a set of expectations that would be continuously updated by ongoing experience. So if you have a terrible flu and must turn over all care of your infant to someone else, it's okay: She may grow anxious and wary during that time but will readjust once you are back to a normal routine.

The idea that a child develops and adapts to a sense of who you are together fits well with research about perception as a highly active process of *prediction*. Every brain, the infant's as much as the adolescent's, generates expectations from experience and uses them to make predictions. If an infant cries or whines, and then sees, hears, or feels a caregiver's face, voice, or body, the nature of that response gives you a little more information about the world and about your relationship with this caregiver. This also fits well with the idea of natural authority. When parents hesitate to scold or somehow limit a child for fear of crying or pushback, they forget that children's dependence on parents can accommodate limits and even anger. This is true, as long as they can trust that they can also rely on their connection with you and your recognition of their needs and their perspective. *(See Chapter Six.)*

Bowlby's first collaborator, Mary Ainsworth, developed the research paradigm of the *strange situation* from research with infants and mothers in Baltimore and Uganda. In these experiments, babies of about one year are separated briefly from their mothers and then reunited. Their behavior on reunion is coded according to the quality of their responsiveness to their mothers to assess, in effect, their internal working model of the relationship as secure, avoidant, or insecure.[36] Many researchers and clinicians attest to the importance of the attachment style of both parties in the ongoing parent-child relationship and its durability, although the claim of universality is not without its critics.[37]

In the everyday rhythms of family life, it is less important to focus on your attachment style than to understand the importance of responsiveness. Your newborn cries to communicate that she needs you, and you pick her up to show that you have heard.[38] Each time that you respond, you add to your trustworthiness as a caregiver, as a source of security and regulation. As your infant matures and your relationship develops, the tricky part is to know how and how much you should respond. Because every parent-child pair is different, I can't give you the answer you want. But by scrutinizing interactions of mothers and infants slowed down to $1/12$ of a second, researchers have learned, as did Goldilocks, that a moderate response is best.[39] As she grows older, her cries or words or behavior communicate in more nuanced ways, and you respond accordingly.

The Natural Authority of Touch

The very first way one relates to a newborn is through touch, the sense that is earliest to develop and perhaps the least noticed, despite its elaborate and acute sensitivity and its eventual nine-pound, 18-square-foot area of skin. Sometimes called an external nervous system, the skin can sense general indirect effects like heat and cold as well as a variety of highly specific sensations through sensory neurons each dedicated to different kinds of stimuli. From the very beginning, the skin and the sense of touch have far more influence on our daily experience than we are conscious of, especially in relation to others. Every child development text includes the devastating photos of infants in Romanian orphanages that show the price paid by touch deprivation.[40] A roomful of young children who had little or no consistent interaction with adults lay curled up in their cribs or rocked back and forth. This is a measurable example of epigenetics, in which the nurturing behavior of human caregivers helps shape developmental outcomes, including changes in the structure and function of the brain and even brain shrinkage.

So important is touch to the health and regulation of a newborn that skin-to-skin contact is encouraged even for medically fragile premature babies hooked up to machines; some newborn intensive care units (NICUSs) require nurses to be trained in touch protocols. In fact, touch may make a difference in their developmental outcomes.[41] Benefits of skin-to-skin contact for infants are legion, from better sleep cycles to fewer infections, especially for preemies in places where incubators are few. This practice has improved the outcomes for premature babies, including a decrease in the likelihood that impoverished mothers will abandon their babies. Studies have shown the positive effects lasting as long as 10 years.[42]

Being held in the big arms of an adult communicates security to an infant not only through pressure receptors in the skin but also through the positioning and muscle tone of the arms. This is because the infant can sense the holder through her skin, as well as her own response, through proprioception, which is one's unconscious perception of one's movement and spatial orientation, coming from within the body itself. I recall the awkwardness of one new father as he held his firstborn with his arms stiffly stretched out in front of him. It can take some practice for a new parent to relax into what can feel like a huge responsibility of holding something so fragile, and the way you hold him, like so much of what you do with your body, does indeed send a nonverbal message. But there is a payoff for you too: Touch stimulates the production of oxytocin, adding to your sense of well-being.[43] Touch is a crucial source of natural authority.

Your more mature brain, then, is a bit like a thermostat for your infant: Invisible neurochemical signals, along with your touch and your voice, continue to help to stabilize and nourish the developing brain and nervous system of the infant. *(See Chapter Nine.)* Even in the Efe culture, in the Democratic Republic of the Congo, where a child may have up to 14 regular caretakers before four months, children still develop a particular attachment to their mothers, perhaps, it is thought, because they always sleep with them—a time when their nervous systems can be in sync.[44] The interaction between you and your infant enables him to in effect *borrow* your nervous system for the regulation of his own immature one. In the period before the activation of the attachment system, the infant, as small and helpless as he is, has the power to make the big people, the big objects, in his life worry about his well-being. Your natural authority is expressed in the reassurance of your touch not only at birth but throughout childhood, especially at times when talking may be difficult.

And touch is not just hugs and caresses. When we arrive to visit our grandchildren, the most likely greeting my husband gets is "I want to rufflehouse!" The episodes of shrieking and rough-and-tumble wrestling can go on for a half hour or more. Given its ability to give joy to all involved, and to require full-body involvement, it is a good recipe for social glue. Hugs, grabbing a kid to lift him up, tickling, and rolling around on the floor are overlooked ways to relieve tension, hurt, and even anger with many children—boys and girls—although some children may be too easily overexcited by it.[45]

Separations

Because attachment is at its core the mechanism for the fundamental human need for connection, the ordinary separations of growing up—going to sleep, staying with a babysitter, transitioning to preschool or daycare and then kindergarten, college, and adulthood itself—give parents sometimes very emotional opportunities for authority.

Bedtime is usually the first frontier, for parents and infants alike, and the issue never entirely goes away. Most children need parents' help making the transitions to sleep, because the stimulation of being awake—light, toys, and grownup attention—competes with the grumpiness of fatigue, especially weeknights when there might be two parents coming home from work. Recent research on interoception—that is, the communication to your brain of your body's sensations—suggests that it might make a difference for parents to not be hungry and fatigued themselves when embarking on the bedtime routine, as they are likely to be more vulnerable to a child's pleas. You have to be able to say with confident authority, "You will be okay without me. I will come back" or "I will be here when you wake up" when your child is clinging to you and screaming, "Don't leave, Mommy! Don't leave! I don't want you to leave," at the door of the daycare center or her own bedroom. How you handle these separations communicates one of the most important messages of growing up: Attachment may be the biological Velcro keeping humans connected, but separations (whether at kindergarten or college) sometimes feel more like ripping off a super-strength Band-Aid. Doing it slowly doesn't necessarily make it less painful.

Even now, when most children have been with caretakers other than their parents long before preschool, many parents and children feel shaky about big separation milestones. Many parents and teachers would advise you to walk away: "He'll stop crying as soon as you're out of sight. Tell him you love him and you'll be back to pick him up." His attachment antennae, as it were, will probably calm down once you are gone and someone else is paying attention to him, comforting him, or distracting him. You may choose, if the school permits it, to ask if you can stay and make the separation more gradual. But if you do, you are implicitly communicating something about the kind of relationship you want to have with your child: perhaps that you want to feel sure that he is secure about your leaving, that you believe that it is wrong to leave him crying, or simply that you can't tolerate it.

You may be anxious about separating or simply be anxious about the experience your child is about to have. You may communicate that anxiety to your child by expressing too much worry ("Are you sure you're going to be okay?"), which can increase insecurity, or too much reassurance ("Don't worry, you'll be all right"), which can be dismissive. You may also communicate it nonverbally with a tense body, a shaking hand, or tears in your eyes. It takes authority to separate, authority to say, "Even if this is hard for me and hard for you, it's part of growing up"—whether kindergarten, a new school in a new town, or college. Those are moments when you remind your child, and yourself, of how much you love them—and that it doesn't mean you have to be together. But whether you are anxious or not, what is often most difficult for parents is a child whose peers seem to have integrated the need for separation but who himself remains anxious.

Periods of separation become more and more tolerable for most parents and children over time. This process will happen naturally as your child becomes more able to regulate herself, and less dependent on you, and as you become more confident about her increasing ability. Different thresholds of tolerance for separation and in beliefs about separation and risk-taking in general are often a point of contention between adults who are co-parents. You and your co-parent may habitually refer to your child being clingy or having trouble separating, and surely some children do have more difficulty. But like the proverbial canary in the coal mine, a child's behavior around separation (or sleep, or going to school) may not be about that at all, but his way of expressing and participating in the conflict he senses.[46]

Paradoxically, the 21st-century technology of cell phones, video chats, and social media sometimes make separation more difficult. You and your child may be able to stay so connected at all times that it is even more of a shock for your child to function independently or for parents to let go. Fourteen years out of preschool, both children and parents often find it difficult to figure out how far from home a child should go for college. In other words, the essence of the relationship doesn't change, but the way the balance of dependence and responsibility is acted out does.

Chapter Three

Habitat:
How You Live

C himps build nests in trees every night; birds build them to lay eggs and raise their young. In the animal kingdom, myriad ways of keeping infants of all species safe have evolved. Rabbit burrows, beaver lodges, and caves: Every animal needs a home base in which to rear young and from which to launch them into the rough ways of the world. Wherever human parents land becomes home for their offspring and for the relationships with which the child grows up. This basic decision is, along with keeping your child physically safe, your most primary act of authority. It springs directly from the very fact of becoming a parent. We use the metaphor of nest freely at both ends of the parenting continuum: The nesting new parents fix up a nursery, and older parents face an empty nest when their children have grown up. But what about the years in between, when the "chicks" are still *in* their nests?

Human Variety

Picture this: A one-room hut made of palm leaves, sitting directly on the sandy beach of an island, a few yards from the water. There are no cars on the island and no animals that treat humans as prey. Children roam freely from this hut to others nearby, occupied primarily by relatives. The main work of the men is fishing; the women grow small gardens, tend pigs and chickens, and take care of children. There is a brand-new one-room schoolhouse, but not all children can afford to buy the uniforms required to attend. The average wages are the equivalent of one dollar a day.

And now picture this: A three-bedroom ranch house on a suburban street without sidewalks, set back from the street with a generous front lawn, a large swing set in the backyard, and a two-car garage. School-age children take a yellow school bus to school. Almost all of the fathers and mothers drive off to work in the morning. Parents drop most of the children at daycare or preschool; a few children spend the day at home with a homeschooling parent or a parent who is perhaps involved in volunteer work or telecommuting, in addition to taking care of the house and kids.

Both of these are human environments. The first is a rough description of the way many millions of human beings live, whether on an island or in a rural village, with many millions more in crowded city neighborhoods where multiple members of a family crowd in together in a small apartment or shack. The second represents suburban middle-class America, an environment idealized in movies and on television. These two human environments could hardly be more different. And yet, the human animal is so enormously adaptable that we can survive, albeit with varying degrees of health and well-being, in both.

Although your options about where to live may be limited, unless you are a refugee or constrained by other forces beyond your control, if you are reading this book, you more than likely have made *some* choice about where and how to live, probably without associating this decision with your natural authority. But even if you moved for economic reasons, you decided it was worth it for you and your family. In other words, by choosing your hometown or a new place far from family or friends, city or country, north or south, east or west, you have begun to activate values and beliefs you have about family life and your children's development. Many other decisions are made on this foundation of authority.

Ecology of Family Life

The concept of habitat comes from ecology, the field of study that has to do with the relation of organisms with each other and their adaptation to their surroundings. I use habitat to include both the physical home (the nest, as it were) as well as the other places children go, or their range. They may move about by foot, bicycle, car, or public transportation, or by means of technology—not only the computer but, at younger and younger ages, the cell phone and other mobile devices.

In every animal's habitat, there are a set of conditions including climate, plant life, availability of water, and the other animals with which it is shared, some of which may compete for the same food and some of which are predators. We can apply the same concept to humans, but with the difference that if we humans can find a way to support ourselves, we can choose where to live. We can choose the conditions that affect us, beginning with climate and geography, but including others that have as much (maybe more) to do with the human world and human history as with the natural world and natural history: city, country, or suburb, apartment or house, busy street or quiet. Although economic and other factors can severely limit how much choice parents have over where they live and where their children go to school, it is parents who use their natural authority to either choose or adapt to these conditions for themselves and their children, shaping a world in which family life takes place.

In Robert McCloskey's classic picture book *Make Way for Ducklings*, when Mrs. Mallard is ready to lay her eggs, she and Mr. Mallard fly over Boston looking for a suitable place to build their nest. They reject various places—one doesn't have enough green grass, another has too many cars—revealing both the values they have about child-rearing and the responsibility they feel toward their future children. They behave in much the same way any couple or individual parent does when contemplating parenthood. They begin to make decisions about what kind of *habitat* will best fit the kind of family life they want to create for their children.[47]

Like ducks, parents have to decide where to "build" their family nest. For many parents, there is little leeway economically: You might not be able to afford to buy a house or apartment, or you might have to rent or buy in a neighborhood without the kind of public school you would hope for. And yet, even within your own particular constraints, you will make decisions about where to locate your nest. It might not matter to one family whether they are on a busy street as long as there is a good public school. Another family might plan to use a private or religious school, so the geographic location will not be as important. Some families seek diversity; others seek a neighborhood dominated by their own ethnicity or religious group. One family might feel strongly that they want only grandparents as additional caretakers and so want to live close to them. These expressions of their natural authority are what we might call *habitat values*, and they underlie all other choices parents make.

The mallards' "starter nest" is on the Charles River: It's quiet, protected, and near water, but apparently wanting a more urban setting, they move to an island in Boston's Public Garden. If you know the book, you will surely remember the drawing of the wild boys on bicycles zooming by, hair and shirttails flying behind them, as the ducks are nest-hunting. "This is no place for ducklings!" one exclaims to the other. But then, just as you might do, they explore the neighborhood a little more: Is it safe here? What opportunities would there be for our children? Are there other kids on the block? How are the schools?

Relating to the Wider World

Habitat includes the routines, organization, rhythm, expectations, and even the feelings that characterize daily life, with sources in the values and experience of each parent and in the wider community, culture, and historical events. Parents' natural authority not only extends to the physical shape and nature of the habitat they create and maintain for their children, but also to the rules and habits of child-rearing, the routines, expectations, and the degree to which children are exposed to religion, the media, and popular culture. Parents bring home their attitudes, their stories, and their stress from this larger world—the pressures of relationships and schedules of work, the anxiety of the economy, the worries about paying for college. All of this is simply what children experience, mostly without knowing why. "You never get home before dark!" a child complains, with little ability to appreciate a parent's commute. "You're always grumpy when you get home. I like you better on the weekend." "Why do we always have to have macaroni and cheese? I want to go to McDonald's!"

A child participates directly in a variety of environments: home, school, sports, church, health services, and stores. She participates indirectly in her parents' workplaces, or in politics, culture, and the media, through the effects of her parents' participation: Do both parents work? What are their schedules? Are they home together? What do they talk about? Children with older siblings have another level of exposure to the larger socio-cultural world through direct interaction with their brothers or sisters or through their attendance at siblings' sporting or other events. [48] With or without a co-parent, you are the coordinator of those movements and this involvement, making decisions on the basis of values and safety.

In our new technology era, you allow or make possible your child's virtual habitat as well, extending almost immeasurably, both directly and indirectly. What media is he exposed to? What do his parents and his siblings watch on television or their devices?

Can he watch TV or movies at will? At what age? Do you monitor his Web presence? What apps is he allowed to use? What games is he allowed to play? Even as recently as five years ago, few could imagine the immense and ubiquitous impact of the media and technology on virtually every aspect of 21st-century family life, how the reach of technology would affect "where" kids could go and with whom they could interact directly; nor could many of us have imagined the degree to which the passive medium of television would give way to the intensely interactive and even addictive world of the Internet and social media.

From the wheel to the iPad, each generation experiences the profound effects of new inventions on family life, some of which not only extend children's habitat range but also drastically alter the nature and frequency of human communication.* Digital technology is not so much a new invention as a new reality, changing the way we use old inventions and creating new uses at an overwhelming pace. Surely being a parent *must* be different than ever before. Don't we need some new guidelines? New rules? New strategies?

Now that phones have become transformed into mini mobile computers, many children participate in social media, and most own or can access a computer or iPad as well. These numbers have exploded since I began this book and will continue to do so.[49] Increasingly, the lives of children are taking place in digital realms and cyberspace rather than in the backyard or the family room or the movie theater.

The core reality of being a parent is a relationship, and the way you interact—or don't interact—with your child, with or without the help or hindrance of technology, shapes that relationship. There has been no change in the human need for connection, but the forms of connection may have implications for

---

* Indeed, some researchers suspect that our very ways of thinking may be affected by the combination of cell phones, email, and the Internet. I confess to being less likely to plan ahead, because with the advent of cellphones in everyone's pocket, I don't have to. Today's kids never did.

both the everyday and the long-term aspects of your relationship. The question, then, is not what rules should I make about cell phones, iPads, and the Internet. The question is, how do I think about technology in the context of this relationship, in this family, given our values about time together, safety, friends, homework, and all the other things that go into family life and growing up, including, especially, the social pressures of the community in which we live? *(See also pp 71-75.)*

Developmental Niche

Research by social scientists in many fields suggests that children who grow up in different habitats, whether physical, cultural, or familial, do indeed develop differently.[50] The concept of "developmental niche" attempts to capture both the changing and interacting situations and arrangements human families and communities generate to care for their children, and the ways children interact with and affect them, even at a very young age. A child's developmental niche includes not only the physical and social settings, customs, and practices of child-rearing, but also the parents themselves, their beliefs about children and development, and their own psychology and experience. As the child grows, parents' beliefs, child-rearing practices, and social settings interact with each other. For example, if parents are religious, they may require children's attendance at religious services, bringing children into contact with other adults who are not their relatives. Those adults may have beliefs about child-rearing that affect the parents' behavior at home.

Moreover, central to the discussion in this book, each child has a different relationship with each parent, shaped at once by gender, temperament, and family position and by the parents' behavior, beliefs, and the habitat of the household. I sometimes think of this as the personality of the relationship itself. Differences in class and race and region also help shape the personality of the relationship.[51]

The developmental niche is so particular that it varies even within the same family. *(See Chapter Seven.)* An oldest sibling is an only child until the next child is born; in a two-parent family, a younger sibling comes into a world with at least three other people older than he is, and the parents have already experienced parenthood for at least nine months. Just ask any older sibling whether he thinks the rules are the same for his little sister as they were for him. Changes besides the family makeup and parents' experience affect the developmental niche or habitat too, from moves across the country to historical events. If a family moves from an urban community to a suburban one, for example, teenagers will learn to drive sooner, with relevant family rules. The terror of 9/11 led many New York families to give their children cell phones.

While large sociocultural forces affect the developmental niche, so too do the age, gender, temperament, and other specific characteristics of the child. My own niche was greatly shaped by being the third of nine children and temperamentally suited to being a mother's helper, a role taken on in many cultures by children as young as three, and by older brothers as well as sisters.[52] The vast range of human arrangements for children's lives is worth remembering when you feel inadequate to the pressures of your own situation. Children can thrive in many different kinds of nests and with many different kinds of caregivers.

Varieties of Habitat Equals Varieties of Authority

Because of the variable conditions of human habitats, human parents' authority varies as well. In *The Evolution of Childhood*, doctor and anthropologist Melvin Konner reviews how the expectations and treatment of children evolved along with human habitats from their hunter-gatherer origins to contemporary modern society. In hunter-gatherer societies, of which a number still exist, there is more indulgence, more holding, and physical proximity, and less emphasis on obedience and responsibility than in agricultural societies. There are interesting examples of exceptions when a child is injured and takes over a sedentary domestic task, or when an older orphaned sibling takes over the care of a younger sibling. With the rise of agriculture, parents needed children to participate. Konner cites a corresponding reduction in play and increase in chores. In modern society, it is schooling that has mostly replaced play. Chores are no longer assumed in contemporary society, and play is not even necessarily the focus of early childhood education.[53]

Countless families in the US and across the globe have been forced into homelessness, migration, or refugee status by economic, political, social, and even climate-caused pressures. In addition to the intense stress for such parents and children of not knowing whether they will have a home again, much less school, and a stable way of life, add loss of habitat. The loss of a familiar physical space and routines of daily life is compounded by dependence on relatives or sharing space with strangers. Human encounters are multiplied, and intimate interactions are exposed to public scrutiny.

What is required to keep your children safe, above all, depends significantly on both physical and social aspects of your habitat: Are there sidewalks or no sidewalks? Are you new in town or do you know everyone from your own childhood? Do you leave your door open or worry about intruders? Do you allow your child to walk to school or take a bus? Imagine the differences in growing up in various American human habitats, ones that come easily to mind. Consider the daily life of a 12-year-old boy in a housing project, a wealthy suburb, or on a family farm. Now add a region: a housing project in Chicago or St. Louis, a suburb of Dallas or New York, a farm in Louisiana or Minnesota. And finally add a family structure: a single mom with several children, an only child of two parents with a stay-at-home dad and commuting chief executive mother, an intergenerational immigrant family living in a small apartment *(See below, Outside the Nest: Range)*.

Even if you know very little about those kinds of living situations or those cities or states, you can imagine that puberty brings not only biological pressures but significant differences in the growing-up experiences of those children in those diverse environments.[54] With different expectations and different risks come different needs for authority. We could generate literally limitless possibilities, not only in the United States but also across the world, including the explosive growth of social media. But every mobile device is in the hands of someone who herself is in a particular school and neighborhood; every television is in a particular living room or bedroom.

Inside the Nest

Any modern home is full of dangers for a mobile infant or toddler: electrical outlets, hot stoves and grills, scissors and knives, paint, glue, cleaning products, stairs, medicines, windows, and more. Your responsibility for your children's safety requires you to decide how to handle these dangers, whether or not to use a playpen to keep your child safe, for example, or to put gates on the stairs, and later, at what age to allow him to turn on appliances. It is a big step to start saying "no" to a suddenly mobile infant, and a big realization 17 years or more later when, your child off to college, work, or marriage, you realize that you can no longer protect him or expect him to take your advice. At that point, you are likely to know very little of his day-to-day life, and maybe even sooner because of where the Internet allows him to go. Growing up is a long process of increasing autonomy for your child and decreasing responsibility for you. There is no set rule, and both children and parents vary: A safe nest can take many forms.

Once settled into a house or apartment, you must make a great many other decisions, many of which may not even feel like decisions. Every decision about technology, for example, has implications about which you are asserting your authority. The first is the cost, and the second is access. Do you have a television and a computer? Is there more than one? Where are they? Do you have cable? What kind of access does your child have to the Internet? Do you monitor his use? *(See Chapter Four.)*

With these decisions made, you answer a number of questions, implicitly or explicitly. When is the TV on? Who decides on the programs? If you have more than one child, is there a difference in who watches what? Will you watch with them? Perhaps you and your co-parent disagree about the answers. How do you decide? Television has been around so long that it may not even occur to you to limit it; it is almost part of the woodwork. Screen time (including television and the Internet) for even very young children continues to increase. But it is not neutral: Language, sex and violence, commercials, what people wear and eat and talk about bring different versions of the world into your household. The Internet and mobile phones and tablets also bring the world to you, and we will discuss them further when we talk about *outside* the nest.

By the time your child is school age, she has homework to do, social life to navigate, perhaps a job, games, or rehearsals to go to. You may be in the living room or family room together, or even in the car, but you are not always actually together: You have an active life on email or Facebook; you have work to do in the evening; you really like playing video games, listening to music on your phone to unwind, or texting with friends. And so does she! It is very possible that there is not only more than one television in the household, but also more than one device on which to access the Internet. Each of you is drawn away from the family room and into cyberspace. Snuggling together in front of a sitcom starts to look quaintly intimate. It is a rare household in the 21st century that does not encompass an active digital realm of activity, from television to mobile devices.

The promise of the new technology is the power of connection, but it instead often separates us from each other. We connect, but less and less with the people who are physically next to us. Perhaps we need to remember that the gadgets with which we live are tools that can be dangerous to human needs and relationships at every stage, and thus they require more intentional and careful use than we usually give them. If you use a "smart speaker," there is, in effect, a new being with whom you and your children interact and a new aspect of behavior to monitor in yourself and your child.[55] *(See section below, Digital Development, Digital Habitat.)*

Other decisions about your household's organization require your authority. If children share a bedroom they will have to work out, probably with your help, what the rules are about whether toys, clothes, and gadgets must be shared or can be off-limits. Similar questions arise when children have their own rooms: Are you supposed to knock? Are you allowed to go in without permission? These are questions about boundaries, a fundamental aspect of family (and later) life, and the cause for many misunderstandings, hurt, and conflict. "She took my pink sweater without asking!" "You can't come in here when I have a friend over."

The luxury of separate rooms and separate mobile devices may eliminate some aspects of conflict but can increase others: They accustom children to a certain kind of privacy and control that may keep them from learning important lessons about getting along with others. What you and your co-parent believe about sharing space, toys, clothes, friends, and time can be communicated implicitly and explicitly, consciously or unconsciously. This, too, is parental authority.

Habitat and Authority

Many of the particulars about your family life and relationships and the authority you need to assert to keep your kids safe depend on the environment in which you live, on your habitat. Studies of present-day hunter-gatherer societies have found that such societies demand little of children and are very indulgent with them. The toddlers in the Kaluli tribe of Papua New Guinea, for example, are allowed to handle machetes without direct adult supervision, but under the watchful eyes of nearby adults.[56] Knives and machetes are integral to the livelihood of this tribe. It is tempting to idealize such anecdotes and wonder if we should all behave that way. In our own world there are tasks, activities, demands, and risks that determine our job as protectors and caretakers. The adults in Papua New Guinea might be more anxious about sources of danger *we* take for granted, ones involving electrical outlets, lamps, and hot stoves. But once a child is mobile, we figure out some way to keep them safe.

In their classic cross-cultural study of childhood, *Children of Different Worlds*, anthropologists Beatrice Whiting and Carolyn Pope Edwards conceptualized development in relation to the child's competence and setting. The lap child, from birth to about one year, is constantly held or closely monitored by parents, siblings, and other relatives. The knee child, from 2 to 3 years old, is still closely watched, but having learned to walk, is able to explore the household environment and handle everyday objects. Like the toddlers in Papua New Guinea with machetes, many toddlers in 21st-century America are given their parents' smart phones on which to watch cartoons or play games. The knee child also begins to have some choice in her interactions with others. Her choice of others depends, of course, on the nature of her family, the nature of her living situation, and the nature of her habitat.[57]

The yard child, from 4 to 5, has even more freedom to explore areas considered safe by her caretakers, and more freedom to play with children outside of her family. Finally, the world expands exponentially for the community child, aged 6 to 10, who begins school, and in some settings, although less and less in contemporary American society, is allowed to travel short distances to do tasks or errands. In the structured habitat of most of America's "community children," with few parents at home in the afternoon, children are enrolled in after-school programs or have play dates arranged by their parents rather than finding playmates next door.[58] *(See section below, Outside the Nest.)* In today's digital world, the range to which children have access via technology could also be characterized by the developmental niche: the texting child, the Instagram child, or the Fortnite or Snapchat child.

But whether the issue is technology, chores, homework, exercise, drinking, or contraception, it is important for you to think hard about what you value, what you believe your child needs, what you want your child to learn for the future, and what you want her to remember about her childhood, topics which we will take up in more detail in Chapter Four. Such intentionality does not come easily. Like Dorothy and the magic ruby slippers that gave her the means to go home all along, as the grownup, you already have the authority that comes with your responsibility. You may feel that you don't have the time or that somehow it will take care of itself. But actively or passively you create a habitat for your family, a habitat that begins with the relationship itself, and includes values, expectations, and opportunities. Your child develops her sense of self and her sense of fundamental security from the accumulation of daily interactions she has in the world, beginning with you. She learns about the world from the world she experiences, but the habitat also requires limits.

As your child gets older, you and your spouse, together or apart, may find you differ in your values or habits of care. *(See Chapter Five.)* One night, when one of my sons was about 15, he had a friend sleep over. After I'd gone to bed, but while my husband was still up, they walked to a neighbor's house to watch a movie. The next morning, when I asked my husband what time they had come home, he said, "I'm not sure." I freaked out. "You're not sure? Do you know if he *is* home?" He wasn't. A phone call assured us that they had fallen asleep at the neighbor's, after my son decided it was too late to call us. But he added, "I was surprised that you hadn't called. Doesn't anybody care where I am?" From his experience growing up in our family habitat, he expected us to keep tabs on him if he didn't keep his curfew. That was the good news. The bad news was that we had not communicated well with him or with each other.

Who Takes Care of the Nest?

Any nest must be maintained, although the degree of care will vary greatly according to the needs, or in the case of humans, the values of its inhabitants. An animal burrow or bird's nest is usually a simple affair, made of mud, straw, sticks, and feathers taken from the surrounding area. For humans, it is a different story: Even contemporary nomads in remote Kashmir travel with blankets, skins, containers, and gear of all kinds. In an in-depth study of family life that we will discuss in more detail in the next chapter, how to manage the family stuff was a significant source of conflict and distress.[59] Whether you live in a small space or a large one, and whether you live sparsely or awash with everyday clutter, someone has to do the dishes, do the laundry, sweep or vacuum or mop the floor—that is, keep the nest more or less clean.

Many parents wonder whether or not they should give their children chores: Don't they have enough to do with homework? Isn't childhood supposed to be a time of freedom? Perhaps they would rather prioritize homework and extracurricular activities, or they don't want to deal with resistance from their children. There has been a shift from expectations that children contribute to the running of the household to expectations that children work for their own academic, athletic, and even economic benefit, especially in middle- and upper-middle-class families.[60] Plenty of families have no choice; they can't afford outside help, and their work, commute, and childcare schedules are such that children must pitch in. Yet many a parent complains about how little her child is asked to do and how much she complains about doing it, apparently perceiving something lacking in their children, rather than in their authority. Who's in charge of this habitat anyway?

Another reason parents hesitate is doubt about their children's ability to do the job. When children *do* have chores, the greatest chore still belongs to you, the parent: making sure that things get done and get done properly. Who contributes to keeping the household clean is a matter of family culture—what you and your co-parent care about—and parental authority.

A child acquires cultural knowledge through practical activities with more experienced others. Any more competent or experienced partner provides *scaffolding* for the completion of tasks or activities beyond the child's current level of competence, including household chores. When the child is close to being able to perform a task but may still need help in organizing it, staying motivated, and avoiding frustration, the parent or any other more experienced person brings the child along until he can do it himself, perhaps in several sessions of receiving less and less help.[61]

From riding a bike to learning how to load the dishwasher, everyday family life is replete with such incidents. The expertise of adulthood is in itself a form of authority in the habitat. Loading the dishwasher is a great example. What more mundane task is there? There is probably no one day when you give the dishwasher lesson, but you show and explain each step of the task as the child increases in care and judgment. Along the way there will be loads with not enough dishes, too many dishes, not enough soap, or too much soap. Your scaffolding includes the implicit message of authority: "This is how it's done in this household" and "This is how I expect you to do it." And you respond with authority if a) he doesn't do it at all, b) he does it wrong, c) he complains about doing it, d) he says he can't do it, e) he breaks a glass.[62]

Cooperation

This stuff isn't easy. Modern family life is rushed and hectic; everybody has too much to do. You probably find that it is easier to take out the garbage yourself than to get your child to do it, even if it is an assigned chore. Just remember that when you do that, you send a number of messages, which might include, "I'm overworked and tired too, but I'll do it" or "This isn't as important as whatever else you're doing" or "I'm afraid you'll think I'm nagging or will talk back if I insist." One implicit message is loud and clear if you do a chore that is assigned to one of your children: Something in this habitat, or something in your relationship, is out of kilter. If there is no particular consequence for children who do not do chores that are expected of them, then the parents have ceded some portion of their power and authority to the kids. Not only does this affect your daily family life, now and going forward, but it deprives your child of a number of lessons regarding how to manage time and how to accomplish tasks that must get done. A new, common-sense conceptualization of family chores has been proposed as "learning by observing and pitching in," encouraging collaboration, belonging, and responsibility by doing.

There is compelling evidence that a human disposition toward cooperation is evident in children as young as 18 months, a disposition that is further refined and specified by the particular conditions of their habitat. Toddlers spontaneously help strange adults who appear to be in trouble. There is similar evidence in chimps and some cross-cultural evidence as well. Young children are quick to recognize norms, e.g., "that's not how you are supposed to do that," along with demonstrating a willingness to show another person how something is supposed to be done. All of this is consistent with the work of others who argue that not only are humans cooperative in child-rearing and the procurement of food, but that it is part and parcel of our evolution as humans.[63]

When you throw your hands up at the apparent laziness or disobedience of the children who inhabit your household, consider your own practices. Not only is it likely that you have not expected chores of your children from toddlerhood, but like the parents observed in their own homes in a University of California, Los Angeles study, you may have put your directives for chores in the form of suggestions, requests, or appeals, accompanied by offers of rewards. *(See Chapter Ten.)* Perhaps more importantly, in the UCLA study, parents often gave up after several tries and did the task themselves.[64] If that's the pattern a child can expect, why should she interrupt what she's doing? You will do it anyway! Many parents are ambivalent about whether or not they should assert authority, so they negotiate instead. The structure of routine expectations, with routine consequences, can save both of you.

Parents: Teachers, Models, and Partners

Everyday interactions, chores among them, are "cultural lessons" that help children learn "what everyone knows."[65] Learning these lessons also takes place as a function of the familial context as well, i.e., not just the interactions a child is directly involved in but what she picks up day in, day out, listening and watching the interactions of others. Do people help each other? How loudly do people talk? Do people eat together? Is the TV on all the time? What happens when someone makes a mistake? Do men and women do the same things? The knowledge acquired through interactions with parents and other family members can encompass both what everyone knows in the wider culture and also what everyone knows *in this habitat.*

It is easy to underestimate the authority of the implicit and explicit expectations communicated through the organization of your household and your daily interactions with your children. Parents and children collaborate, at least implicitly, in their choice of activities, taking into account children's abilities and interests, as well as time, finances, and transportation, but parents are the guides in their children's participation, helping as necessary by structuring the necessary steps. When baking with children, for example, scaffolding is the way an adult might put a hand over a 2-year-old's hand as he puts in the sugar, give the measuring cup to a 5- or 6-year-old to pour in herself, and allow an 11-year-old to measure it and pour it in without help. Adult guidance is a form of authority, since for much of childhood, as our society is organized, a child does not choose his activities or companions without adult input and support.[66]

It is a commonplace of 21st-century discussions about parenthood to talk about "helicopter parents": the hovering, anxious people many parents seem to be. Many contemporary parents feel so uncomfortable asserting their authority, and yet paradoxically, they do more to arrange their young children's social lives than ever before, a significant example of authority. There is another paradox as well: In many families, both parents work long hours, often at more than one job, and continue to work on mobile devices of one sort or another at home. Guilt-ridden parents who fear rejection may abdicate much of their parental authority, seeking friendship with their children instead. But many parents hover over their children's every activity and piece of homework, both indulging them and pressuring them to succeed. The child gets contradictory messages: Am I supposed to be able to do my homework and manage life by myself, or am I supposed to wait for my parents' help? If my mom is my buddy, then why should I obey her? She might do it for me if I wait long enough.[67]

If you are always or even often present at your child's activities, or involved in his homework, he is less likely to feel able or inclined to do by himself the things you expect or ask him to do and in which you don't want or intend to be involved. Authority relies in part on acknowledgment of and respect for the generational and experiential boundaries between you and your children. There are some things that parents do and there are some things that children do. Children need and deserve your support and attention, but not every minute of the day and not for every task or chore or activity.[68]

Outside the Nest: Range

Peter Rabbit disobeyed his mother when he was outside the burrow. He not only got the fright of his life from Mr. MacGregor chasing him with a rake, but he also lost his coat and shoes and had to go to bed without supper. Like Peter, young children can and do try to leave the nest, and one of the steep learning curves of parenthood is adjusting to the need for constant vigilance regarding the whereabouts of young children, especially on the street or near a swimming pool or body of water—but really anywhere. There is an especially risky time when children seem to have developed some degree of judgment about what is safe but may stray further than they—or you—can handle.

As your child grows and changes, he has the capacity and interest to interact with and develop relationships with more people, and the ability to get to and *be* places by himself. What is his *range*? What are the parameters of his physical world beyond the safe nest you try to maintain for him? What is he allowed to do? Why or why not? Who decides? Are your decisions in sync with your neighbors and friends? How do you talk about it? You may not think about it this way, but even a lap child has parameters: Who is allowed or encouraged to hold him? For how long? Do you leave him with other family members? Neighbors? A nanny? A 13-year-old babysitter? How do you decide when he is ready to do something new? How much scaffolding does he need? *(See Chapter Four.)*

It is the question of where kids can go, how they get there, and how much contact they are required to be in with the headquarters of home that puts parents' authority to its severest test. Other issues, like rudeness, disobedience about chores, or avoidance of homework, don't rise to the same level because safety is not being threatened. Safety is also the area where parents may be most anxious and may have the most conflict with each other—sometimes (but not always) related to the gender of the parent or of the child, and sometimes related to the parents' own experience. There have been a number of stories in the last few years about parents who were reported because their children were deemed to be too young for the independence the parents had given them, part of a cultural conversation about "free-range parenting."[69] A growing number of parents are resisting the helicopter culture of the last twenty years and, in effect, using their natural authority as parents to make decisions based on their values and their judgment about their child's competence and confidence, rather than adhering to current conventions and norms.

I have had many a parent confess that because they kept a lot from their parents, they fully assume that their children must be keeping things from them. And for the child's developing autonomy, that may not be such a bad thing. At the same time, if you keep your head too much in the sand, your child's safety can be threatened—drugs, pregnancy, venereal disease, cyberbullying. There is plenty to worry about.

Digital Development, Digital Habitat

Technology straddles the inside and the outside of the nest: How much screen time is allowed inside the nest? Where are your children allowed to go outside via the Web and social media? Technology also means different things for children of different ages and with different personalities and levels of competence and maturity. Limits are adapted to the degree of independence or responsibility that you deem appropriate to your child's age and capacity for judgment, no matter what the neighbors do. Different forms of technology have different implications and require different decisions: The connection afforded by a cell phone and email may make it harder for a child to separate, while access to the Internet may allow her to grow up too fast. The need for talking about limits, permissions, and the experience of the child away from you has never been greater. Yes, it is technology, but above all, you must come back to authority. If you don't want texting at the dinner table, forbid texting at the dinner table. And don't waver—take away the phone if you need to. You are the parents; you make the rules, and you enforce the rules. As it happens, kids are so dependent on their phones that it gives parents a powerful tool for setting limits.

One of modern Western parents' child-rearing decisions is whether—or, more likely, *when*—to give their child a cell phone or other mobile device. This involves not only decisions about parameters in relation to the Web, but also about who pays the cost of purchase and the monthly bills. Additionally, are there restrictions on using the phone? How does it interface with school work and life at school? Many parents argue that a phone is a safety measure. "She can always call me." "I'll always know where he is." What does this do to your relationship? Instead of relying on a child to go where he says he's going, a phone allows him to be a free agent, and your knowledge of his whereabouts depends either on your relationship and mutual trust or on location technology.

I am sure that you have thought about how these changes have affected your relationships with your children: the relief you feel at knowing that you can reach your child by text wherever he or she may be, the jokes you make with friends about trying to keep up with what your 10-year-old knows about the computer, the fact that texting is the new email and email the new snail mail, your fears about bullying on social media.[70] What else should parents think about? And how should they think about it?

Twenty-first-century technology has added a whole new dimension to the question of family habitats and their boundaries. The decades-old question of how much TV is now expanded to include all varieties of media and devices under the rubric of "screen time." The Internet is not a physical place, but it is still a place you can go, a place where you can meet people and do things; it almost immeasurably increases a child's potential range, and it is much harder to monitor than the neighborhood or the mall. As technology races ahead with video conference calls, smart speakers, and who knows what else, family habitats will continue to change.

Children may be more tech-savvy than their parents, but children's dependence means parents must make decisions about their children's range—on land and on the Internet—adding the necessity for conversations with your co-parent about your values and about the maturity and temperament of the child in question. Cell phones, iPads, and laptops extend the possibility of being connected elsewhere, for both of you. This doesn't mean that you must be focused on your infant or your child at all times, but it does mean that you should think about how your behavior may affect her and be intentional not only about her screen time, but your own. As you become accustomed to things that once seemed miraculous, never forget that while technology can be an aid to human connection, it is not a substitute for it, and in fact can be a barrier to it.

Social beings above all, all of us, young and old, have become used to being able to reach each other at all times, in all places. Because we *can* do it, we *do* do it, sometimes to the point of addiction and with little regard to where we are. It is easy to forget that all of us need not just digital contact but real, human interaction. When we video chat with our grandchildren in other cities, we joke about sharing a banana or being able to hold hands, but young children don't yet understand this, and their innocence about it should perhaps be cautionary for us. When we were video chatting with an 18-month-old grandchild a few years ago, he went to get a book for his grandfather to read to him, reinstated himself on his mother's lap, and stretched out his hand to the screen with the book in it. His mother told him that the book couldn't go through the computer. Perplexed, he got down again and walked around the table to look behind the computer. Of course, unlike in *The Wizard of Oz*, no one was there.

Friendship and Danger on the Web

Although the world has always been (and will always be) dangerous for children, the Internet expands both danger and temptation, and cell phones may create the illusion of safety. Now the importance of two parents working together (even if they live in different houses) comes in. It is your job—both of you—to help your children internalize principles of safety and judgment and to continue to help them adapt to new levels of competence and new technologies. You are his guides and his bosses in relation to the Internet just as you are in relation to curfews, drunk driving, and taking out the garbage. Technology dramatically changes the scope of his social world and how he accesses it, but it doesn't change the fact that he is just a kid and still dependent on you.

As the pull of peers and social networking starts to play tug-of-war with your authority, you begin to use the cell phone to stay connected, often under the rubric of safety. "I need to know where you are—that's why I'm texting you!" Did kids in fact get into more trouble before parents could call or text them anywhere, any time? Without a mobile device to stay in touch, parents had to trust more in their child's obedience to limits agreed upon ahead of time, and sometimes had to rely on other parents to verify their children's whereabouts.

Faster even than the spread of the flu, younger and younger children and older and older adults have joined the college kids who first embraced social networking. Being in the same social world, even online and even one with over a billion users, means you need to think about boundaries. In my office, young adults complain about their mothers wanting to "follow" them, and parents and kids alike want to know how to deal with the revelations they may have stumbled on in each other's social networking pages. Many young people choose Snapchat or Instagram Stories as a way to erase their social media activity. The answer to questions of technology still lies in your relationship, part of which is being conducted online: How much do you want to know about her? What do you want her to know about you? How do you want to find out what you know? How will you cope with her shutting you out?

Once the kids are old enough to be out of the house on their own, the effects of technology shift: There continues to be the need to set limits and keep kids safe, but suddenly you're the one who wants and needs more contact. Oddly enough, the risks to your relationship shift from allowing technology to come between you to allowing technology to keep you too involved. Does it help your child for you to remain so present in her life? Or do you do it for yourself? How and when will the separation finally occur, if at all?

In her book *Girls and Sex*, Peggy Orenstein makes the point that while there are very significant risks in the virtual world online, most of them are versions of risks parents have always had to consider but existing now in more exaggerated, virulent, and accessible form.[71] From predators with fake profiles to easy-to-access porn, from middle school sexting to videos secretly made and sent, the domain of sex and sexuality requires serious effort from parents in the realm of monitoring, discussions, and boundaries. But it is not just sex: Simply tallying likes on Instagram can heighten a child's anxiety. Again, these are different challenges requiring different sources of advice, but the essence of parenthood stays steady: You are the grownup; your child depends on your authority.

The influences of the family habitat you create and sustain are deep and wide, and the implications for your relationship, your child's development, and your authority are great indeed. The questions about technology are compelling ones; but keep connecting face-to-face at home or in the car, which is where your natural authority lies.

— Chapter Four —

What Matters?
Gaining Clarity About
Your Values and Beliefs

In the Broadway musical *Man of La Mancha*, the prostitute on whom Don Quixote has focused his affections is confused to the point of anger at the motives of this eccentric noble. She sings to him "Why do you do the things you do, why do you do these things?" It is not a simple question! In fact, it is the core question not only of the social sciences but also of much of everyday human conversation.[72] Why did he do that?

If you were to ask your child that question—and many of us do—she would almost certainly have no idea. She is being herself—whether a 3-year-old who spends two minutes creating a disaster area with paints and walks away, or a 10-year-old who loses her homework, again. Such miniature crises, and many much bigger ones, force you to make a judgment: What do you do now? You may get triggered to shout even as you know it won't help to overreact: Three-year-olds make messes; this 10-year-old often loses track of belongings. Should a 3-year-old be told to clean up the paints? Is she capable of that? Shouldn't you have known this would happen? Your frustration mounts. Or the lost homework: Is she old enough to tell the teacher herself? Should you write a note excusing her with a white lie? Does it matter?

Everyday Decisions, Everyday Assumptions

Each of us lives amid a tangle of influences, from the intimate pressures of working things out with or without a co-parent to those of extended families, cultural conventions, religious traditions, social media, or just plain gossip among parents at soccer practice or on Facebook. Having children changes you: Whatever your schedule of work and family time, your children's constant presence and changing needs force you to discover what is important to you. You make judgments. And in those judgments, you activate your natural authority, from the thoughtfully considered choices about schools and daycare to the offhand answers to questions like "Can I use my iPad now?" "Can I have seconds?" "Can I have a cookie?" "Can I stay up later?" "Can I take the car?" Your job as parent encompasses judgments about how involved you need to be, when to intervene, what to allow and what to prohibit, how to enforce rules, how to respond to violations, whether or not to punish, and how. From those choices, you develop habits of behavior you and your child both come to rely on.

You have natural authority because you are the grownup; the foundation of your authority is the home you create. But you also have a foundation of values or assumptions, some way that you decide what to do when confronted with all of the possible alternatives presented by virtually any trying moment of parenthood. And why does it matter? Embracing your natural authority is only part of the process: I am convinced that thinking about it and better understanding how it emerges and works itself out in your family will strengthen it. Why? Because, whether you know it or not, you have a vast repository of thoughts and feelings and ideas about what matters; you will learn about them as demands are made on you to make grownup decisions. The more you think about what you care about, the more you will be able to trust yourself and the choices you make. The buck, after all, stops with you. You are the grownup; you must have and communicate clarity to be effective as the authority your child needs.

The most fundamental conviction you need as a parent is that it is *your* job, *your* responsibility, and *your* evolutionary role to keep your child safe and secure. That conviction must infuse any directive, prohibition, or penalty you give with clarity and authority. But conviction alone isn't enough: If you haven't thought enough about your guiding assumptions, every moment has the potential to evolve into an internal debate or, worse, an open negotiation with your child. If you are not sure about what to do or what to think, how can you communicate convincing limits and boundaries and rules to your children? If you create a household resembling a military base, with what seems like a hard and fast code of behavior, you will still inevitably be required to make impromptu decisions because of the inconstant nature of family life. If you are committed to talking things through, the buck still stops with you about what is possible, what is tolerable, what feels okay. In the end, you must trust yourself, but understanding how you got there can help you live with your decisions, important especially if your child disagrees or is upset about the results.

Your Children Know What You Care About

Even if you came to parenthood without a clue about curfews, diet, or chores, your kids—and you for that matter—know what matters to you from the decisions you make and the actions you take. Sometimes values are explicit, for example, a saying like "God gave you a gift, now use it," as my father-in-law used to say to his children; or a heart-to-heart talk, like the one many parents dread, about sex. This is what my parents care about; I know it because they told me so. But as we saw in the previous chapter, your kids also learn your values through the organization of your household, the expectations, curfews, chores, rules about calling home, and so on. This is what my parents think is important; I know it because I'll get punished (fined, yelled at) if I do this or don't do that. And finally, this is what my parents think is okay, what I often refer to as your family "ethos." I know because we spend a lot of time doing it (watching TV, cooking, arguing, swearing). Children know what is permitted, and what is prohibited or barely tolerated, just by the way you are, the way you behave with each other, the tone of your voice, or the look on your face.

The assumptions that affect your decisions, ideas, or feelings are often hard to put into words and sometimes harder to put into action. They go by many names: values, beliefs, principles, codes, ethics, morals, standards, norms, convictions, tenets, rules, ideals. But whatever name you use, it is inevitable for parents to generate a set of tacit assumptions about family life, a sort of everyday morality. What motivates *you*? What do *you* care about? What makes you stop short? I want to bring your attention to the judgments that both allow you and spur you to act—the choices, big and small, that constitute the foundation of what your child experiences as your authority.

Origins of Natural Authority

Your natural authority is activated and tested by concerns as primordial as your child's safety or as passing as whether to allow a snack. Being a parent requires enormous patience: The child who stonewalls a serving of vegetables or the one who comes out of the bedroom repeatedly at night, changing reasons with abandon—a drink, a hug, a pee, a nightmare, chapped lips—can exasperate the most patient parent among us. Although you may consult the experts or other parents, in the end you have to listen to yourself, relying on something on the order of gut feelings to make many judgments. These judgments come from some intricate interweaving of your partnership with your co-parent (or lack thereof), your family of origin, your culture, your social class, your religion, and, as suggested by recent research in neuroscience, by the evolution of your brain. Whether you are fully conscious of them or not, much of what you do, you do *because* of such convictions, shaped by the behavior and messages around you.

Traditional theories in psychology were based on the development of the child's ability to reason: A toddler doesn't know writing on the wall is bad until you get mad at him for doing it, and even then he doesn't understand why it's wrong. By the time he's an adolescent, he understands it is wrong to destroy property and would probably only write on a wall as graffiti or social protest. The function of all emotion is to guide us to adaptive behaviors, which, when integrated with complex motivational mechanisms of reward and punishment, help us decide what to do next. The field of moral development has expanded to emphasize the role of social connection and relationships in decision-making. In the case of marks on a wall, an adolescent would know what a toddler would not: Someone you care about has to take the time, money, and effort to repaint that wall.[73]

Along with studying children, developmental psychologists and anthropologists study parents, their psychology and cognitions, their beliefs, and the effect their beliefs have on their behavior.[74] Any situation can be looked at from many angles, cultural, personal, and developmental: Your belief about what a child can do at 6 or 16 may be influenced by how much your culture values independence. But it is also affected by your personal experience. If a first-grader falls down and scrapes her knee, you may know if she is capable of picking herself up physically and carrying on, but because you didn't like the way your parents didn't help you when you fell down, you are quick to help. In some cases, your judgment involves both what you value and what you believe a child can do. You may value chores even for young children, because your closest friends do, and you believe that a child of 6 years old can make a bed. You might be very concerned with appearances or believe that your child can learn from her social group. When your teenager comes to kiss you good-bye in the morning, you may stop and say, "You are not going out of this house dressed that way" and mean it; or you may comment with a smile, "I doubt that the dress code police will let you get away with *that*." You know that how to dress is an appropriate decision for a teen to make, but you have to decide if a lesson in social appearances is in order. All of these are values in the everyday sense of what feels right, what fits into your worldview, your sense of who your child is and what you want for him, and even what matters to you about what others think.

Culture: What You Know Without Being Told

Most of us are so embedded in our culture—from the intimate culture of marriage and family to the wider culture of religion, region, class, and country—that we don't recognize its implicit effect on much of what we do; we just think this is the way things should be. If you have thought about social or cultural norms before, it was perhaps hearing the phrase "cultural practices" in the context of a college class in sociology or anthropology. My guess is that you didn't think about it applying so much to your own life as to the lives of those different than you. Culture can be as big as a nationality and as small as a family, with lots of layers in between. There could be some values we all are likely to agree on (say, civility, generosity, and respect), whether everyone acts on them or not, but even such common values may get a different emphasis in different families.

Sleeping patterns present one of the most telling examples: Until the recent popularity of "co-sleeping" among some groups, parents in the United States were advised to train their babies to sleep in a separate crib or room if possible, as if this were an unassailable standard. In fact, children the world over are much more likely to sleep with their parents and/or other children as well. Other cultural forces that are particularly germane to our discussion are the value placed on cooperation, beliefs about the nature of control and discipline, and attitudes toward teasing and shaming. Parents are on the front line of transmitting these values.[75]

Cultural differences regarding expectations of children were the subject of a 2009 anthropological analysis of responsibility across childhood in three different societies, the Amazon rainforest in Peru, Samoa, and Los Angeles.[76] The Peruvian and Samoan children are expected to do simple chores without adult assistance from an early age, a cultural practice reflecting some of the values of their society. In the tribal society of the Matsigenka of Peru, laziness is to be avoided at all costs, and even then, the way infants are held, e.g., facing outward to the group or inward toward the caretaker, is intended to show them how things are done. To achieve another cultural value, self-sufficiency in everyday work, by the time they are toddlers, Matsigenka children are expected to do small tasks that contribute to social well-being. The consequences for disobedience and laziness can be harsh and include public shaming. The Samoans too expect children to do work of significance, learning by watching, trial and error, and correction by adults. Praise is rare, but those who support the efforts of someone else to be responsible are encouraged. In contrast, you might ask your toddler to bring you a dustpan, but it would be in the nature of play, sharing in your activity and perhaps teaching him the word for dustpan, more than an expectation that by doing so he would actually be learning how to sweep the floor.

Immigrant parents often have to make difficult decisions about which cultural values to emphasize, and it can be even more complicated when co-parents come from different cultural, religious, or economic backgrounds. But it can be useful for all parents to consider how their values, whatever their origins, influence their decisions, especially if they conflict with what "everyone else is doing."

Local Culture: Family and Neighbors

We humans spend a lot of time, money, and energy measuring, matching, or distinguishing ourselves relative to the norms and practices of our communities. And community can be as local as your immediate or extended family or your next-door neighbors. Despite the advent and dominance of social media, which we will discuss more below, most of us still have people close to us whose opinions about child-rearing are communicated explicitly and implicitly. I remember the people, usually older women, who used to address my children in the stroller on a cool day in fall, saying, "Doesn't your mother know you need to be dressed up warmly?" It may be that you are making decisions expressly in opposition to the way your parents ran their household. My mother kept a diary when she was 10 or 11 of the things her mother did that she didn't want to do. When you encounter an especially difficult moment or an especially big decision, you may turn to your parents, in-laws, or other relatives or close friends for advice. But in the end, your natural authority encompasses being able to make a boundary between what they would do and what you will do: You are the one on the front line, with or without the support and cooperation of a co-parent. *(See Chapter Five.)*

With your first baby, even if you have had experience with babies, everything is new. You are exhausted from getting up in the night, and when you talk to another parent at your birth preparation class reunion or in a Facebook group, you find out *that* baby is sleeping through the night, or nursing only every three hours, or taking four naps a day like clockwork. Yours, on the other hand, nurses every two hours 24/7 and her naps are random if they happen at all. Or vice versa. Who is right? Who should feel bad? Nobody, of course—but easier said than done. And what about how clean your house is, whether your baby is crawling or talking yet, or whether, as time goes on, your children are getting good grades or making goals on the soccer field?

The messages around you can be loud and might even be coming from your own children. Any parent whose child brings a lunch from home hears a lot about the better food other kids bring—or at least are reported to bring. In the children's book *Bread and Jam for Frances*, Frances refuses to eat either the nice dinners her mother makes or the packed lunches.[77] She becomes fixated on what her friend Albert brings. Finally, in exasperation, her parents decide to give her only bread and jam, since that's the one food she will eat. Soon enough she gets sick of bread and jam and clamors for what the rest of the family is having for dinner. Her parents have deftly given her rein to make her own decisions even as they surely suspected she would come back to the values of the more nutritious family meals.

Your kids may tell you their friends don't have to do chores. And that might be true! Their reports only matter if you are more concerned with what people think of you than you are with your family habitat. Regardless of what everyone else does, you might be surprised at how well children respond to your having well-defined values and directives based on your natural authority. As one 9-year-old boy said to his mother in our session: "Sometimes I *want* you to tell me what to do." But we humans are very sensitive to the opinion of our social group. On the one hand, it can be hard to be more demanding of your kids than other parents are because you want your kids to like you; but you also are likely to worry that the other guy keeps his house cleaner, has kids who are more obedient, more successful in school, and so on. It's a lifelong battle.

Peer Pressure for Parents Too: Social Media

One of the hardest parts about being a parent is worrying about whether you're doing right by your children. And one of the ways you judge "rightness" is by the community around you. We'd all like to think peer pressure ends in high school, but in every human community there is pressure to behave in a certain way—regarding dress, school, and other activities—and there may be family pressures too, about everything from discipline to churchgoing. These pressures are not easily dismissed. Parents too are deeply affected by the actions and judgment, imagined or expressed, of others. In today's hyper-connected world, peer pressure is amplified through social media, exacerbating the natural inclination one has to see what the other guy—and the other guy's children—are doing. Contributing to the anxiety is a cultural atmosphere of intense competition for college entrance, jobs, and success.

Peer pressure can be acute for divorced families in which parents run separate households with children going back and forth, and especially when the "other" family is actually your former spouse in a new family. If you are a single parent without an involved co-parent, you often make your decisions without the benefit (or sometimes the stress!) of consultation with the other parent. You probably seek out advice from family members or other adults, but there is risk in such outreach.

Being shunned by one's social group is a painful experience for many primates, humans among them. Learning local social norms and practices takes on emotional power because of the fear of being shunned if one violates them.[78] Long before social media, one of my children took social exclusion into his own hands when he wasn't invited to the birthday party of a neighbor, one of a group of five boys who played together frequently. He picked up the phone and challenged his friend to justify himself: "Why didn't you invite me to your birthday party?"

There are always going to be differences, for better or worse, between your kids and the other kids, or between your approach to the problems of family life and what other parents do. On the other hand, there is a lot to learn from what other people do: You might find out about a new book or website that tackles something you've been confused or perplexed about, or you might receive advice from someone who has had good luck with something you have found difficult. Even social media can play a constructive role if you keep it all in perspective.

You Were a Kid Once

My parents required us to clean our rooms and make our beds, without adult help. With my own kids, I cared enough about order to want the rooms eventually cleaned up, but not so much that I needed it done regularly or on their own. I didn't have complete confidence in my kids' ability to do it well themselves, partly because we hadn't trained them early, a decision I suppose my husband and I made by default: Neither of us is great about putting clothes and books and shoes away ourselves! And why was I the one helping and not my husband? I wasn't the only parent, after all. Like many women, I may have thought it was my bailiwick, but to be honest it wasn't something my husband seemed to care about a whit: It was my value and my assertion of authority. My decision to help them clean their rooms reflected a value perhaps influenced by the culture of my generational cohort: By making it a project we did together, not only was I able to lend some organizing advice and modeling, we also got to spend time together.

As your child ages, the stakes get higher. Your phone rings at nine on a Saturday morning. "I have to tell you something," says the mother of your son's friend. "I'm very embarrassed. I should have told you sooner, but Joe and Trevor drank some whiskey when Joe slept over three weeks ago." Joe is 14. You march into his room and wake him up to confront him. "Did you drink whiskey at Trevor's?" He panics and sits bolt upright. "It's true. I'm sorry! I'm sorry! I'm sorry! I just wanted to know what it was like. I'll never do it again." What do you do? And how do you decide what to do? You've got the upper hand not only because you're the parent but because you're awake and on your feet. But you're upset too. Personal influences may come to mind first: Perhaps you had an alcoholic parent or uncle; perhaps you grew up in a very strict household and rebelled with alcohol or drugs yourself. How you react carries on or perhaps rebels against the values and beliefs and habits and practices you grew up with, your version shaped by the particulars of who you are. This is moral development in practice. It shows the power parents have, by virtue of being parents, to shape their children's character, passing on both household rules and conventions of the wider society, including the idea of respect for authority itself. [79]

Biology in Decision-Making

But where does that power come from? How do *you* know— or at least decide—what's okay for your child, whether about food, friends, or the Web? The most basic motivation for any animal is keeping one's offspring safe and healthy. This motivation helps make many contemporary parents vulnerable to fears and anxieties of all kinds, from what their children eat to sexual predators. Joseph LeDoux, one of the leading researchers on the neuroscience of both fear and anxiety, distinguishes them this way: If there is a present threat to your child's safety, you will experience fear. But if you anticipate the possibility of future danger, you will be anxious, a feeling exacerbated by all that you don't know. And of course, people vary, including co-parents, together or apart. One parent might allow a brand-new driver to take his little sister to get ice cream, while another might require a probationary period. And another might prohibit ice cream altogether! One source of such differences is parental temperament and your different thresholds of worry. It helps to recognize that your perception of safety, whatever its source, determines your actions, and work to resolve differences with a co-parent if necessary.[80] (*See Chapters Five, Six, and Seven, and below, Different Parents, Different Attitudes.*)

You have your own inner voice about your child's welfare, whether about sheer survival or about health and psychological well-being. As the big animal in charge of small animals, it is normal to be at least somewhat protective, to want to keep your child out of harm's way, or to keep *her* from experiencing anxiety. The parental brain is motivated by oxytocin and other hormones to nurture, protect and bond with offspring. [81] And as we saw in Chapter Two, a primary function of attachment is to keep track of the other's whereabouts, which has the potential to increase your anxiety. The state of your own attachment helps you decide where a child can go and for how long, to a friend's house, to summer camp, on an out-of-town school trip. Research suggests that fear related to separation is distinct from fear related to threat. Fear and anxiety can play a significant role in your authority, as you grapple with what limits are appropriate. [82] *(See section below, Safety and Independence.)*

Of course, it is not only physical fear that can trigger difficult decision-making. For example, the amygdala, which is associated with fear and anxiety, is also associated with disgust, including disgust at the behavior of people who violate social norms. A simple version of what happens, which we will discuss further in the next chapter, is that a sort of neurobiological dialogue takes place between your prefrontal cortex (your executive and evolutionarily most recent brain) and your amygdala, which needs calming down because it is trying out all the different possibilities and how you might feel should one of them take place. [83] If I call my neighbor and complain that her child is using bad language around mine, how is she likely to react? Will it mean an end to play dates? Will it mean I can't borrow an egg if I need one? Do I care? These inner dialogues shape your authority.

Areas of Authority

In recent decades, social and psychological anthropologists have taken to field studies within their own cultures, a trend exemplified by the study of 32 families by the Center for the Everyday Life of Families at UCLA from 2002 to 2005. Seeking to understand "how members of a family act, think, and feel shifts with the winds of prevailing values and practices across generations and communities," the CELF study took an unprecedented look at the intimate interactions of a group of diverse middle-class families. Unscripted video taken throughout each family's time at home over the course of one week was analyzed in detail by anthropologists, psychologists, and education researchers. With the luxury of such comprehensive and intimate documentation and the ability to scrutinize interactions frame by frame and word by word, they were able to reach an understanding of what parents valued and the degree to which, in the rush of hectic everyday life, they were able to enforce their values.[84]

This study provides a rich example of the wide-ranging nature of parents' authority and need for decision-making. How clean a room should be and when and where a new driver can safely drive, the domains of parental responsibility—and therefore values and beliefs—are as varied in scope and importance as life itself. You could make the list in a minute: eating vegetables, homework, health, sibling conflict, sex education, bedtime, toys, gadgets, screen time, chores, and friends. While appreciating the holistic reality of the families' lives, the research team extracted a variety of themes and situations from the data, from everyday greetings and homework supervision to dinnertime conflicts and how families managed their "mountains of stuff." Their analysis suggested that the combination of a child-centered parenting philosophy and the stress engendered by the sheer magnitude of what parenthood means for working families conspired to shape these parents' behavior around authority. It should also be noted that researchers were struck by the affection and support given to children by their parents, despite their stress and frustration, and the conscientiousness with which they approached their job as parents.[85]

Regardless of their philosophy, parents' beliefs can be classified into several categories, including beliefs about development, beliefs about their own and their child's responsibilities, beliefs about behavior and relationships inside and outside of the family, beliefs about money and work, to name a few. Parents have spoken or unspoken goals about their children's development: what they want their children to be like, what they want them to learn, and what they want from them. Parents have different views about the course of development and what they believe influences it, including the importance of parents. It is in the nature of parenthood that the parameters of such beliefs will overlap. For example, a goal that your child knows how to get along with others would probably overlap with ideas about the development of self-control.[86]

Your goals and expectations for your children imply different responsibilities for you. If you believe in talking things over before, during, or after conflict, then you will likely feel a responsibility to guide your child in how to talk about her feelings. If you believe that talk is not as important as making a quick parental decision, or if the issue is a familiar and well-rehearsed chore or routine that you have already talked about too many times, then you won't stop to focus on feelings but will be more task-oriented for both of you.

The Social Domain

As a parent, what is your responsibility for your child's social life? When do you intervene in your child's relationships with others in the family, in the world? If one child borrows a sweater from her sister without asking, is it your business? What do you do if a parent calls to tell you your child has been mean to a peer? If your child reports being bullied on the school bus, do you work with her to understand the interaction and guide her to stand up for herself, or do you call the school to intervene? This area of decision-making is complicated by the online social world, not only the extremes of cyber-bullying or sexting, which overlap with safety, but more apparently benign calculations of "likes" on Facebook or Instagram.

In everyday life, the lines between different domains of authority are decidedly blurred, as they are in this example: A father worried about a friend of one of his children, then in seventh grade. The friend reminded him of kids he'd known growing up who came to no good—drugs, jail time, early fatherhood. He fretted about what to do, but finally gave his child a lecture about the importance of friends and the influence they can have on you. He didn't forbid the friendship but warned of its possible consequences. The caution is a common one: In the children's book, *Best Friends for Frances*, Frances the badger's mother did the same when she reminded Frances to "Be careful!" when she went to play with her sometimes mean friend, Thelma.[87] In most relationships, this father would have encouraged kindness and inclusiveness, rather than avoidance; and this was a neighbor, a part of his family's community. But his concern was ultimately about his child's safety and about whether or not the child would exercise good judgment at that age, concerns that trumped the social considerations in this discussion.

Other decisions you have to make are directly related to your situation in the larger world: Who cares for your child? How will your child be educated? Such decisions require significant advance planning, usually including financial commitments. Despite the huge social shift toward most women working that has taken place in the last 50 years, there continue to be parents, even on tighter budgets, who choose to have one parent stay home with children and make the financial sacrifices necessary to live on one income. Others do not have that choice, but still must make decisions consistent with their means. Similarly, in urban areas especially, the days of everyone going to the neighborhood public or parochial school have evolved into a wider set of choices, including magnet and charter schools, and a growing movement of home-schooling. Many would argue vociferously for the rightness or wrongness of one side or another, but the choice is yours to make with consideration of a wide array of both values and concerns. Here is one place where parental consensus is required, however difficult it is to achieve.

Safety and Independence

Questions of safety raise many of the issues that underlie almost any moment of parental authority. In the iconic example of how a parent reacts to a child running toward the street or a child struggling in a swimming pool, the reaction is universal: You run or jump in and grab him. But parents—including parents of the same children—differ widely on what they consider dangerous, and for whom, and what to do about it.

Even if you are clear about what is important to you, you may still wonder how you know your child is ready for more independence. From the first day of your baby's life, you dress and feed her, and decide where and when she will sleep, but as she gets older you are constantly confronted with the question, "Is she ready? Can she do that by herself?" In making these kinds of decisions, you take into consideration both what kind of protection you as a parent are obligated to provide and what you know about your child's temperament, competence, and confidence. Whether consciously or not, in the problem-solving that is everyday family life, you will consult your beliefs about that child, if only fleetingly, every time you say yes or no.

When is your child ready to take a risk to her physical safety without your supervision? Once a child becomes old enough to be at other children's houses and then, eventually, out in the world without adult supervision, she will be relying on her own judgment and on her own ability to restrain her impulses or, if she is less sure of herself, on what she thinks you would say. One of our kids went to a preschool at which, because we were living in California at the time, the kids spent most of their time outdoors. According to the school's philosophy, kids were allowed to climb on anything—a chair, a tree, a roof—that they could get onto and off of without help. The school's approach forced me to reconsider and modify my own more cautious attitudes toward risk-taking. I came to believe a good place to start was each child's sense of what each thought he could do, even if it was something I was afraid to do—like riding a roller coaster—or something I was afraid to let him do.

But beginning with the child's judgment doesn't mean ending with it: You are the parent, you are responsible, you are in charge. Sometimes the danger was great enough that we parents had to talk through the risks and necessary precautions or conditions. And there were exceptions, times when what they wanted to do, whether they felt ready for it or not, was dangerous or illegal or even just inconvenient. There were other times when I knew they were ready and they didn't quite feel it, so they needed a little push. At least when kids are still mostly under your roof or under the care of other adults, the decision is finally yours or yours with the other parent. *(See below, 96 ff, for changing issues as children get older.)*

Different Parents, Different Attitudes

Parents often differ about safety, with one pushing the other toward fewer restrictions around safety or advocating a looser routine around bedtime or eating. I have had more than one parent worry that if her young child doesn't get enough sleep it will affect not only mood and school performance but vulnerability to infection and illness. Although parents of young infants, especially firstborns, tend to be vulnerable to social practices about their decisions in relation to sleep, once the child is older or there is a second child, they hit their stride—unless of course the second child is so different in temperament that the old protocol just doesn't fit.

In our house, one difference was in relation to violence in movies: We never came up with a consistent policy but waffled back and forth, although we discussed it periodically over the years. Clearly neither of us felt quite strongly enough to insist, but I remember taking the youngest out into the lobby when we ended up at a movie I wish we hadn't chosen.[88] When parents disagree, at least three relationships come into play: the relationship between the parents themselves and the relationship between each parent and the child. Complications quickly follow. A parent readier to let a child be independent can help the other let go just a little bit more. If an anxious parent lets go, it is not just that instance but successive instances that will follow; you will relinquish not only control but a version of your relationship, a degree of dependence. It can work the other way too: The safety concerns of one parent can persuade the other, and that too resonates in their relationship. *(See also Chapter Five.)*

This kind of decision fits into what the anthropologist Beatrice Whiting called the "dependency conflict," that is, the conflict many American parents feel between the cultural ideal of autonomy and their fears about letting their children be on their own. Others have taken it up since then.[89] The dependency conflict is an expression of ambivalence on the part of both children and parents: For parents, a desire for but a fear of control; for children, a desire for autonomy and freedom but fear about leaving the safety of parental protection. You may recoil from being the kind of parent who says, "that's the way it is in our house," but clear rules and routines about family rules reduce the need for negotiation, which often leads to conflict. Such routines can be developed through discussion and negotiation, and changed as circumstances and capacities change, but as long as they are in place, it is up to you and your co-parent to consistently enforce them.

Parents have always had opinions about their children's future, but as modern life has generated more expansive opportunities and gotten more competitive, preparation for whatever future you envision may carry more weight in parents' sense of responsibility and bear directly on authority. According to Annette Lareau, class differences may be the primary determining factor in how parents handle homework and expectations about grades, with parents who don't expect their children to go to college having lower expectations than parents who do expect or want their children to be college-bound. But even among that group, beliefs about what children can or should be able to do on their own, and how parents handle homework, may vary. You have to decide, and peer pressure is likely to play as big a role as your philosophy. A related goal is the ability to manage money, which might lead you to give your child an allowance, along with guidelines about whether they have to do chores in order to receive it, what they're allowed to spend it on, and whether some of it must be saved. This becomes part of your family's culture.

The Role of Gender

Perhaps the most fundamental area in which parents pass on mostly unconscious beliefs is in regard to the sex of their children. Despite few measurable differences, the question "Is it a girl or a boy?" has enormous salience in conversations about pregnant bellies and newborn babies. Where there is compelling data about the difference, however, is in how differently adults, whether male or female, father or mother, teacher, relative, or stranger, respond to children whose sex they know. This suggests that their expectations of gender-linked characteristics is shaping their responses, rather than inherent differences they perceive. From how steep an incline their infant daughter or son can climb down to expectations about toy preferences, adults pass on cultural, community, and family values and beliefs: Girls are worse at math, boys are worse at reading; girls like clothes, boys like sports. This is, of course, another major and unsung role for parental authority: What are your assumptions about sex differences? Are you interested in knowing what science says about the issue? Do you have strong beliefs about gender roles? Do you and your co-parent agree?

Gender will probably always be a lively and controversial area of research. After years of concern about discrimination against girls, alarming differences have been found between girls and boys from a variety of environmental influences.[90] As society becomes more accepting of homosexuality, transgender people, gender neutrality, and nonconventional expressions of gender, parents from all classes and political persuasions are being confronted with the need to explore their own values in regard to questions their parents and grandparents would not even recognize.

Changing Assumptions, Changing Rules

The changing nature of the parent-child relationship across development means that what people make rules or have ideas about changes too. Unfortunately, changes don't necessarily come when you are ready for them. It can be hard enough to say good-bye at the door of the kindergarten room that first day, even when you have known from the day your child was born that she would go to school. Many situations will catch you by surprise, and you have to consider, sometimes on the spot, whether you really think anything could go wrong: Are there streets to cross? Does she know the way? Was it really dangerous, or was I being too careful? You can be too protective of your kids, and it is easy to let your own fears cloud your judgment.

My spouse and I encountered moments of decision around independence with all of our kids at roughly the same age: We allowed our oldest to bike to school at 9 and we let the second walk from school to his piano lesson at 10 (although only after repeated rehearsals with me driving alongside him in the car because I wasn't quite convinced he knew the way). The third was allowed to ride his bike to baseball practice and the fourth to move from house to house within a certain group of houses without telling me each time where he was. I realize now that these examples are perhaps not only about safety but also about a time of change for each child, a time for moving out into the world. I remember it because they were turning points for them and for us, although they're transitions none of them are likely to remember.

We didn't have a hard-and-fast rule to follow: Each child was a little different, and we lived in several different cities in different kinds of situations. But in each case, they were out-growing their need for our help and feeling ready to be in the world more on their own. They were simply growing up; we had to let go. Which brings us back to our relationships: If I was the parent getting the request, I had to judge that child for that task in that spot at that time. I had to feel okay about it. If I chose to say no, I knew I could explain that it was for safety's sake—that the child in question wasn't ready, wasn't old enough—but I had to be ready too.

What if you're a worrier? How do you find the balance between your child's developing competence and your own anxiety? You may have to tell your son or daughter you're not ready to change the rules or routine today, but you'll think about it. Talk with your spouse, talk with your friends and neighbors. Look for clarity: What are you afraid of? What do other people do? Does it make sense? Figure out how to build in some safeguards. My kids were cruising around before cell phones, but they could call from their destinations. In today's world you can always arrange for a call. A young child can borrow a cell phone; an older one may already have one.

In my case, even though I wasn't particularly adventurous by temperament, my spouse was, but both of us valued independence. On the other hand, my spouse was more of a worrier. Sometimes I had to make myself be a little more careful than I tended to be. If you and a co-parent disagree, about this or any other value or belief, you will serve both yourselves and your children best if you can either hammer out a compromise or agree to disagree and let the other parent handle it her way. It is important enough to support the authority of the other that if you have chronic fights about particular children or situations or about child-rearing in general, you should consider getting outside help.[91]

When the Stakes Get Higher

The assumptions and judgments you bring to bear will probably stay surprisingly consistent as your child grows up, regarding the kinds of places she should be allowed to go and with whom, what she should be required to do around the house, what standards you have about language, schoolwork, or manners. But the kinds of situations of course change: While a 9-year-old may be riding a bike, a 16-year-old may be driving and will most likely have access to alcohol or drugs.

As children become more independent and more likely to be in situations you can't control and may not even know about, problem-solving with your co-parent is still necessary but is more difficult. When drugs, alcohol, and sex are involved, you may need to do research (is marijuana really a so-called gateway drug? Some parents prefer that their kids have sex at home rather than in a car or in the woods—should I?) and grapple with what makes sense to you before broaching it with your child. You will also want to have serious discussions with your co-parent, if possible, to find common ground from which to generate guidelines for discussions with your child. If that is not possible, or if you and your co-parent are at cross-purposes, conversations with peers or other trusted adults at the child's school or your church, or with a mental health professional, can be helpful in sorting out how to handle these kinds of differences.

Talking to your child may feel just as challenging for many reasons, ranging from your shyness about talking about sex with your teenager, your awareness of *his* self-consciousness, your ambivalence or uncertainty about what is right for him and for you, and any and all of the forces of influence we have been discussing in this chapter. The #MeToo movement on campus and in the wider society has undoubtedly increased parents' worry about both girls and boys in different ways and suggests a need for conversations beyond the birds and the bees and contraception. The goal is to figure out what matters most to you and to trust both yourself, your co-parent, and your child to come to decisions that you can enforce and she can accept.

It is my conviction that there is more continuity than not in the values you rely on, but exactly how that applies in a given situation may take some intense thought and discussion, especially when the stakes are higher and the child in question is more able to argue with you. As you grow together, your child will undergo a process that involves both internalizing your family's values and developing her own sense of the world, including whether your assumptions fit *her* life. A mother recounted a story about her daughter's request for birth control pills. From the mother's point of view, it was a discussion about permission, with an embedded question about both readiness and values. From the daughter's point of view, it was a conversation in which she was telling her mother that she had made a decision, that she felt ready, and that she thought it was the right step for her. When the mother expressed some hesitation and said she wanted to talk to the child's father, the daughter responded, "How do you know I won't just go ahead and do it? I can, you know." The mother answered, "Because of our relationship." In other words, they had a relationship of openness and trust; each expected the other to respect her views. But they had also reached a turning point in the girl's development for which the mother was perhaps not quite prepared: The girl had a boyfriend with whom she was having discussions about values and relationships too, and a school clinic where she could get the pill without her parents' permission.

When children are old enough to leave home, like many contemporary parents you may be confronted with decisions about how much support to give them. True at all economic levels, this is one of the most challenging areas of decision-making for parents. Whether or not or to what degree you help your children financially depends, first of all, on your own economic situation. But whether you can afford $5 or $50 a week, most parents I work with and many I know personally or read about in the media seem to be inclined to help pay their children's way, even well into their 20s and beyond, often by having them live at home rent-free and sometimes even chore-free. My guess is that they don't consider this a question of values, but it is.[92]

Such help—to any degree—also reflects the deep sense of responsibility you have as a parent. Even if a young person succeeds in landing a job after finishing school, she may not have benefits or may not earn enough to pay rent or pay off loans. More and more children either don't leave home or return home, often for economic reasons. And in much of the world it is entirely normal for children to live at home until they are married. Your response may be, "We have to help her." What you do in this instance, as in many others, is in effect an expression of a value and a belief, namely that it is your role or obligation or a cultural expectation that you help your child and that you believe your child needs it. But in doing so you may undermine other values you surely have about your child being able to make it on his own. As long as you are there to help, your child will be slower to develop self-reliance, whether financially or by never learning to unload the dishwasher or cook. Almost every child will eventually be completely on her own. Your decision as a parent comes down to when that happens; every child and every parent is different. Many parents are surprised to learn, once their children are grown, that they continue to confront parental decisions: whether or not to tell them what you think, whether or not to bail them out of a tough situation. And they're surprised to realize, in retrospect, that their parents must have struggled with the same decisions.

— Chapter Five —

The Web of Authority:
Interdependent Family Relationships

"**B**ut Mom said I could!" …Have another cookie, stay up late, have two sleepovers in one weekend. As sure as the tide comes in, as sure as your dog will find the muffin you left in your briefcase, just about any child will use one parent's word against the other. And often it works, especially when the target parent is left alone with dinner to prepare or is preoccupied with work he needs to get to after the kids go to bed. If parents are divorced, then the possibilities for such strategies multiply. Maybe Mom did say he could do whatever it is he wants to do, and maybe Mom didn't. What should *you* do?

Besides being a pair of particular someones, both of you are functioning in a web of relationships, a web that means support but can also mean conflict, confusion, and complication. What most often brings families to therapists' offices is the canary in the coal mine of family life, that is, a child who is acting out at home or at school, sometimes with academic problems too. Or to quote Miss Clavel in *Madeline*, "Something is not right!"[93] Some therapists want to see the child; some want to see the family. I want to see the parents because conflicts between parents—whether living together or apart—underlie most "parenting" problems I encounter. In more cases than not, although parents disagree about how to handle the child or report ways in which they handle him differently, their conflicts often do not reflect differences in values, goals, and expectations. Instead, they reflect the sometimes bewildering and infuriating differences in style and threshold for tolerance between parents. Those differences in turn shape the relationships between the parents and between each parent and the child. That is the web of authority in which your child grows up, learning moment by moment just how sticky it is.

Two Parents, Two Approaches

Paradoxically, being a parent with someone else may be the hardest thing about being a parent, even when you live in the same house. It should be easier to have two parents to earn income, do laundry, calm down screaming toddlers, and discipline rebellious teenagers. But despite the human propensity for cooperation, anything that two people try to do has the potential for disagreement, and children manage, even at a young age, to learn who is likely to say or do what and to take advantage of the dispute. While you two fight about what to do, I'll keep screaming. Then one of you will give in just to get some peace, and you can continue to fight about that.

Choosing to rely on the word of your child rather than on family rules and routines or a check-in with the other parent puts you in dangerous territory. Parenting books and magazines are full of good strategies and techniques, many of which may be identified as effective for a particular age or a particular situation, but if one parent uses a highly recommended strategy and the other parent consistently—or even randomly—does something different or expresses skepticism, the strategy will very possibly not work. The effective implementation of household chores, homework time, and other family routines depends to a great degree on how much co-parents agree, but even more importantly on how they deal with their disagreement. Unresolved differences or a relationship in which one parent's authority is regularly challenged or dismissed by the other diminishes the authority of both.

Although most couples recognize their difficulty as one of communication, they usually consider communication in a limited sort of way. Yes, it matters what you say, and it matters a lot whether the other person listens. But because household organization is only as effective as those who manage it, you may need to step back and take a look at the workings of your habitat. If you don't support the other parent's approach, or if you don't respect the relationship the other parent has with the child, authority is weakened, regulation may be disrupted by conflict or bad feelings, and an everyday incident may develop into a problematic pattern of interaction. And in virtually every case—even if the stress is an external one—resolution will only come if both parents work toward it, or at the very least don't undermine each other. It is a central dilemma of being a parent that you must both work together and respect the boundaries of the other relationship.

Most authority scenarios of the everyday variety—brushing teeth, taking out the garbage, deciding what a child can wear—don't require two parents, and for more than a third of children in the U.S., there is no second parent in the home.[94] It may be a relative or a babysitter who shares the authority that creates and maintains the child's habitat, the authority that is communicated in daily interactions and ongoing relationships. Authority in those daily interactions emerges from myriad choices and decisions, each shaped, mostly unconsciously, by values, personalities, and the particular history of your family and relationships—and what each parent, if there are two, brings to the family. The effectiveness of your authority is shaped by the functioning of the entire family system, itself shaped by the relationship and interactions *between parents*—between their personalities, their values and experiences, and often their differing identification with a child because of gender, temperament, or birth order.

Parents and children are connected to and affect one another in the ongoing moments of interaction in daily life, i.e., through emotional regulation, coalitions, and the inevitable differences in how an incident is experienced. A 3-year-old's tantrum can get you and your spouse into a fight, or conversely, your fighting may seem to trigger a 3-year-old's tantrum. You know that resentments build up and fester and spill over into other relationships. But how does this happen?

In some seemingly mysterious way, even very young children manage to exploit the differences between their parents. You know it well, and you'll say, marveling, "She really knows how to play us against each other." But in fact, it is not that mysterious. Emotional regulation, the capacity to sense and anticipate the mood and probable behavior of others, takes place constantly at a nonverbal and unconscious level between and among human beings. *(See Chapter Nine.)* It helps humans get along with each other; it helps create functioning families, communities, and even democracies. But it also gives humans, old and young, big and small, powerful tools with which to generate or exacerbate conflict and tension.

Remember Michael who wouldn't come to dinner and Samantha who wouldn't come home from a sleepover? I can guarantee you that their interactions—and their relationships—with the other parent would be different simply because their parents are different people, with different temperaments, experiences, and expectations. The relationship between each parent and each child has a different history, a different feel, a different personality, if you will, much of which would be hard to put into words but which helps shape the behavior of the child. This is the stuff that fills novels and psychology books, but it is often forgotten in the rough-and-tumble of everyday life. One mother told me that the most important moment in several years of family therapy was when I said, "Your kids have a different relationship with their father than they have with you, and you must accept that and not try to rescue them or change it."

She was right; this is a hugely important message for parents. It is guaranteed that you will be irritated, disbelieving, or occasionally furious at something your co-parent does. Like you, each of your children will have a story to tell about growing up, and it might include unflattering descriptions of your or your co-parent's behavior. And there will be many more things that you are glad they don't remember. They also won't remember the thousand times you read *Goodnight Moon* or fell asleep while you were reading it. That's okay. They'll stay up late with their new college roommate and compare notes: "My dad was such a perfectionist about grades; he used to freak out when I didn't do well in math" or "My mom couldn't stand it when I violated my curfew, she would rant and rave and then just admit she had been worried."

Parents Don't Have to Agree, But...

In many couples, one parent is often more direct, more demanding, maybe less patient with negotiation but more able to be decisive, while the other finds it more difficult to confront the child and assert authority. This is a clinical observation, not a scientific finding. But when it is the case, it holds true whether the issue is kids fighting, clearing the table, rudeness—you name it. Perhaps opposites attract, or at least are complementary, but when it comes time to be parents, differences in approach must be understood and acknowledged, if not resolved. For a parent who grew up without yelling or overt conflict, or who prefers to exert a quieter authority, watching kids get yelled at by the other parent can be painful. A common presenting problem in my office is a child who reportedly "listens to my spouse but never to me" or who will go to bed for one parent but not the other.

One theory holds that the main difference between parents is a difference between pragmatism and idealism. The idealist wants to teach lessons of character, like sharing, while the pragmatist just wants to make things work. The pragmatic "whatever works" approach tends to come from the parent who is most involved with the children, while the more idealizing parent has less contact with the demands of everyday family life and can afford to think in more ideal terms.[95] The overworked or more involved parent not only feels oppressed by too much responsibility but annoyed by criticism from the one who isn't. In principle, this can be solved by dividing household and family tasks more equally, but there are usually at least two obstacles to overcome: a backlog of resentment about the differential in time and effort expended and the far trickier reluctance of many of the overworked parents to relinquish control. This has probably always been a dilemma for couples. In a Bohemian folk tale in which a competitive couple, each convinced that their work is harder, decide to switch chores for the day, the husband, as you might expect, ends up in a mess of housework gone awry and pleads to be allowed to go back to the fields and plow.[96]

Despite these built-in stumbling blocks to working together, most parents make some effort to present, or at least give lip service to, a "united front," psychological folk wisdom that everyone seems to have picked up somewhere. Family therapists call it the "parental alliance" or "parental coalition," but the soundtrack of daily life tells a different story: "You know she doesn't like strawberry jam, she likes raspberry!" Or "You let him go out? He was grounded! You're a pushover." You can hear the dismissiveness in your voice; you know you sound irritated, and you don't mean to be critical, but still, you can't seem to help it. It is hard to stay united. But the importance of finding a common voice that demonstrates mutual support and respect between parents cannot be overstated, and it is not only important in situations of conflict about child-rearing or the assertion of authority. If it means turning a blind eye to the mess the other parent makes or accepting a different way of doing things, that too may be authority.

You and your co-parent don't always have to agree, but it is of utmost importance that you be aware of the joint nature of your natural authority. The two of you are the grownups, and each of you has a relationship of authority with your child, however violently you may disagree. As such, you both bear a responsibility to work together and to maintain a firm and clear boundary around your subsystem, working hard behind the scenes to resolve your differences or agreeing to disagree.[97]

Differences between parents can become serious, especially when a child is physically ill or presenting with disruptive or worrying behavioral issues or a psychiatric diagnosis. The intense conflict between the parents in one separated couple I worked with had its roots in significant cultural differences about the involvement of the extended family in decisions about and care of a seriously ill child. Another separated couple's conflict emerged from a woman's illness, during which she hadn't felt cared for by her spouse. Most common are vigorous, and sometimes bitter, differences about blame and management relating to children who seem out of control: Running away, substance abuse, and failing in school are all common teen behaviors with many possible causes and a strong need for mutually supportive parental authority. Just when the child needs your common voice and agreement on what you value and what you expect, it is often fear that intrudes, and a shift in focus from the child's need to conflict between parents.

When Two Becomes Three or More

Once you add a third party to an interaction between parents, whether a sick third grader or a sullen teenager, things quickly become more complex, more stressful, and in all but the rarest cases, more conflicted. The increased complexity, stress, and conflict come in large part from the fact that each person is functioning simultaneously in at least two relationships, and therefore being affected not only by all the powerful but invisible forces between herself and each of the others, but by the forces she perceives and experiences going on between them. This is the family system.

Whatever form authority takes, it must be clear, persuasive, and consistent to be effective. Two voices saying the same thing are clearer than two voices saying something different, and they're far stronger than when one voice undermines, scorns, or puts down the other. The united front of parents is more than a chorus in unison; it is the voice of authority in a system of relationships in which children rely on parents not only for the tangibles of food, shelter, health, and education, but also for emotional security and emotional regulation.

Key to thinking about families as systems is the idea that there is nothing final about the way families function, made up as they are of individuals and relationships. This is easy to agree on but harder to live by. Just when you get used to something that seems to work, it changes—sometimes for the better, as when your kid gets his license and can not only take himself to soccer practice but might be able to do some family errands too. Maybe he'll be able to take his sister to her practice, which will give them time together and add a new element to their relationship. But a license brings more difficult and unknown changes too. Perhaps driving is a source of tension between you and your co-parent, and it spills over into the relationships with your son. There is a need for new rules to govern his use of the car; maybe you won't agree on the rules or how to enforce them. Who can he take with him? Will he buy his own gas? The whole system can potentially be affected, depending on how the individuals and relationships within it react to these changes.

What goes on in a family system can be seen as a group of jugglers in the circus, with balls, bowling pins, and plates all going through the air, all while people also balance something on their noses or heads. Things are fine when they are in balance. Even if one juggler drops something, a skilled performer can reach down and pick it up, and his skilled partners will compensate until he is back in the swing of things. A family system cannot possibly always be calm, but family members will make subtle adjustments to ensure that the imbalance is fleeting and not disruptive. Sometimes, however, disruption is precisely what is necessary as not every pattern of interaction is adaptive.

Under the Hood: Understanding and Interrupting Patterns

It is a rare driver who actually understands how his car works, how all the parts of the machine work together to make it go. Maybe you have some vague notion of spark plugs and combustion, but generally most of us rely on our cars in ignorance, be they old or new, hybrid or conventional, until something goes wrong. Your family is not a machine, but like a machine, its moving parts—individuals and relationships—work in ways largely invisible and unconsidered until something doesn't work. Families have, in effect, always been wireless, and perhaps it is time to marvel at that. Despite all the words, what matters more are boundaries, emotions, and nonverbal communication, evident from studies of our relatives, the primates.[98]

The work of a therapist in early sessions with a family is something akin to the conversations with an auto mechanic: The parents will tell me what they've noticed and what they're concerned about—the human version of strange noises or the car not responding as it's expected to. Then, like a good mechanic, I ask questions to try to pin down where the problem might be. There are mysteries, of course, even in car repair, but even if the mechanic can't discover the problem from words alone, he can look under the proverbial hood. Not so easy with families, but not impossible either.

I rarely make my hypotheses explicit at first, but would, in effect, raise the hood and explore the perspectives of each parent, including both the history of their relationship with the child in question and a blow-by-blow account of a recent interaction. Solutions can often be found simply by helping one family member change his or her behavior, which in turn affects, and can change, the behavior of other members. This is the most fundamental principle of a family system.

Let's say that a young teenage girl consistently goes somewhere different than where she said she was going or is allowed to go and evades detection by turning off her cell phone. Her behavior drives her father crazy because he worries incessantly that she will get hurt. He usually can find out where she is or where she's been because she either tells her little brother where she really was or lets something slip at dinner. He wants to ground her or otherwise take away a privilege. He argues about this with her mother, who worries less and who doesn't want to punish her daughter. The mother thinks that they could pretty easily solve the problem by insisting that their daughter allow them to speak to a parent in the household she is visiting (another family rule is that a parent must be home). But that embarrasses the teenager, and it embarrasses the father too, who thinks it shows that they can't handle their own daughter.

A change in any of their behaviors could change this pattern. If the father could admit his embarrassment about talking to other parents, if the mother were more aware of her fear of alienating her daughter's affection by punishment, if the daughter didn't feel she would lose face by following her parents' rules—any change would disrupt the pattern in which they are stuck. But if the father admitted his embarrassment, he would need to be supported by his wife and feel confident that she wouldn't make fun of him. If the mother admitted that she worried whether her daughter would still love her, she too would need to rely on her partner's support. Both might need to explore the ways in which their own experiences—with each other and perhaps long before they were married—contribute to these fears.

It's not easy to change, nor is it easy to believe that change will make a difference. Additionally, it can be hard to figure out what you feel and harder still to admit it to someone else, especially if you fear criticism or rejection. And yet it is these undercurrents of emotion—fear, shame, self-doubt—that keep relationships stuck in harmful or at least ineffective patterns of behavior.[99] Even if you know intellectually that the family works in an interdependent way, it is difficult to keep that in mind. Each of us tends to be so immersed in our own subjective experience in each relationship that it takes effort to understand that our behavior is having an effect or that we are responding to someone else's behavior, which in turn might have been a response to ours. How much easier it is to blame the other guy! This work is much of what therapists help individuals and families do, to answer, in effect, "How did that happen?" But you can do it too, if you take the time.

Small Interactions Can Upset the System

It helps to try to break down a series of interactions into smaller parts and explore where each person is coming from. Is one parent afraid of something or afraid of admitting she was wrong? Like a novel that tells its story by getting inside the head of a different character in every chapter, in family therapy it is common to ask each family member in turn to describe their feelings or motivations or understanding regarding a certain difficult interaction. In fact, you probably do something like this every day when working something out with your co-parent or with one or more children. "I thought you were criticizing me," your child might say to explain her irritable response to your unsolicited advice about how she was chopping vegetables for salad. "No, I was just trying to explain that there might be a different, safer way to do that." Since she feels proud of being able to handle a knife, she is a bit touchy; your offer of help felt intrusive to her. Now you know that. And she can keep on chopping, probably a little more carefully than she did before.

Family life is full of such seemingly trivial interactions. A parent corrects or scolds, and a child complies or objects. A child disobeys and one parent or the other, or both, will respond with a threat or a consequence. There will be an answer to "what happens next?" And what happens next in that instance will affect what happens the next time. Chances are no one will change and the pattern will continue. This is homeostasis, a second principle of systems.

Homeostasis or "stable equilibrium" is from the Greek words for "same" and "standing." It originated to describe the physiological balance in your body's system. *(See Chapter Nine.)* This sounds like a good thing, and in a sense, it is: Systems seek stability. In a family, however, stability doesn't always feel good to those who maintain it. Homeostasis in a family means that for better or worse, the same patterns repeat themselves: the same conflicts, the same avoidance of conflict, the same falling apart in response to conflict, the same misconceptions about competence, the same martyrdom in doing things for others, even if they don't want or need it, the same patterns of intervention or lack of it, the same alliances, the same blame. No one likes it, but it is easier not to change. Families, individuals, and relationships all resist change. When you feel frustrated with a child or your spouse because they can't seem to or don't want to change, you might resist thinking it is their fault. It is the nature of the beast—or the system.

What this means for parents' authority is that children get used to patterns of interaction and behave accordingly. If you are the one who usually makes sure a thank-you note gets written, your child is less likely to take a directive to do it from her other parent. If there are chores in your house but no one does them without repeated nagging, that will keep happening, no matter how much you complain about it, until you stop nagging but still expect chores to be done and enforce the expectation with a consequence (say, an allowance for doing chores or a loss of privileges for not). You may think you "would give anything" for your son to get up on time for school by himself, but as long as you keep waking him up, he has no reason to get up on his own. These are examples of homeostasis.

The Family Ethos

Homeostatic patterns become, in effect, family rules for behavior. These repeated patterns create a feeling of what it's like to be in a family, what I call the *family ethos*. Some of the family's habits, practices, and values we have attributed already to the family habitat. While those too contribute to the ethos, I use ethos here to describe something less concrete and more interpersonal and emotional. The ethos is less about the structure of the family and more about the process, about what goes on between people, including, of course, parents' authority or lack of it. The family ethos answers the unasked question, what is it like to be in this family?

There is an invisible set of functional demands that organize the ways family members interact—in other words, the interactions that determine the family ethos. The Argentine psychiatrist Salvador Minuchin, one of the founders of family therapy, conceptualized two kinds of constraints on what he called *transactions*, ways families have of "organizing the data of living together." There are *universal* rules governing family organization, especially the power of the parents, and there are *particular* rules that are active in particular families. (There are of course class and cultural forces affecting both.) This does not mean rules about curfews and chores, but rather ways of being with each other—"explicit or implicit contracts," habits, what I sometimes call family "arrangements." A husband's criticism reminds a wife of her father, who used physical punishment when she disobeyed. Her husband has never, and never would, be violent, but her fear of it keeps her from challenging him. Their child "knows" this, so tends to go to his father for permission when his mother has turned him down. They are used to this unconscious adaptation and will continue to use it as long as it seems to function well enough in their family system.[100]

As the family members interact according to a set of implicit rules, their interactions create patterns to which newcomers, whether infants or in-laws, must adapt, just as the family must adapt to them and the rules and patterned behavior they bring with them. Think about the first time you visited your prospective in-laws. You were probably able to tell in a heartbeat that the other family worked differently from yours; it felt different, unfamiliar. Not just the house or furniture or food or when they got up in the morning and whether they drank coffee or tea. Something else: the personality of the family, the "vibe." Your family may be crazy, but it's your family; you know how it works, consciously and unconsciously.

When my husband and I had differences, especially early on, it helped our marriage to wonder together, what was it like to be in his family compared to mine? It wasn't just that my husband had only brothers, whereas I had sisters and brothers, that there were four of them and nine of us. Or that they lived in a suburb while we had always lived in cities, or that they were Irish-Catholic and we were Protestant, or that they considered interruptions normal and that we were always told interrupting was rude. It was all that, and a lot more too, but more importantly, it was also the mix of all that, along with the particular personalities of each family member and the many relationships within each family that made them *them* and us *us*.

The family ethos means different expectations, different habits, and different experiences. But "what it's like" for your child to be in your family includes, importantly, how you and your co-parent relate to each other around being parents and around authority. And it can mean real clashes between you, which brings us back to the question of the united front and what family therapists call "subsystems" of the family.

The Family Structure

The structure of the family was so central to Minuchin's theory of family systems that he called his work with families "structural family therapy." Fundamental to this approach is a belief in the natural hierarchy of the family, with parents, simply because they are the grownups, the dominant and most naturally powerful subsystem. This approach has deeply influenced my work with families and my thinking about authority. But there are more indirect ways in which all of us use power, and one of them has to do with the structure of family relationships. When a 2-year-old seems to be running the show with his demands, he is standing on the shoulders of at least one adult.[101] In other words, one or both of them has abdicated their responsibility to be parents and given it to him. This can be true even of a newborn. Who has the power in the family?

Every family, no matter how small, consists of at least two subsystems, the parent subsystem and the child subsystem. If there is more than one child, then there may be older and younger children, and if more than one gender, boys and girls. With separation or divorce there may be more than one set of parents, stepparents, grandparents, alloparents, and so on. Subsystems can reflect organization by generation, age, or gender and can be consciously created or recognized.

Each subsystem is protected, as it were, by a boundary, with rules that determine who is in and how they are expected or permitted to behave. Invisible though such boundaries may be, members of a given family have a sense of their permeability. The consistency and sharpness with which subsystem boundaries are defined is one of the primary sources of that different feeling you get from one family to another. But it is important to note that the degree to which family members are able to cross boundaries does not necessarily imply family dysfunction—there is no one correct degree of permeability. In one family it may be quite normal for a child to tease a parent, for example, while in another that would be seen as rude. How then do you know when the hierarchy of the subsystems has been violated? How do you know when teasing has gone too far or when the toddler is standing too tall in the system?

Boundaries of authority are the point at which you assert, by word or deed, the fact that you are the parent and your kid is the kid. In order for parental authority to remain effective, boundaries must be clear. The limit varies from family to family, and it is an implicit aspect of your natural authority that your children know it by your verbal and nonverbal responses to their behavior. You knew just how far you could push your own father before he would say, "that's enough." You knew how many times your mother was willing to joke about your lax performance of your dishwashing chore before she got irritable, told you that you were being fresh, and threatened to fine your allowance. If you stop to think about it, you also know what your own child knows about *your* boundaries—and whether he can get clemency from one parent in regard to the demands of the other.

The issue of boundaries is one of the most important aspects of the natural authority of parents. Like Minuchin, I see the family as a natural hierarchy, in which the parents have the responsibility to wield the power that comes with their role and experience, whether children like it or not. There has been a shift in our society in recent years toward increased autonomy for children within the family, or at least for more democracy, more reasoning, and more negotiation. But autonomy does not have to conflict with the exercise of parental authority if the authority is not intrusive and doesn't undermine the child's motivation, sense of competence, or relationship with the parent (and, I would add, if the authority of one parent doesn't undermine the authority of the other).[102] This brings us back to the parental unit. It is often difficult for one parent to tolerate the exercise of authority by another parent, and unfortunately, this often pushes the uncomfortable parent to intervene on behalf of the child. Such an interaction is known as *triangulation*.

Family Geometry

Since the triangle is a stable figure in geometry, it is a useful metaphor for what happens in families, and popular psychology has readily adopted it (when, for instance, one friend or family member gossips to another, he or she may apologize in advance for "triangulating"). The application of triangles to the question of parental authority is particularly apt. A dyad is stable as long as things are calm, but if the relationship between two people becomes stressed, that stress can be reduced (and the relationship stabilized) by adding a third leg to the stool, i.e., by seeking another family member to connect with you over your complaints. If the stress is great enough, then other interlocking triangles may be generated; in other words, the person you are in conflict with seeks an ally.[103]

Stress on family relationships can come in many forms, including anxiety, anger, frustration, and sadness. One person might experience such an emotion and then ask for help from another, implicitly or explicitly. In that case, the dyad remains a stable unit. But the feeling of anger on the part of one person often creates anxiety in another: Is he going to leave me? Punish me? Make me feel guilty? Any organism can tolerate a certain amount of anxiety, but when anxiety or tension is chronic or sustained, then the organism—or relationship—looks for relief. The triangle is a reliable form of such relief, one that you and your child use every day. It is as if you say to yourself, "I don't like this feeling. I've got to get rid of it. Who can help me?" I spend a lot of time in my therapy office helping people recognize feelings of anxiety or anger or hurt and teaching them to let spouses or other family members know about the feelings directly, rather than indirectly: "I feel anxious when...." If a person is easily made anxious, any system of which he is a part will also be easily stressed or will require the investment of a lot of energy into alleviating that stress.

For example, a mother has said "no" to an advance on a college-age daughter's allowance, worried about family finances and about her daughter's ability to manage money. She worked her way through college and thinks her daughter should be working. Her husband, however, thinks his wife is too tough: He thinks they can afford it and thinks she has time to learn. This is a topic they have always fought about, and the daughter is well aware of their differences. What happens?

The daughter is on the phone with her mother, talking about guy troubles, and brings up the allowance question. Her mother says, "No, absolutely not, you'll have to wait until next month to buy the boots you want." The daughter, while still on the phone with her mother, texts her father, who is out of town, visiting his ailing parents. "Dad, I just saw these awesome boots, but I can't afford them. Can I get an advance on my allowance?" The father knows that his wife would probably object, but he feels sympathetic and is flattered to be asked for support. He texts back, "Sure." So the daughter tells her mother that Dad said it was okay.

The mother is now furious—not at her daughter as much as at her husband, so she texts him in capital letters: NO ADVANCE! NO BOOTS! Just to complicate matters, he is in the midst of a face-to-face conversation with his mother, tells *her* what's going on, gets her support for his position, and texts it back to his wife. "Ma thinks we're too tough." Now there are three interlocking triangles: father, mother, and daughter; father, mother, and grandmother; father, daughter, and grandmother. And if Grandpa weighs in on one side or the other, even more triangles pop up. Lest you be quick to judge the scheming daughter and hapless father, stop and think about the last time you told someone about a conflict you were having with someone you both knew. Even relatively innocuous gossip is a form of triangulation, i.e., making sure someone is on your side in a stressful situation.

Triangles often function to create coalitions or alliances, which, like my scenario, may cross the generational boundaries of family structure. This is where parents often get into trouble. A mother and daughter ally with each other against a father who is often forgetful, clumsy, or quick to blow up. Such an alliance may take the form of teasing and may, from the point of view of the teasers, be well intentioned. They may be using a joke to communicate something they know will inflict some pain but couch it in humor to make it palatable. Baboons are probably not capable of making jokes, but extensive observation of baboon troops has shown that they are very aware of who has aggressed on or mated with whom lately and act accordingly. We come by our triangulating tendency because we too are social primates living in groups.[104]

Triangles also contribute to the system's homeostasis. Equilibrium is not disturbed as long as the parents continue to disagree, alliances are stable, and everyone feels the comfort of a familiar pattern. This may seem counterintuitive: Isn't this kind of pattern dysfunctional? But homeostasis doesn't make positive or negative judgments. It just seeks equilibrium. Perhaps this father can tolerate conflict more easily with his wife than with his daughter, or maybe he gains a feeling of power from the two against one. Neither the mother nor the father is motivated enough to finally resolve their differences about money in relation to their daughter, so they seek refuge in their long-held positions. Each feels that they have the moral high ground: The father sees himself as more generous to the daughter, while the mother believes she is helping to build her character. Had the father refused to give in on the boots and instead referred his daughter back to her mother, the system would have been destabilized for the better. He might have finally decided that his wife was right, enabling them to resolve their differences, or he could have opted to avoid another fight, which would have surprised his wife, perhaps leading her to soften her stance and be more willing to see his perspective.

Every interaction, big or small, has the potential to create a triangle, but especially when a parent has given a child a command or a punishment. And it doesn't have to be a child who brings in a second parent. It is common for a parent to intervene on a child's behalf—maybe when a call to bedtime means getting off a video game, or when a chore hasn't been done. What do you do if you feel undermined? Rule number one: Do not start talking about it in front of the child involved. Remember, you don't want to reinforce the triangle. You want to reinforce the parental subsystem.

Conflict in the System

Although conflict in marriage is normal and unavoidable, families vary when it comes to the frequency and intensity of conflict and attitudes toward it. Many couples feel uncomfortable fighting in front of their children, but regular conflict can be a part of a family's culture. Research on marital conflict suggests that children's perception of the meaning of conflict—both verbal and nonverbal—makes a difference. Children's reactions to parents' post-conflict behavior showed that if parents can resolve their conflict, even behind closed doors, and demonstrate a shift from negative to positive affect, children's distress is reduced. Conflict per se is not a risk factor, but when children lose confidence in your ability to support each other, they are not only likely to feel less secure in general but also less likely to trust parental authority.[105]

Stress in your relationship makes triangulation more likely. When a child feels she has to help one parent in a conflict with the other, for example, the subsystem boundaries are blurred, and the authority of both parents will be compromised. But the most common pattern in my work with parents is the "acting out" child whose behavior is a red flag waving on the train tracks of the parents' relationship. His behavior around separation (or sleep or going to school) may not be about that at all, but his way of expressing and participating in the conflict he senses. It is not necessary to disentangle cause and effect, i.e., whether the identified "behavior problem" started because the parents' relationship has become stressed or whether the stress in the relationship makes it impossible for the parents to work as a team. I have seen a 4-year-old who couldn't be potty-trained, a 12-year-old who refused to stop burping at the dinner table, a 15-year-old who let her schoolwork go. In each case, there was at least inconsistency if not deep disagreement between the parents.

Children are rarely acting intentionally, but their behavior is a powerful tool to get the attention of the adults on whom they depend.[106] This is particularly true when parents either fight or actively undermine each other in moments of explicit authority. Even if you think you have a better way to get those shoes on and get the family out the door to that longed-for Friday night pizza, your intervention is a triangulation and undermines the other parent, making it far more likely that the scenario will repeat itself. In my husband's family growing up, it was his mother saying, "Wait till your father gets home!" She was abdicating her authority even as she attempted to call in a hypothetical reinforcement. This kind of dynamic is not reserved for older children. It is easy—and common—to triangulate with a toddler or even an infant, whether by invoking a child's perceived distress to blame a co-parent for lack of care or involvement, or by not being able to work out a consistent response to night-waking, feeding difficulties, or separation anxiety.

Not only is a child of any age affected by the parents' disagreement, but the parents react to each other's presence too. There are detectable changes in the behavior of one parent when the other parent is present.[107] In one study, fathers seem to become more authoritative and mothers more nurturing when both of them are present. The content of the change is less important, though, than that it reminds us that we affect each other even when we are not trying to, sometimes simply by our emotional states, perhaps through an expression, tone of voice, or even touch.

There are other issues to consider: Is there one parent or are there two? If the parents are separated, are they negative about each other to their children? Do they enforce the same rules about behavior or bedtime? Are there alloparents—relatives, babysitters, friends—who share responsibility for the child? Do these adults also share values and ways of handling daily life? Do they support each other, or do they undermine each other? Do they communicate well with each other? Can they keep their own conflicts within their own relationships, or do they use the child to further their own agendas? Sometimes conflict is triggered by external events like job loss, or even the loss of social support, as when a close friend moves away. But just as often, change internal to the family system, and even change that is totally expected, can be a source of stress.

It is natural for parents to want to intervene in sibling conflict: No one likes to hear their kids fight with each other, and many parents may feel it reflects badly on them if their children do fight, especially in front of others. Sibling conflict is an area where it is imperative that parents work hard to be consistent, since otherwise you will surely trip over the many interlocking triangles you have constructed together. One of the most common instincts of parents is to blame an older child if a fight breaks out, but the principles of family systems, as well as the power of blame, suggest that caution is in order. An example:

Two kids are building a sandcastle together. Suddenly, there's a sand fight. "Stop it! What's going on?" you shout.

"He took the shovel I was using."

"Don't take his shovel."

"He was hitting me with it!"

"Don't hit your brother!"

And so on. Each turn gets you deeper into the morass of he said/he said.

Children learn what is likely to happen next through experience, day in and day out. As with so much else, you and your co-parent, or other regular caretakers, decide when and how you will intervene in conflicts between your children. But bear in mind that putting the weight of your authority on the side of one child breeds resentment in that child toward the other. Remember that what is at stake, more than the decibels of screaming and yelling, are relationships.

Developmental Change

"What will happen next?" is a question most family members can answer, so well do they know how their system works. But change is constant in family life, including what family members need and, therefore, the patterns that correspond to those needs. Normal developmental changes, like a child learning to dress herself, touch everyone in a family system. She may need more time to get dressed; there may be conflict when she takes too long; whichever parent used to help her may have trouble letting go of her dependence or may not like the clothes she chooses. Looking at families over time, family therapists work under the assumption that even normal developmental steps disrupts family structure. For example, when the first of two children graduates from high school and leaves home, the second is suddenly the only child at home, for better or worse. How do we survive the turbulence of even small changes, much less births and deaths, divorces and new families?[108]

Many children complain that their parents are far more permissive with a younger child than with an older one—later bedtimes, fewer chores and responsibilities. This is practically inevitable as parents learn how to be parents the hard way, by doing it. They come in with all sorts of ideas and ideals that reality knocks down. Or as they have more kids they simply pay less attention. Having four children across an 11-year spread, I was acutely aware of the way in which our family had to reconstitute itself each time someone left for college: There was a new oldest each time, and finally my youngest was the only child at home—an enormously different habitat and system.

As families and relationships, like individuals, develop and change, those changes amount to another kind of environment, an environment of time, if you will.[109] This is also true of historical time. Baby boomers like me grew up under the fear of the Cold War and the atom bomb; today's children grow up with the specters of terrorism and climate change. Then there are other less anticipated transitions, like moving, changing jobs, a college graduate returning home. There are big, predictable changes to systems, of course, as time passes. Family members arrive by birth or adoption or marriage; family members leave by going to college or moving out. There are big, less predictable changes through divorce, serious illness, or death. Each transition requires adjustments in relationships as well as changes in the habitat. Who is going to take the trash out now that Al has gone to college? Who gets to use the car first? These are especially important times to look under the hood and pay attention to how the system is functioning.

A newborn comes home from the hospital. The older sibling, 3 ½, wakes up in the night because of the crying of the new baby. She gets up and goes to her parents' bed, where she has gotten used to expecting a groggy, sometimes grumpy, reception, and one parent taking her back to bed with a hug and a kiss and maybe a little back rub. But this night, she comes in to find her father changing the baby, her mother in the bathroom, the lights on, and a curt "go back to bed." No one intended it, there was just a lot going on, but she feels hurt and confused. This time she goes, but she wakes up again a couple of hours later and calls out. No one hears her at first; they are just too tired. So she turns up the volume. Her dad comes in, gives her a kiss, and rubs her back, but he leaves before she has gone back to sleep. The next morning, she is grumpy and has a hard time falling asleep that night, which in turn ratchets up Dad's irritation. She has trouble getting up the next morning and whines while she gets dressed and ready to go to preschool. And so on. Even if her parents worked hard to prepare her for her new little sister, there is no way they can really prepare even themselves for the changes, big and small, that having two kids will bring to their family system.

At the other end of the family life cycle, a child goes to college or gets married or has a child, bringing an in-law into the family system. The remaining child or children and parents will inevitably—albeit unconsciously—adjust their behavior. A second of three becomes "the oldest"; a second child becomes an only child; a youngest is displaced by a niece or nephew. Both positive and negative stress affect us all.[110]

In one family I worked with, an 8-year-old boy was hitting more than seemed warranted. When we looked under the family hood, it turned out that his older sister had had lots of doctors' visits because of what turned out to be a serious allergy. Her parents were worried and tense and rarely scolded the sister for anything, perceiving her as fragile; the boy was sent to friends' houses to play rather than going on the doctors' visits but became unwelcome because he was hitting so much. His hitting was communication: Something is wrong here! Help me! Get me out of here. I want to be home. I need attention too! Once the parents "heard" his hitting as a message, they were able to make some adjustments and break the pattern. *(See also Chapter Seven, for effects of developmental change on relationships and authority.)*

It can be overwhelming to consider all of the ways that a family system can be affected, all of the patterns that seem entrenched, and all of the forces influencing family members from both inside and out. With each parent coming from a different family ethos, there are many places for disagreement. Some of these are related to temperament or external stresses, some come from ethnic, cultural, or religious practices, and many emerge from parents' *own* family systems. Your child too is a person, navigating *her* way forward in your family system.

Chapter Six

Who Are You?
Self, Emotion, and Authority

To celebrate my turning 6, my parents took me, alone, to see the newly re-issued *The Wizard of Oz*. It was my first movie. Four siblings, two older and two younger, were left at home. It was a big deal to be given this special attention, pulled out of the family system, as it were, for a solo birthday outing. My other birthday present was a doll with a dog, which I had named Dorothy and Toto. I was in a heightened state of expectation and excitement, securely seated between my parents in the huge, dark theater, unfazed by flying monkeys or the Wicked Witch of the West. But when the big hot air balloon worked loose and took off without Dorothy, who was left bereft on the ground clutching Toto as the Wizard flew away, I fell apart. Triggered into a full-fledged meltdown, or what my mother described in her personal slang as an "NB," for nervous breakdown, I insisted that we leave the theater. I was so upset—angry, sad, betrayed—that I took action. The minute we got home I immediately renamed my new doll Diane. The doll is long gone but I remember the moment vividly.

A Feeling of Being You

Any child is *someone*, a person who, in the routine moments of family life, in a relationship with you, acts and interacts from her own developing sense of herself and the way the world works. And you, a someone too, consider who this child is, what it is like to be with her, and who you are in relation to her, filtered through *your* experience in the world. But you can't know what it feels like from the inside for her. My behavior at the theater probably didn't surprise my parents, who surely would have described me as sensitive, but renaming my doll was a less predictable choice, something I came up with by myself. We will look closely at temperament and other givens in the next chapter, but first let's consider the important and often forgotten reality of you and your child being two individual people or selves.

You each develop in the context of a culture, a family, a time and place. Whatever the influences that have shaped your perceptions and experiences, each of you maintains a feeling of being *you*, of being a self. And what does it *feel* like to be one of those selves? What is it about one self that gives it natural authority in relation to the other self? How does it feel to be the authority and to tell another person what to do? How does it feel as the child grows and changes? It mattered how my parents responded to my outburst at the movie theater because they were my most intimate partners in developing my sense of self.

Truly believing that your child is another person with a subjective experience, a mind, a body, and a perspective—and her own strategies to handle stress—is fundamental to your natural authority. A screaming, oppositional 3-year-old, or a passionately upset child of any age, can be very powerful. You want to go out; he refuses to put on his shoes and kicks them out of the way. "No!" he shouts. "I won't!" What is it like to be *him* in that moment? And how do you bridge the gap that such an outburst creates?

As it happens, my parents and I left the theater and went home. Even though I don't remember how long I was upset or what we talked about during the 20-minute drive, the experience as a whole still resonates with me, now a grandmother of five, more than 60 years later. They could have tried to firmly calm me down in the theater and insist that I stay; they could have taken me out into the lobby and talked it through, hoping we could all go back in. Depending on my past experience with them, I might have done just that. They could have punished me or given me the cold shoulder once we got home for making what must have been an embarrassing scene for them. With five children and 10 years of experience being parents together by that time, their habits of authority were probably well-established. Their choice was to respond to my passionate objections and let me make the decision. This is consistent with other high-emotion moments I can remember in my relationship with them having to do with sex, politics, and life decisions, like taking time off from college, moving in with my boyfriend, or getting married. That was their approach to natural authority, our relationship, and my developing self.

The Self Is the Body, the Body Is the Self

Most of us would agree that gradually over the course of early childhood, each of us experiences himself or herself as someone. William James, the 19th-century philosopher who is often called the father of American psychology, described the self as both the one who knows, "I," and the one who is known by others, "Me." This distinction makes intuitive sense: You feel like someone who can know and act and feel, and you feel like someone whom others know and with whom others interact and share feelings. James further divided this "Me" into several kinds of selves, one of which was social and as variable as the people with whom one had relationships.[111]

Increasingly, neuroscientists see the self as intimately interwoven with the entire body, as a stream of perceptions, feelings, sensations, and thoughts that make up one's experience in the world, rather than a particular entity in some part of the brain. Some argue that a primary role is played by a region called the anterior cingulate cortex, which is where the brain processes sensory information from the body (more about this below).

Memories of one's experiences, and one's reaction to them, create a sense of self that although constantly changing retains a central sense of being felt in the body, even as it thinks, acts, and interacts with others and with the world.

If you don't think about the self being in a body, it will be harder to feel and express the authority you use both to keep your child safe and to help him develop the judgment he needs to keep himself safe. When a toddler says, "no brush teeth," she is an active self whose will has to be reckoned with by a dad with toothbrush in hand. Depending on how much she feels or means by her declaration, she will squirm, or kick, or perhaps collapse on the floor if her father insists on her teeth being brushed. You each have a perspective, a will, being acted out in this context and with each other. That will, acted out with the body, is not only present in what she expresses but also in the proprioceptive feeling she gets from her tantrum. You make guesses about what she feels, needs, and wants from what you know about her and your relationship with her, hoping to relieve her stress.[112]

The newborn can do little but move his arms and legs in a random way, suck on a bottle, breast, or pacifier, burp, cry, pee and poop, and take in the sights and sounds of family life. He is primed to learn patterns in order to enhance his survival; his actions are largely instinctive and not yet under his control. The 3-year-old runs and climbs; falls down and gets up again; builds towers out of blocks; walks up and down stairs; rides a Big Wheel bike; throws a ball. His fingers know their way around your iPad, and maybe he can put on his own jacket or at least try. Only five years older, the 8-year-old might seem almost a different creature from either of her younger siblings. She is competent in many of her movements; she has developed control over her body enough to handle tools and follow rules; she is capable of reading and thinking more analytically. Physically, her limbs may have elongated enough to make her look like an older child, and she may even have hints of adolescent features and moodiness.

What Happens Next? Sensing, Feeling, Reacting

Most people locate their subjective feeling of being someone right behind the eyes, the location of the prefrontal cortex, the brain's center of organizing and planning. However, evolution tends to build on old structures and systems instead of inventing new ones, leading some to argue that the human sense of self is in fact rooted in the need to be ready for action: to get food, to escape prey, to reproduce, to protect our young, and to maintain homeostasis.[113] In this view, the self emerges in the motor parts of the brain and then interacts with both external and internal stimuli to provide the foundation for all other forms of consciousness.

Consider a worm that senses the earth along one side of its body as it wriggles along looking for dead leaves to nibble on, feeling, on the rest of its elongated body, the air temperature, breeze, and moisture. Now think of a newborn stretching and rooting and crying, experiencing the sensory multi-ring circus you and I take for granted. From inside the watery womb to air and light and noise and human touch, his first—and his continuing—experience of the world is of being held, but also of himself moving and acting in it, and of the responses of humans and eventually objects.[114] As a living being, his body, like yours, is not only always interacting with the environment but also never stops changing: A toddler falls repeatedly while she learns to walk, or a gangly adolescent might have grown six inches in a year and has to figure out what to do with his long arms as he awkwardly flirts with a girl on the school steps.

The sensations of any given moment, the messages from your five senses, your muscles, your skin, and from what you sense internally in your viscera are collectively known as interoception, or what one neuroscientist calls "the global emotional moment" creating the experience of "the I in the feeling self."[115] The sensations are communicated to the brain via nerves networked throughout the body and encoded together in a moment of time.

This is your subjective experience of self, the way your brain represents the neural activity of any given moment, that is, what is happening now. This is what makes it possible for the body and the brain to interact with and adapt to their environment. But it also makes memory: The connections between neurons that were active at the same time are reactivated together again. By renaming my doll when I got home from the movie, I tried to cut off this process, hoping to quash my memories of the troubling movie with Dorothy and Toto.[116]

When two people interact, your memories of past interactions influence you. Your brain predicts what might happen as neuron networks representing memories are reactivated to influence your perception. A child wonders, "How is the way my mother's voice sounds or the way her face looks similar to other times I have heard or seen her? What happens when she looks like that?" Meanwhile, the parent considers, "Will this child have a meltdown if I reprimand her here in the grocery store? I don't think I can handle a tantrum." Or, "This is the third time he has violated his curfew, but he just got an upsetting text from a friend. I don't want to upset him more." None of this has to be conscious, though some of it may be. Not just your brain but your body itself remembers. Some of what it remembers we feel as emotion, which we will come back to below. But let's look first at the joint development of body and self.

Recognizing a Self in Others

A fundamental aspect of being human is being able to perceive and think and feel, and to understand that the other people we interact with must also perceive and think and feel. Parents and children attribute motivations, thoughts, and wants to the other person in order to anticipate and make sense of the other person's behavior. Perhaps most important for parental authority, there is an emotional—or as psychologists say, *affective*—aspect to what we guess about other people, which means that we come to know and to act on the knowledge that the other person has feelings and *that they may be different from ours.* Note that knowing or guessing what the other's feelings might be does not necessarily imply empathy, the ability to understand and share the other's feelings.[117] Because you can never truly know what the experience of the other person is—and in fact may have difficulty articulating your own experience in a way that is understandable and convincing to the other—your guess, at any given moment, has a large chance of being wrong. Even when you are feeling very attuned to someone, it is impossible to literally know what it feels like to be that person. You are separate selves, with separate perspectives, shaping each other through your interactions.

Of course, you have (or had) parents too. But it is likely that it took until well into adulthood before you could begin to consider your parents as people with feelings, needs, and worries, especially ones that might not concern you. *Your* self continues to develop as you and your children grow older and have more experiences together. As you age, it may slowly dawn on you, often in difficult moments as a parent, that there were reasons for your parents to behave the way they did. Times when they seemed not to pay you enough attention, for example, may have been because of stressors in their own lives and relationships.

The limits on our ability to truly consider the perspective of the others with whom we are so deeply intimate goes in both directions. There is so much to think of when you are a parent—whether in the early days of learning to burp and diaper or the later days of rationing screen time—that it's easy to lose sight of the deeper currents of relationship running between you and your child. It may be only in the most heightened moments of great togetherness or great distress that you can appreciate how much this other being is herself a person, someone with a brain and a body, a will and a mind, albeit a younger and less experienced one.

How one thinks about other selves is influenced from the earliest moments by cultural beliefs and traditions. What feels natural for you may not be natural for others. For example, it is not the practice in every culture to speak directly to infants. Societies with a collectivist philosophy are far less likely to emphasize the self, focusing instead on the needs of the group.

Mind the Gap

Voices coming over the loudspeaker in the subway systems of many large cities remind riders to pay attention to the gap between the platform and the train. So too in human interaction, and especially for parents and children. It is often in situations in which parents are actively exercising authority that gaps in understanding emerge and cause trouble, from the early days of figuring out sleep and feeding to the oft-dreaded developmental hotspots of toddlerhood and adolescence. The fact that your child's brain is still developing leads to many of the conflicts plaguing relationships between parents and children of all ages. In some moments, you may treat your child too much as an equal, too much as another person more like yourself than he is, and expect behavior and understanding of which he is not yet capable.

Inevitably, some of your interactions will be conflicted. You may think that your daughter is purposely pushing your buttons when she doesn't come to dinner and she may feel unfairly and meanly treated, when in fact *she's* having a hard time making the transition out of what she's doing and *you're* tired and exasperated. Each of you tries out the behavior stimulated or triggered by the other. And you may have a hard time feeling sympathetic.

Or take a 13-year-old who can get around alone on a bike or bus, who can mow a neighbor's lawn, who can make a playlist on iTunes—doesn't he have a pretty well-developed brain? Why did he end up texting with friends instead of unloading the dishwasher, as he knows he was supposed to? Does he really think he did an adequate job of folding the laundry? What was he thinking when he "forgot" his phone and "forgot" that he was supposed to be at his music lesson?

Unfortunately, it is the parent's lot as the grownup (however stressed) to figure out how to move past these kinds of difficult situations. That can be hard, but your child can learn from you that each of you has a different perspective, and the more you can understand that, the more in sync you will be. He may need you to help him structure his time or come up with strategies for remembering what he is supposed to be doing when he is supposed to be doing it. The kind of help you provide depends a lot on your relationship, what you have learned about him, your temperaments, the expectations and organization of your habitat, the balance of power in the family system, and so on. There are different ways to use your natural authority. You may decide that age- and task-appropriate consequences are in order to help him remember; you may prefer to sit down and work with him to develop strategies. If defiance is the issue, not strategies or memory, your work may have to do with your own past responses and his expectations.

At the other extreme, you may underestimate your child's emotional or cognitive capacities. You know quite well that little though she may be, she has a will of her own, but you may forget that she has feelings, opinions, and an emerging theory about *your* mind based on your relationship so far. Just as you have expectations and attributions about her, even a 3-year-old has expectations and attributions about you. She has a sense of whether or not you will be angry if she climbs up on a chair to get a cookie out of the cookie jar. She may have a memory of something that happened last time, or of observing you with her older sibling when she had a snack right before dinner. She knows, even if she can't say so, whether or not you will be angry if she doesn't pick up her toys when she is told, whether or not you will let her use your iPad to play a game at bedtime. That doesn't mean, however, that she yet has the self-control to behave accordingly, and an important aspect of your authority with a child of any age is to respond to your child's behavior in a way that takes her temperament, perspective, and capacities into consideration.

Two Selves, One Authority

One of my sons, at 4 ½, begged to take piano lessons like his older cousins. At first, I said no; he seemed too young. But he kept insisting and I finally gave in. He soon changed his mind and refused to practice. What to do? We had decided early on that all of our children would take some kind of music lessons. Doubting my own authority in the face of his vehemence, I worried, "If I let him have his way, I will never be able to get him to take piano again." I opted to make him continue, and continue he did, complaining off and on for the next five years, at which point he and I negotiated a switch first to chorus and then guitar. True to his early interest, he became a musician. I see now that he was indeed too young to grasp what taking lessons required. When he said, "I hate piano!" what he meant was, "I like how it sounds and how it feels to play piano, but I don't want anyone to tell me what to play." Too insecure about my own capacity to revisit the question when he was a little older or to find another way for him to engage with music, I ignored his perspective (what it was like to be him, a 4-year-old who liked music) and insisted on my perspective (our family's belief in the value of music lessons and my own self-doubts), creating needless stress for both of us.

Being able to accept the other's perspective even as you use your natural authority begins with the understanding that the other self may not see or experience things the way you do: You are in different bodies, and you have different experiences and different abilities to understand what you experience. Conflict sometimes emerges because of the parents' greater ability to look ahead. My 4-year-old son had no way of knowing what it would mean to take lessons over time. As the parent, you bring to bear your sense of what's important along with an awareness of implications for your child's development and for your relationship. Each incident in which you balance authority with the other's perspective adds a new layer to your changing relationship.

All Experience Is Emotional

A big part of who you are in the world, both in your subjective experience and in how your *self* comes across to others, is emotion. A current theory of emotion suggests that there are not particular identifiable universal feelings or systems of emotion, but that humans construct emotion from the interoceptive sensations described above. This is a rapid, automatic process engaged in by your brain to make meaning of what you are sensing. But the most important point for our purposes is that emotion is a bodily process fundamental to survival itself, a process human beings use to adapt to experience, sometimes in extreme ways. Feelings cause us to take, in Darwin's words, "actions expressive of certain states of mind."[118]

For a parent, this is nowhere more evident than in a toddler's tantrum, when an entire nervous system is wracked with rage or distress. Imagine an older sibling is going on a play date. "I want to go too! It's not fair!" shouts the younger one. At such moments, your child literally cannot understand what you are saying, however calm you sound. Her brain's alarm systems have gone off, as if she will be left behind in a dark cave. But emotions are not only experienced at the high pitch of a tantrum. Against a bodily backdrop of internal processes that maintain one's essential safety and integrity, or "the body carrying on," everyone also experiences and communicates, mostly nonverbally, "background emotions." These are full-body feelings like calmness or tension, contentment or irritability, from waking up on the wrong side of the bed to a general sense of well-being.[119] Even a young child can sense another's mood, although he might not be able to say why. Part of a therapist's work with parents and children, or with co-parents, is to help them become more conscious of what they sense in themselves and in the other, and to more consciously use that information to understand the other's perspective. *(See Chapter Eight.)*

There is much more to emotion than the two extremes of meltdowns and the background hum of an emotional state of mind and body. Through the experience of emotion—your experience of what is going on in this moment—your *self* is prompted or motivated to act. If you feel tense already and your child interrupts a phone call, a more acute emotional sensation, which you might identify as anger, both suffuses your body and prompts you to do something. You scowl, shake your finger, hiss "shhhh," or even blurt out a retort you may later regret. Despite centuries of belief in universal emotions, like sadness and anger, current research suggests that there is great variability in how people react to the same stimuli and how they interpret what they experience.[120]

Lisa Feldman Barrett's theory of how we *make* or *construct* emotion regards affect as a combination of the level of arousal we feel in our bodies and the value we give to that sensory experience. I vividly remember a time when we had a family over for brunch; two of the children present were about a year old. One was my son, who took a large box of Cheerios and dumped it out on the floor. I did nothing as he and the other toddler gleefully grabbed fistfuls and stuffed them into their mouths. I decided I might as well wait to clean up until they had had their fun. The visiting father looked at me in disbelief: How can you stand watching them make that mess?[121]

We tend to pay less attention to the ongoing level of arousal we experience but are acutely aware of specific stimuli. A stimulus can be the sight of someone you love, a smell, a song, a reprimand, a memory, or a rumbling in your stomach. An infant finds herself standing on her own and smiles broadly at the sensation as well as the excited reaction of a roomful of adults. A

10-year-old sits on the piano bench at his first recital and is so overcome that he can't play. An adolescent sees an old boyfriend across the street, in front of the coffee shop where they had their first date, and feels like crying. A parent reads a homesick email from a child at college and gets weepy. Or the stimulus can be an action by someone else, such as a parent who stops a toddler from touching an outlet by calling out a sharp "no!" The toddler's body and brain take note: I have been thwarted! I want to touch this; now I can't touch it. Any stimulus, familiar or unfamiliar, evokes bodily sensations and associations based on your history with a place, with other people, or with a similar past experience.

From Feeling to Action

Sensations become part of the brain's ongoing process of assessing the need for action: Can I tolerate what I am feeling now? Do I need to respond to this? How should I respond? What does this stimulus mean for me? Will it stop me from getting what I want? Will it injure me? Will it get me something I need? What did I do last time this happened? This assessment is neither instinct nor conscious thought but a multifaceted response specific to your experience and expectations. The brain engages in its habit of prediction and correction to decide if this stimulus is what we think it is and to act accordingly. In the classic example, a stick on the path looks suspiciously like a snake and you startle. Once you realize it is a stick, you relax. Or, in the words of Feldman Barrett, "you feel what your brain believes."[122] If it had been a snake, you would have responded in a way related to your level of comfort or distress with snakes. Closer to family life, if your daughter hears a loud noise, she too instinctively starts. Once she learns that the noise was her little brother knocking over the elaborate block tower she just constructed, her reaction becomes emotional. She runs to the scene of the crime to yell, to cry, or to hit him.

That increase in arousal causes the brain to send messages to both the bloodstream and neural pathways in the form of electrical and chemical signals, which in turn act on neurons, muscle fibers, and organs to cause involuntary responses of the body like blood flow, muscle tensing, sweating, or a change in voice quality. They are part of what constitute the body's regulation of its homeostasis and affect the way the brain continues to process incoming stimuli, including what other people do, translating the stimuli into responses visible to others as nonverbal behavior. *(See Chapter Nine.)* If the girl's brother continues to mess with her blocks, she will undoubtedly get more upset, running back to you to complain or hitting or pushing him. Any state of mind and body has many possibilities for action, actions determined in large part by history, both evolutionary history (what will keep me safe?) and, if another person is involved, personal history (what can I expect from this person or situation?).

Note that we are talking about changes in the body, that is, behaviors and thoughts elicited by the physiological feeling of emotion. Note also that the word emotion encompasses "motion": Your young toddler at the outlet might withdraw his hand when you shout "no," and might also start crying or run out of the room, so new is he to being scolded. The big sister whose block tower went down might rush in with her fists clenched in her angry response, creating a trigger for the offender to respond himself with fists or screaming. This is the body's motor system acting by movement or communication, both verbal and nonverbal.

An adult enters the room seeking to calm the situation down. "What's going on here?" The unconscious feeling of each child comes into awareness, and the processes going on in body and brain are interrupted. The adult's presence and words connect to thoughts and ideas and values. Two children learn another lesson about feeling sad or mad or glad; they learn words for the feelings they have; they gradually develop more complex thoughts in relation to both you and others. Both implicitly and explicitly, they learn what is okay to express in the language of words and the language of the body in this habitat of their family. Natural authority, then, extends to the myriad ways in which the more mature emotional systems of adults help develop those of children. What should she react to? How should she react? What should she do? What should she do with the feelings she experiences? These implicit lessons about emotions, learned through interaction, conversation, and everyday family life, are a large part of what constitutes the self in action. *(See Chapters Eight and Nine.)*

Authority, Emotion, and the Developing Self

The inseparability of thought and emotion has practical implications for your authority. What you probably find difficult, but painfully frequent, is the necessity to assert your authority—to be the grownup—at times when you yourself feel emotional, or when your child feels and shows emotion. It is often *because* you are very upset about something that your child has done or is doing that you have to assert authority: Your teenager violates her curfew, making you both furious and frantic with worry; your 11-year-old has bullied someone on the school bus and is suspended for three days, which embarrasses you and obligates you to take time off from work or find a babysitter. Even relatively insignificant interactions, such as getting your kids out the door in the morning, can evoke enough stress to threaten to undermine your authority. Each of you will express yourselves one way or another, in language or action or simply mood, because that is what human selves do. But such interactions bear some risk.

Like all parents, you have probably reacted spontaneously with impatience or anger or frustration more often than you care to remember, and perhaps you worried later that you had caused harm or hurt feelings. And you may have, in that moment. And you will again. It is this risk of disruption of the relationship that inhibits many parents from asserting authority with their children. Luckily, it is the *patterns* of interaction, rather than isolated instances, that are more important for your relationship, your authority, and your child's development. If, for example, you feel repeatedly frustrated with your child for whining or taking forever or being forgetful or obstinate, these interactions will accumulate to constitute an important part of your relationship. To change the pattern, you must, as the parent and the authority, see the pattern as a function of the relationship between you, not as a characteristic of or bad behavior by your child. But it is not an equal relationship, and your two selves don't bear equal responsibility. You are the big object with enormous emotional power, and your brain and self are far more developed and far more able to understand what's going on. You are more capable of changing your behavior and getting some distance from the situation. A child depends on interaction with you, even if you are sometimes inconsistent and irritable, to become a person with a sense of self, whatever his biological inheritance.

You know this unconsciously, which is why you act with an infant as if he is a person. As he grows older and his brain becomes more like yours, the interaction becomes more equal. There is the sharing of joint attention, as when your gaze and your child's gaze follow each other's, or the sharing of intentions, say, when you play jokes by pointing a spoonful of applesauce toward your mouth when it's meant for his or thrusting his bottle toward you to drink. Perhaps most importantly, there is the sharing of emotional states, as when a toddler has just fallen down and hurt himself and looks up but doesn't cry until he sees your reaction. Sharing emotions is what human beings all do most of the time. Even early in life, emotions are both the means by which we communicate and what we communicate about. These shared emotional states continue to one degree or another over a lifetime and have great bearing on your relationship, on your authority, and on your child's developing self.[123]

All parents—myself included—can remember moments in which they wish they had responded differently than they did. I can attest to having doubts like this for decades. But I reassure myself that it is not any one awful moment that counts with your children, it is a lifetime of moments between you that matter. But whether in divorced families in which children go back and forth between households, or in intact families with two parents in one home, children demonstrate resilience and adaptability.

Shame and Guilt

Anger isn't the only way attunement breaks down; shame can precipitate a version of the freeze response, a shutdown rather than a meltdown. Shame and guilt are part of the same emotion family, the so-called social emotions. They share a number of features, including similar kinds of triggering experiences, similar behaviors (such as facial movements, bodily actions, and vocalizations), and similar though not identical interpersonal functions. They also serve important functions in the regulation of behavior and relationships. Researchers have distinguished them in this way: Shame is more self-focused, i.e., you feel silly, embarrassed, inadequate, or worse because of something you have done, and the feeling makes you want to move away, whether to another physical space or by slumping, looking down, or otherwise withdrawing from interaction with others. Guilt is more other-focused and functions to motivate you to make amends or reparations to someone else.[124]

Infants can do little to regulate themselves and aren't yet sensitive to shaming. As your infant becomes more mobile at the end of the first year, she learns what she is allowed to touch, where she is allowed to go. You induce shame in a number of ways. Because the visual system is so powerful and, when positive, a source for the release of dopamine, a scowling facial expression may be enough. But because she is often not looking at your face, you must repeatedly say "No!" Adults have been observed to give a prohibition as often as once every nine minutes. This necessary socialization to the environment is also one of the ways an infant learns self-regulation. Through repeated experiences of disapproval, the child gets small doses of shame and disconnection, which, when followed by reconnection through a smile or a "that's okay," give her the opportunity to feel safe again.[125]

Other experiences of shame, e.g., being scolded for peeing on the floor or crumpling up a sibling's drawing, teach the toddler what matters to the adults in the household and what happens if she violates those rules. An older child's transgressions are more likely to be interpersonal, yelling at or hitting a sibling, stomping out of the room. She may get more than a look of disapproval, perhaps a time-out or a scolding. After each incident, each of you in effect updates your "working model" of this relationship, and the child's brain grows increased connections. Because shame is effectively a reaction to the loss of attunement, it is important to repair the break and reconnect, in order to allow the child to return to a feeling of autonomic and emotional balance.[126]

Imagine a 4-year-old going with his mother to visit someone whose house has lots of novel objects to look at and places to go. The hostess glances up from what she's doing and sees the child in the act of picking up a treasured picture framed in glass. She calls out, "Be careful with that" in a louder and harsher voice than is either intended or appropriate for the situation. The child looks up with a startled expression, puts the picture down in silence, and turns away. The little face crumples, lips quiver. The child feels ashamed, and the hostess feels guilty, not only toward the child but toward her visiting friend. It will probably take a few minutes of gentle approach, offers of stories, apologies, and assurances until amends have been made and both parties are "regulated" again. There are no magic bullets for making amends and no foolproof protocols; as in so many cases, what you do depends on your relationship.

The experience of shame is among the most powerful a person can have and in fact is thought to underlie much interpersonal conflict and rage.[127] Even my dog feels something like it when I catch him in the kitchen with the cheese I forgot to put away. Making a child feel ashamed is an easy trap to fall into. If, like my dog, a child has snuck something forbidden out of the kitchen, or lost his shin guards yet again, that feeling of exasperation can easily take over. Feeling ashamed yourself about your perceived failures as a parent, often including having flown into a rage, is another trap for parents, and it can be lifelong.

Feelings of shame and guilt affect not only people's behavior but, over time, their self-assessment, both in relation to specific others and in general. This can be true whether the feelings are triggered by your own thoughts about yourself after you do something that violates a rule or by someone else's response to your actions. Parents are as susceptible to shame as children, perhaps more so. You forgot to do something for your child that you promised to do, and you feel both ashamed of your forgetfulness and guilty about how the child may feel. You blurted out an angry or scornful remark when your teenager got under your skin, and you realize afterward that you had let your own mood get in the way. You swore in front of a child and you have house rules against swearing. You're human, as well as a parent, but you feel ashamed.[128]

Emotional Scaffolding

Your child and you are each in a body, in a moment in time, and in an environment that often includes both of your bodies. Each of you interacts with and experiences not only your surroundings but also each other's presence, including what you remember and feel about each other. But you don't rely only on what you have learned or on what John Bowlby called your internal working model; you also continue to sense the other, checking your current perceptions against the past.[129]

This perception of each other and your capacity to imagine the other's perspective are key to the trust in your relationship and to your authority. A crawling nine-month-old needs a caretaking adult to be ready to grab her should she get into trouble. The 18-month-old who hates having someone put a toothbrush into her mouth can't understand why it is important. She therefore needs a physical sense of both authority and trust that you won't hurt her. An older child who is hovering on the edge of tears needs a gentle touch on the arm to keep him steady.

This is not news to you. Every day you treat your child as the person he is, but you also help him with what he can't yet do alone. This is scaffolding, the psychological equivalent of the supporting platforms builders use when they need to work and stay safe at a height they can't reach. We encountered another version of this in Chapter Three when discussing chores. This type of help is perhaps easiest to see in language, where you can actually hear development happen from one day to the next. You instinctively correct or expand what you think he is saying, probably without hesitation. You know that you are the language authority, at least compared to your young child. So too with emotion.

Something akin to scaffolding, applied to emotional and interpersonal understanding, helps build your child's emotional self. This is natural authority. You lend your experience, your nurturance, and your nervous system. You do this without thinking when you help a toddler—or a teenager, for that matter—work out a conflict with a peer: "Toys have to be shared so everybody gets a turn," you might say calmly in a play group when a fight breaks out over who gets the truck. Or you might say to a rejected teen, in a low sympathetic tone, "Have you tried to talk to Joe about the fact that you feel hurt?" Some interactions communicate your values and beliefs. Others soothe feelings, while still others set limits or model behavior.

In any interaction with your child, who you are, the self you have become over your lifetime, interacts with and helps shape the child's developing self. Of course, this is also true to some degree of siblings, peers, teachers, and others. Everyone with whom your child has a relationship can influence who he becomes, for better or worse. But as the parent, the big object in your child's life, your influence looms large. And this is true whether you are helping him with other relationships or working on the one between you.

Such influence is not a one-way street. It bears repeating that the influence, the shaping, is mutual. How you behave with one child or another, including, prominently, the ways in which you assert your parental authority, depends a lot on what you have come to know and expect from her and on the relationship you have developed with each other, a relationship made of accumulated interactions, many of them repeated over and over again. It is partly because of this relationship history, for example, that there is less similarity between siblings than you might expect: Despite growing up in the same household, despite all the effort you may make as a parent to treat children equally, each sibling has unique relationships with each parent and with her siblings, in which she may seem to be a different person. What is different in each pair is not so much the person as the relationship between you, distinguished by different experiences and perspectives.

Change and Continuity

As your child gets older, her brain of course is catching up, as is her ability to think, act, and have opinions and a life of her own. Once she is grown up, you'd think it would get easier to resolve conflict. Not necessarily. You remain a big object emotionally for her, and she remains, in your eyes, someone to take care of, guide, or even tell what to do, but in a very different sense than she was as a child. My practice is filled with young adults whose parents have trouble relinquishing their authority. It is complicated enough for two unrelated adults to work out differences. Like any two people, a parent and child have had literally thousands of momentary experiences together, shaping their attitudes and responses to each other, but they have also had a shifting boundary of authority and autonomy across childhood that means they must constantly adjust to new responses in each other.

I have a photograph of my mother and me discussing my wedding menu. I was 23. I don't remember the details, but the looks on our faces show that it was not an easy conversation. In the many conversations that a parent and child have while planning a wedding or any big event, there is potential for intense emotion and conflicting feelings of ownership. The two prospective spouses have definite ideas about what they want: It's their wedding, after all, and they're grownups, aren't they? But perhaps the parents are very traditional and expect to be very involved. The parents and their children, of whatever age, have a complex of shared experience with each other in addition to the feelings and expectations each brings from elsewhere, the parents from their own wedding and perhaps their parents' interference, the children from the weddings of friends. It's the kind of intergenerational emotional force field that therapists often see. In my own situation, our often-rocky relationship surely contributed to this moment, as hard as we tried to connect. Interactions like these can be extremely stressful for both parties, in part because of the impending separation. The child has grown up, and yet many parents find it hard to let go. I call it the binoculars problem: As the parent, you keep your child in close focus, with your relational binoculars on high magnification. But for the child who has become an adult, the binoculars are turned the "wrong" way: You and your co-parent look far away.

Chapter Seven

Particular Selves:
Everyone Is a Little Bit Different

A 10-year-old comes home several days in a row complaining about the kids on the bus; they are teasing him, he says. They make fun of his hair, his backpack, and his shoes. His father talks it through with him, and they agree on some strategies. The strategies don't work, although the father has no way of knowing for sure which ones he actually tries. After a couple of weeks, the father suggests that it might help if he talked to someone at school, a suggestion that makes the boy collapse in a heap on the floor, hiding his face in his hands and shrieking: "No, no, no! I don't want you to talk to anyone! That will make it worse." Not long after, his younger sister complains of her teacher being unfair. "Shall I talk to her?" his father asks. "Yeah, I guess so." A 13-year-old girl reacts to her father's request to put her clothes away with a shrill "I will! Stop telling me what to do!" This has been her style of response since toddlerhood, so much so that her parents regularly admonish her to stop being overly dramatic. "I'm not overly dramatic! You guys just don't understand me." Her brother rarely gets upset.

Born Different

People differ, and that starts from the beginning. There are differences in the ages, genders, birth order, and situations of these pairs of children. But they are siblings, with the same parents, living in the same house, and going to the same school. How can they be so different? The level of embarrassment triggered in the first child by the idea of his father talking to the teacher compared to the "whatever" response of the second is very likely due to individual differences in temperament, or those qualities of being in the world and with other people that shape both how it feels to be you and how others feel being with you. Being someone means being so much at once: a self, a mind, a gender, a child, a parent, a sibling. The many answers to the fundamental question "Who are you?" when applied to you and your child, have a significant effect on your relationship of natural authority.

From birth, it is patterns of sleep that grab parents' attention first: Your neighbor's baby seems to fall asleep easily even as a newborn, while yours needs endless rocking. And as to the parents, one sleeps through frequent wakings; the other startles at the slightest stirring of the infant. Sleep is a factor that distinguishes humans early, but it is only one manifestation of the way in which our experience of the world and how we respond to it is shaped to a measurable degree by our biological inheritance.

When my first child was an infant, T. Berry Brazelton's *Infants and Mothers* had recently popularized the concept of innate temperament. Based on then new research, Brazelton's book explained that temperament is essentially a profile of a child's level of activity and reactivity to the world around him.[130] As a relatively isolated young mother with what I learned was a sensitive infant, this book helped me understand the ongoing adaptation a primary caregiver may need to make to the very particular baby she has. What is it like to be *this* baby in the world? How do *I* get through the day with this child, being who I am? And once there was another, and then two more, the concern was not only about each baby and me, but about how all of our different ways of experiencing life were going to function together.

Temperament is one of the givens of development, what in everyday conversation one might call "how you're put together."

Although there is far less consensus about what else in addition to temperament makes you and your child particular someones, there are at least three other givens: birth order, developmental change, and with some caution, to some degree (given the current burst of possibility and variable expressions of gender identity), gender. These factors bring a particular form to the self as a body in the world, to the brain systems that process and respond to the experience of each moment, and to what triggers its actions and reactions to people and situations.

Temperament as a Baseline

The birth of a second child can make much of what you think you have learned about being a parent seem almost irrelevant, so different can two babies be. This is an experience shared by many, if not most parents. "I treat them just the same way," you protest, exasperated, "but one is so easy and the other is always complaining, getting in my face." Because the focus here, above all, is on the relationship between you and your child, it is crucial to remember that the differences may be in you as a parent as well as in the babies. If you have two or more children, you were by definition older and more experienced when each successive child was born, even if it feels as if the experience gained with one doesn't help much with the other.

Life events such as the illness or death of a family member, a move, or unemployment also affect children of different ages in the same family. Not only that, you too have a temperament, which means that part of getting to know a new baby is working out how your ways of being in the world fit together, what is called goodness of fit.[131] Any consideration of your relationship must be mindful of how you and your child interact from moment to moment, that is, what you trigger in each other. When you add the temperament and behavioral style of a co-parent or other adult caretaker with whom you must negotiate parenting strategies, the situation becomes complicated.

A body of late 20th-century research has established that different children growing up in the same family do indeed have very different environments, at least some of which must be due to the different fits between parental and child temperaments, the working out of differences between parents over time, the presence of other children in the house, and a host of other influences. My own family of origin, while extreme, is a good illustration: By the time my youngest sister was born, my oldest sister was in college; they were bookends for the baby boomer generation, the oldest and youngest of nine.[132]

A pioneering longitudinal study of 100 families from infancy into adulthood underlies contemporary research on temperament. This study came up with three types: easy, slow to warm up, and difficult. For many years this was the conceptual framework for both temperament research and related parenting advice and was enormously helpful to me as a young mother when my firstborn wasn't much of a sleeper. In the succeeding decades, home observations and parent questionnaires have been supplemented with a range of biological measures that have allowed researchers to demonstrate some of the biological mechanisms that appear to underlie temperament.[133]

Although academics continue to debate how to classify temperament, the assessment is usually based on where one falls on six dimensions: behavioral inhibition, irritability/frustration, positive emotionality, activity level, attention or persistence, and sensory sensitivity.[134] These qualities show up in infancy, remain consistent over time, are at least somewhat predictive of later personality, and have a biological basis with parallels in nonhuman animal behavior, especially primates.

Temperament is the baseline around which a personality hovers throughout life, helping to shape but not determining how one develops. Think of the child's nervous system as a filter for experience, so that the very same experience, say, a consequence given for a chore undone, may register differently with different children. There may be some outlier moments;

a shy person can train himself to be less so, and a bold person can learn to temper his audacity in some situations lest he come across as disrespectful, but your neurobiological profile remains essentially the same.[135] There are now decades of research about temperament and many different ways of explaining this fundamental phenomenon of human development. I will illustrate temperament here using two major approaches, one with two major types and one with three major dimensions.

Analyzing Temperament: Two Types and Three Dimensions

Research on temperament has identified two primary types, *high-reactive*, or inhibited, and *low-reactive*, or uninhibited, which are believed to be the expression of two different biological systems. The brother in my opening example would be *high-reactive*, aroused to the point of agitation by the possibility of being exposed to school authorities as a victim of classmates' bullying. He is reacting to uncertainty and the risk of an unfamiliar situation, not to mention the possibility of being bullied again. It is novelty or surprise that triggers his amygdala to react, with a deep evolutionary advantage: "Watch out! What's up ahead?" The visceral feeling of vulnerability—maybe a queasy stomach, maybe a racing heart—leads him to make an interpretation based on his experience, perhaps having seen someone else ostracized for tattling, or a more general feeling that being the center of attention or being forced to speak to someone in authority is fraught with unknowns. "What will happen if the principal knows this happened to me?" he wonders. "What will people think of me? Won't things get worse, not better?" The inhibited child is cautious, timid, and far more likely than other children to develop anxiety.[136]

His sister is the uninhibited type. Novelty does not trigger her; in fact, she goes toward it. She is more likely to explore and take risks, to talk and smile more. The uninhibited child has a higher threshold for distress over uncertainty. It takes more to make her worried about what's behind the rock, and she will probably go look and see. The uninhibited child doesn't experience the same vulnerability, although she may encounter risks if her judgment doesn't keep up with her energy. There is of course a great risk for parents in having children of such different temperaments: The squeaky wheel gets the grease, as the saying goes. But in fact, squeaky wheels *need* more grease; this is part of what is meant by the nonshared environment of siblings.

From Low to High on Three Dimensions: Extroversion

Another approach identifies people on three primary dimensions: extroversion, sensitivity, and effortful control, each with a continuum from low to high. The first dimension ranges from extroversion at one end to introversion at the other. Levels of activity, impulsivity, and intensity of pleasure and anticipation range across this continuum from smiling and laughter on one pole to shyness and timidity at the other.[137] Not long ago I met two babies, each around six months old, both strangers to me and striking in their friendliness. I met one baby on a playground. He stretched out his hands to come to me from his mother's arms only seconds after I greeted his mother, a casual acquaintance. I observed his need to be closely monitored as his mother chatted with other adults and kept an eye on an older child. He grabbed at someone's coffee; he grabbed another baby's toy away from him. I smiled at the other in an airport baggage claim as her parents and I, complete strangers to each other, waited for our bags. She looked at me with a great big smile. She seemed not just to drink in but literally to gulp down the environment around her, but she had no impulse to reach out to me.

Like the younger sister in my first example, these two babies were both high on extroversion. They were going to become children who run, who show great excitement, who like going high and fast, who favor change and intensity. This is the 4-year-old who runs from the slide to tell you he has made a new friend, the 6-year-old you know you need to watch closely because she's always climbing to the top of ladders and walls, the teenager you worry about once she has her driver's license. If you are timid yourself, you may not only marvel at your child's approach to life but would want to restrain her.

By contrast, an infant low on extroversion (and high on introversion) would be slower to smile on meeting a stranger and more hesitant even to look up; when she did she would be watchful, cautious, or easily startled. As she got older, she might want you to come on play dates or want a new friend to come to her house; she might delay getting her driver's license. If you are more on the extrovert end of this continuum than your child, you may be impatient with him. "Why can't he just get over it?" you think to yourself. "There's nothing to be afraid of!" But for him there is something to fear: His filter may be different from yours, not to mention his being much smaller. You've seen the child who runs to grab a blue-jeaned leg at a barbeque, only to look up and see the wrong giant looking down at him. She was looking for reassurance and now has to deal with a stranger.

Low to High: Sensitivity

The dimension of sensitivity includes levels of fear, anger and frustration, sensory discomfort, and sadness. Later to develop than other factors, fear shows stability only after 10 months of age. This timing coincides with the emergence of the attachment system. Fear regulates by putting the brakes on as you approach situations that might be threatening or harmful. Part of what you can do as a parent is help a child learn what is truly threatening—but at the same time remember the filtering quality of each individual's nervous system. It really *is* scary for me to jump off a high diving board, and no amount of persuading by my high-in-extroversion, low-in-fear husband will get me to do it. I have forced myself, however, with the support and coaching of others, to jump off a medium high dive.[138]

The child high in this factor would be quick to get upset by an unknown or loud sound, for example, an interruption of an activity, or frustration at her inability to accomplish a task or assignment. She will be hard to soothe, easily disappointed or frightened, and have more difficulty recovering. This is the child who you may hesitate to scold or discipline, for fear that she is so easily hurt. A father recounted a lesson he learned early on: His daughter, who spoke very softly, seemed almost to cringe when he scolded her. When he made an effort to temper the degree of irritation in his voice, she responded better. Her sensitivity meant that she would respond to even the slightest indication that he was upset with her. This is the child who needs your calm authority and encouragement to take more risks, or who may need help developing coping strategies to manage her fears. A child low in sensitivity would be slower to feel discomfort or frustration or fear and easier to soothe or distract, or would have more capacity to self-soothe.

Twins offer parents a sometimes uncomfortable study of temperament in real time. When my youngest son was 2, he barely hesitated when I dropped him off for the first day of a new playgroup. Somewhat sensitive to new environments myself, I found myself thinking he should hesitate. Meanwhile, a woman standing near me was peering through the glass in the classroom door practically in tears: She had twins, a boy and a girl, one of whom was happily exploring the room and the other of whom was sobbing uncontrollably. It was clear that this mother had at least one child who was very sensitive. She clearly would have to respond to them differently.[139] I saw this mother after an interval of nearly 30 years, and she confirmed that what I had noticed in those early moments of separation stress had persisted as temperamental differences.

In a somewhat older pair of twins, age 4, and also a boy and a girl, separation at daycare goes well enough, but evenings and weekends are stressful. The mother has a long commute and gets home with just an hour before bed. The boy is happy to get home to his toys and take advantage of playtime before bed. The little girl, however, is often restless and agitated. She whines, complains, clings, and interrupts the parents' conversation. She refuses to settle down for bed. There is never any obvious proximate cause for the behavior. It may be that she is, in effect, thirsty for more soothing mom-time. Your natural authority—in this case knowledge of her temperament, your relationship, and whether more time together helps—is required. And these factors are easily entangled: What might have been a higher need one week can easily turn into a hard-to-break habit.

Low to High: Effortful Control

The last dimension, *effortful control*, like fear, is not usually apparent before 10 months. As the child's brain develops, so do the ability to focus attention, plan, and suppress or control actions, and the ability to perceive and get pleasure from less exciting or intense stimuli. At the other end of the continuum is poor persistence in attention or low ability to control distraction. I am reminded of my dog, Bobi, a beagle mutt, who would go after the smallest crust of pizza on the sidewalk or react to the slightest characteristic pre-walk movements that we made. The trouble was that he would lurch for the crust, or jump up and down and run around in circles until I had his leash ready to snap on, like a child who asks the same question over and over: Are we going for ice cream? Are we going for ice cream? Bobi was high on perception but low on self-control. Like some of the children in the now famous marshmallow study, in which participants were allowed to eat a marshmallow but would get two if they could wait 15 minutes, the child high in willpower can sit for long periods of time drawing, doing a puzzle, or just watching the world go by from a parent's lap.[140] The person high in effortful control has more flexibility because he is able to regulate his reactions to the world and make more choices about what he does. It is possible, however, to have too much control, to be impossible to pull away from an activity or too dependent on plans or certainty.

Temperament and Authority

Each dimension of temperament varies in what it takes to trigger it (latency); in how strong it is (intensity); in how often it is activated (frequency); in how long it lasts (duration); and in what it takes to recover (recovery). The two babies I met shared an uninhibited temperament but expressed it differently, one with extreme friendliness, the other with reaching and grabbing. There is a quality you recognize, but its trigger or threshold for distress, and how it shows itself, varies; sensitivity can emerge as an upset stomach or as agitation. The wide variation in early childhood experience also affects the expression of temperament: A child at home with a nanny or relative is probably exposed to fewer unfamiliar people than a child in group daycare; the world of a firstborn or only child is far different from a second, third, or fourth child. [141]

Aspects of temperament identify distinct, measurable factors or types; they are also very much related to one another. One factor may inhibit or facilitate the other. For example, fearfulness or self-control may inhibit aspects of extroversion, but extroversion itself may inhibit fear. I was extroverted and sociable, but I was a scaredy-cat. One memorable time this got me into trouble. I followed a group of children up a tree and found myself paralyzed with fear about getting down. My father climbed up to rescue me, but he might have been able to use what he knew about my sociable nature to help me overcome my timidity myself. Or he might have reminded me that I shouldn't always follow the group! It may be tempting to favor extroversion and activity, but remember that these factors are descriptions, not value judgments. In fact, children high in extroversion may have difficulty with self-control and may need a stronger hand of parental authority to learn what is appropriate and what is safe. Extroversion is an accelerator and sensitivity, the brakes. Children need some of both, and you may need to lend your own brakes to your child while he develops his.

It is easy to mistake a child's behavior as an inherent characteristic when in fact it may well have another source. And it is far too easy to pigeonhole a child or a co-parent as unchangeably difficult. Consider the parent who called me with this concern: "I don't know what to do with my 4-year-old son. He throws things. He is so stubborn and angry. I've heard that some little boys get aggressive at this age, but maybe something is wrong with him." I discover that there is an older brother and a brand-new little brother in the house. "Maybe he's jealous of the new baby; maybe he's feeling caught in between." Good hypothesis.

"What happens?" I asked. "Well, it is usually when I'm working, and I'm usually in a hurry." He paused. "Maybe I should take him outside and throw a football around." I agreed. "And he could bring you the hammer or the nails. You could teach him how to hold a saw." Aggressive, angry kid? Probably not. Impulsive, sensitive kid? Maybe. Kid who needs activity and feels a little left out? No doubt. Solution: Take your son's interest in you and what you're doing and exploit it. But let's say this little boy was in fact high-reactive and did tend to be impulsive. The environmental factors would still help shape his behavior. Still, there is good evidence that the responses of parents and other adults can both moderate and exacerbate the constraints of temperament.[142]

Whether the issue is activity level or sensitivity, being the parent means helping your child cope not only with the world—which includes you—but also with his own impulses, fears, temperament, or disability. You do it all the time; this help is your authority in action. The 2-year-old crying on the first day of preschool would probably benefit from an extended period during which you would be allowed to be with him in the classroom or some practice with a shorter day. You know that the 6-year-old who bolts to the top of the climber will probably be fine; how you react will depend in part on your own level of adventurousness. But you will probably remind her of the dangers of falling or of the possibility that she might accidentally push a less confident child on her way up; you might stay close enough to coach or to intervene when necessary. A light touch to guide her foot down will probably help.

Touch is a powerful tool in relation to temperament, and not just in infancy. Although it may work best to stay calm when a child is agitated or anxious, where touch is concerned it is more effective to match your physical tone to hers: firm pressure for an outgoing, even defiant child, ever so light and tentative for a more sensitive child.[143] When a child can soothe himself, the onset of a behavioral reaction will be less stressful for him and his parent. I watched a 2-year-old boy who moments before was prostrate on the sidewalk and dragged into the house go to his toy box and get out his xylophone and start to play. An older child might turn on music or immerse himself in a video game.

Beyond Temperament: Do You Need Outside Help?

If you feel stuck in a pattern of negative reactions to your child, whether worry, impatience, frustration, or anger, you may need some help to get out of it. Help may be as close as your co-parent or a friend or relative. If you are a single parent, get conflicting advice, or want someone more objective, a therapist or parents' group can be a good resource. With some ongoing collaboration, you and your co-parent can be helpful to each other, stepping in when the other is about to lose control or regularly taking on a responsibility that triggers the other's impatience, such as putting on boots and mittens. If you do want the help of the other parent or another adult, it is probably best to consult out of earshot of the child in question, unless it is unsafe to do so.

Ultimately, it is important to develop some self-awareness of your own reactions and the habits of interaction you have with this child. Much of what you do as a parent is based on what you have done and felt before, for better or worse. A spouse may not always be helpful, of course. That's another dyad in which you must function, one that also influences your relationship with your child. Because you are the parent, caretaker, and big object, part of your parental authority must take temperament, fit, and circumstances into consideration, including conflict with a spouse. *(See Chapter Five.)*

Some children develop behaviors that are beyond the norm of intensity and difficulty in adaptation, for example, persistent attention deficits, excessive tantrums, or oppositionality. Your natural authority puts you in the position, with your co-parent or other supportive people in your child's life, of investigating and implementing strategies appropriate for your family. You may need professional help to determine whether there are strategies that you can implement yourself with some guidance or whether you need outside intervention to alleviate what is happening in your family. Seeking help takes time and a measure of humility as you say to yourself or others, "We are not sure we can handle this," or "We want to make sure we are doing whatever we can." It never hurts to check in with a professional if you are not sure.

Whatever resource you choose, keep in mind the core idea that whatever is taking place is taking place in the context of a relationship between two people in a particular family and cultural environment. Although the titles and some of the content of most resources will conceptualize problems in the child, whatever the source of your child's difficulties in behavior and adaption to daily life and interaction with others, your role as the parent and the relationship you develop are essential to his well-being and ongoing development.

Parents Have Temperaments Too

It is not infrequently the case that difficulties parents report with their children can be traced back to differences in temperament or parenting style between them. Say one parent is very anxious about a child and the other simply isn't, as is frequently the case with couples who come to see me. Consider an extremely picky eater. One parent worries about whether the child will get sick or not do well in school because she isn't getting enough to eat. The other makes comments like "She's not starving; let it go." If the child eats different foods for the babysitter, a grandparent, or a divorced parent, then the dynamic can become difficult. I usually try to break the problem down, to ascertain whether we are really talking about sensory sensitivity, for example, or behavior that has been shaped by adults' responses or marital conflicts being worked out on the child's plate. Don't try to sort it out at the dinner table.

If you are shy, you may really appreciate that your child is bolder than you are, but your differences can make for conflict: Perhaps you like to plan ahead of time and your child often reacts to your plans with the complaint, "I don't feel like doing that right now." High intensity in both parent and child, for example, can cause conflict too: "He's a chip off the old block; that's why they can't get along." As the parent you can—and you must learn how to—make changes in your approach or your expectations that will make for a better fit. You are the parent. You can avoid a lot of frustration or unhappiness by anticipating situational factors that might cause difficulty and, if necessary, getting help from your co-parent or someone else if you end up in a rut of mismatched interactions. I found it hard, for example, when my oldest was about 2 and could never decide which Popsicle he wanted. I wanted him to be able to choose, but I got impatient with his not being able to, although—or perhaps because—I found it hard to make choices myself. My husband's solution: Give him a limited choice, orange or green. It helped me use my authority and it helped my son accept it.

Responding to Temperament

Is it all relative, then? If my daughter is very active and hates to sit still, does that get her out of Sunday school? Or if my son would prefer to stay at home rather than attend big neighborhood or extended family events, should he get a pass most of the time? These kinds of situations can be tricky for parents. Different temperaments do respond differently to their environment, and relationships with children vary tremendously according to many, many factors. And yet parents are told over and over again that they should be consistent.

It always comes back to the relationship between you: your responsiveness, your child's ability to trust in your care, whatever form it takes, and the experiences you have together. The answer may be yes, in the instance of Sunday school: If she is truly so active it is hard to sit still, it may not make sense for her. But if Sunday school is nonnegotiable for your family, then you need to work out some strategies to try to make it work. In the second instance, if your son will be so miserable in a crowd that he makes your life miserable, then maybe it is okay for him to stay home when the rest of the family goes out. There may be some family events that you decide are simply too important for your son to miss. As the parent, you will have to make that choice and you will also have to work with your co-parent and with your child to help him tolerate it. Many parents so fear the reaction of an easily aroused child that they are not firm: Sometimes the simple fact of your authority and the way you express it will help a child reach for ways to manage what is usually a difficult situation—and grow in the process.

Although temperament is very important to the development of personality and plays a big role in how people get along with one another, temperament is not destiny. Temperament is sensitive to environment and circumstance. You may wonder how much you can or should try to influence a child. How much should you adapt to him or should he adapt to you and your household? Research on this question has been done with children who at four months are assessed as behaviorally inhibited and whose brains show a certain pattern of activity.[144] Although virtually all of the children showed the same neural patterns at age 14 months, some of them no longer showed the behavioral inhibition. Conclusion? The brain doesn't always necessarily change, but behavior can. Because timid infants often develop into children with anxiety, and children with anxiety often have more social and other behavioral difficulties, it behooves you, as a parent, to do what you can to encourage that child to find other coping strategies for the increased arousal he feels.

Whatever her temperament, a child will need to learn rules of behavior—household rules, peer group rules, society's rules—some of which may come more easily to one temperament than to another. One father described getting his young son to comply by keeping at him until the boy gives in. In their case, it is a pattern that gives the child a sense of control even if he finally gives up. But whatever your child's reaction to a situation, he will learn from the reactions of his environment to his attempt to cope. He may decide, upon evaluation of the situation, that he would like to change his behavior in the future; to do so he may well need your help. Your authority plays a role in reacting to his behavior and in helping him learn another strategy.

Gender: Not Necessarily a Given, But Still a Factor

You may wonder why I haven't said anything about sex differences yet in my discussion of "being someone." Surely gender contributes to one's sense of self, and even apparently simple clothing preference can be a way of saying, "I have some ideas about who I am, and what I wear affects my sense of myself, so don't think you can just ignore it." There has been radical change in the expression of and attitudes toward gender identity. But how does this change affect the relationship between parents and children, particularly when it comes to authority?

There is no data that can tell you how a mother or father should respond to a son or a daughter, nor data from early development to suggest any significant differences on fundamental developmental issues such as attachment. In a meta-analysis of 200 studies of gender and behavior, girls were higher on self-control and boys were higher on extroversion.[145] This is not evidence, of course, that the differences are biological. An individual of either sex can prove any generalization wrong. One memorable witching hour, all four of my sons were present in the kitchen, aged perhaps 6 to 17, and there was such a tapping and bouncing and sheer level of activity and noise going on that I found myself thinking, "Ah, for a roomful of daughters." But that led to memories of my own noisy battles with my mother, which may have had nothing whatsoever to do with my gender or hers but are a good reminder that the grass is always greener on the other side of the generational—or gender—divide.

What is important about gender and authority is not that your parenting technique might be different with a girl or a boy (though it might be) but that, like so much of what I have written here, it is what you make of the differences and how they affect you and your relationship with your child. Does your family make a lot of your daughter being "Daddy's girl"? Does that affect your authority with her, whether you are the mother or the father? Do you make allowances for one or the other child that are linked to your expectations of what girls or boys do or should do? You can choose to do any of these things, but it is important to know that with such patterns of interaction, you are helping shape your child's expectations of himself and others. Every parent has values and beliefs about gender, even if what they value is to abolish differences.

Finally, in this age of increasing openness about fluctuating gender identity and wider acceptance of gender reassignment, many parents will be confronted with a child whom they thought they knew but who, at a certain age (and it can happen surprisingly early), expresses discomfort with their body and assigned gender. Happily, there is much public discussion and research to make what can be a complicated and painful process more positive for parents not sure how to weigh in, especially if their own values and beliefs make them uncomfortable with gender fluidity. What is most important for your child is that you be accepting and supportive of the process of exploration in which they are engaged.[146]

Does Birth Order Matter?

The Darwinian approach to birth order argues that siblings compete by divergence, for example, choosing a different career path than their brothers and sisters, or by different attitudes to authority. This is not simply a case of competing for attention, but rather competing for the parental resources of investment in their future. Eldest children, for example, are thought to identify more closely with parents and to accept their authority, while younger siblings are "born to rebel." Despite the conviction most of us have that there *must* be differences related to birth order, studies have consistently found a surprisingly low level of influence that could be attributed to birth order among either genetically related or adoptive siblings on either personality or developmental outcomes. In one of the largest studies of its kind, measures of personality given to 20,000 adults from the United States, Britain, and Germany were analyzed for evidence of statistically significant differences among birth order positions in the so-called "big five" of personality traits: extroversion, emotional stability, agreeableness, conscientiousness, and openness to experience. None were found.[147]

Other studies assess sibling similarities in personality traits rather than differences but find little. Again, our intuition that there must be similarities is hard to quantify; they had the same parents, didn't they? Researchers go so far as to say that there are more differences among siblings than among strangers, even if differences cannot be attributed to birth order! Those differences are attributed instead to other aspects of the so-called nonshared environment, such as external events like divorce, accidents, or changes in family situation.[148]

As the third of nine children, I have trouble fathoming how it could not alter your experience if you are born into a family first or arrive when one or two or more siblings are there already, and whether there are two or five or nine. But a difference in your *experience* is not what psychologists have measured, except in the case of disparate treatment by parents. In observational and video research of mothers interacting with different children at the same age, the mothers' behavior was consistent, which means a particular mother would be equally affectionate and responsive to successive children at age 1, for example, but perhaps less so when each reached age 3. The implications for children's perceptions and feelings are significant: The 3-year-old sees her mother cooing and cuddling her 1-year-old brother but perhaps being abrupt and demanding with her, not realizing that she got the same cuddling when she was a baby.[149]

This kind of difference is perhaps most relevant to authority: Many parents' decisions about chores, consequences, and the general attitude of "You should know better!" pertain to whether a child is an older brother or sister. Common sense may suggest that such differential treatment is inevitable to a certain extent, but in the form of different expectations and demands, it can be treacherous not only for your relationship with a child but also for the relationship between your children. Sibling relationships are a place where the power that comes simply from being a parent is amplified: When you place your approval or punishment on the side of one child and not another, it is less likely to make the child angry at you and more likely to make him angry at the sibling who has gotten your support or your real or perceived favoritism. If it helps you to know what biologists and psychologists have made of gender or birth order or sibling relationships, by all means discover what there is to learn, but be careful not to limit your expectations and your behavior on the grounds of either gender or birth order.

The Certainty of Change

Temperament and sibling position are givens in development. Gender still is for most children, although clearly less so than a generation ago. A very different kind of given, and a more paradoxical one, is change, which is always in tension with what seems stable. A child is the same extroverted active person he was at 5, but what he can do as a teenager has changed, and what is required of a parent may feel different too.

The stresses from the brain's bursts of growth can be trying for parents and children. It is a commonplace for parents to allude to the difficulties of developmental transitions and emotional growing pains: "She's having a bit of a hard time because she just started middle school." Doing so seems to reassure parents that they haven't created a monster, that there is a reason for what may be outrageous and out-of-character behavior from their once cuddly son or daughter. Even when a child is very young, with new abilities come new dangers and even new interactions, like grownups saying "No!" in a loud voice. Such interactions, many of which are an expression of your natural authority, serve the process of regulation; they may include physical cues like touching and visual cues like facial expressions. They aid not only in the return to a calm state when a child is agitated, but also in the growth of the brain itself.[150]

How can it be that your child, or you for that matter, can feel like essentially the same person—with the same shy or impulsive or sensitive way about him—and yet be so much bigger, so much more competent, so much older, or so much less likable? As a student of child development, I never managed to memorize the characteristics of a given stage; in fact, I was always rather resistant to the idea of stages at all. Development seemed to me then, and still does, to be much more of a process, and a messy, inexact one at that. You can say unequivocally that a child changes, but as soon as you try to describe even the earliest phases of development, you have to make qualifications in when things happen.

The most important developmental norm to consider is the norm of change itself. There are things a child of 5 can do and things he can't; there are ways he is more or less likely to act because he is 5 years old. A child of any age can be hypersensitive to criticism, but a 2-year-old is more likely to collapse on the floor because he doesn't yet have the capacity to reflect on his feelings or to express them in words. Even if change is the only reliable norm, somehow two 7-year-olds can seem amazingly more alike than either of them seem like their former 4-year-old selves.

The Persistence of Natural Authority: Big Kids Are Still Kids

As important as they are, developmental norms are only part of the picture. Parental authority—whether household organization, responsiveness to a child's needs, or limit-setting—is the core of the relationship between parent and child. What may surprise you is that the key concerns of parenthood remain essentially the same despite the enormous changes in a child's capacities over the course of childhood, adolescence, and young adulthood and despite the less predictable changes that arrive in every family's life, whether moves, deaths, or change in school or employment, which may also have an impact on individual development and family relationships.

As the ratio of your child's dependence and independence changes, the nature and degree of your responsibility and control must change. And both parents must experience a growing separation if he is to become a functioning member of the wider society. Easier said than done. It is painful, even embarrassing, when your formerly affectionate 12-year-old no longer is willing to hold your hand in public or your smart, hard-working, polite daughter wants a tattoo or purple hair. One of the great parent-child exchanges of my life was on a family trip to New York. As we drove through Greenwich

Village, I pointed out three teenage boys sitting on a bench, all with spiked hair and all wearing black leather clothing and Doc Martens shoes. "They're not very original," I said. "They all look alike." "Yeah," said my oldest, who was about 13, "but they don't look like their parents!"

Adolescents and parents differ sharply when it comes to areas of legitimate authority. Teens tend not to believe that their parents should have much say in the personal domain but do believe their authority makes sense in the domain of safety. In other words, don't tell me what to wear or who to go to the mall with, but I will begrudgingly agree that there should be a designated driver leaving a party. "I may not agree with you," he is effectively saying, "and I may not do what you say, but there are topics I consider fair game for you to talk to me about." If your son wants a tattoo, he may consider it a personal decision, but because it is a permanent change to skin with clear social and possible medical effects, and because permission is required for minors in every state, you have the authority to say yes or no.[151]

Change Brings Vulnerability to Children and Doubt to Parents

What does all this change mean for your authority? It is the insecurity most mothers and fathers feel about that question that fuels the parenting industry. It can be very helpful to know that the new, sometimes weird-seeming behaviors and activities your child is engaging in are seen as normal, or at least that a lot of his peers are acting the same way. While many of your fears about the terrible twos or adolescence are well based, there is no one for whom the unpredictability of these periods is more difficult than your child herself. Consider the world even a 1-year-old encounters once she starts to walk: The adults or older siblings who carried and cuddled her now may scold her and restrict her sometimes reckless movements. By the middle of the second year, verbal requests, commands, and rules will become more common.[152]

Feeling vulnerable themselves, preteens and teenagers can make you feel very vulnerable to your own doubts about making the right judgments for permission or punishment. You too are adjusting to new dimensions of authority and how best to communicate it. And it can be difficult to hold fast to your judgments. Drinking, doing drugs, staying out late, hanging out with kids you don't know or of whom you don't approve: As your adolescent increases in competence, autonomy, and exposure to the world outside your family, you are likely to change your ideas and behavior in relation to parental authority. This doesn't mean that a stubborn and rude 13-year- doesn't need your limit-setting. It does mean that her brain is constantly maturing, in the context of interactions in which she is learning about the implications and consequences of your values and beliefs. Hang tough; most kids will grow out of such attitudes. If she doesn't, you may need to consider your relationship: Does she know why you don't trust her? Are you consistent and clear about boundaries? Have you talked with other parents or with teachers and coaches about your concerns?

It is these changes in both cognitive and physical autonomy, and your changing responses to them, that make these periods of development stressful and emotional for both parents and children, especially around your authority. Mobility and communication stoke the engine of change. The toddler runs; the adolescent moves around in the community at will—by foot, by bike or bus, in a friend's or the family car, or on the Internet. In both cases, depending on the child, a parent must develop a new voice of authority for a child who has become capable of significantly different abilities in the service of communicating what she wants or needs or feels. The toddler's cute words become sentences; the adolescent begins to develop skills of reasoning and persuasion that make her sound as if she's been going to law school at night.

Change is at once inevitable and stressful. Your child changes, you change, your relationship changes. Change goes on all the while, but some periods of change are harder than others. The terrible twos and adolescence intimidate most parents, and not without reason. What one does as a parent during a child's first year and a half requires staggering physical, psychological, and practical adjustments to a very different way of life. But when a child starts to walk and talk, the demands of the early months may take on a misty air of the good old days. (Not for everyone, of course: Some newborns are colicky, a new mother may have a difficult recovery.) By a year, the cuddly baby becomes more fully human because he has developed a will; he is able to express and to act on his own intentions. During the course of the second year, as cute first words begin to build into two-word phrases and then sentences and, simultaneously, cute toddling steps turn into confident running, the child's consciousness will engage with yours. Now you are truly two people, in a relationship for life. As time passes, your responsibility shifts, expanding in some areas and shrinking in others. The help and the limits your child needs have changed. You need not compare your child unfavorably with your neighbor's, nor, I hasten to add, take much delight in how angelic your own is. If there is one sure truth about being a parent, it is that things can and will change—and not always for the better. *(See also Chapter Five, for the effects of change on the family system.)*

Chapter Eight

Being Together:
The Rhythms of Everyday Life

A s I rode a crowded subway train early one morning, a woman took the seat next to me. She sat down and told her young son to take the seat beside hers. A sturdy 5-year-old, he rather ostentatiously went in the direction she indicated, bumping into me on the way. She nodded to me by way of apology as he stretched himself out, halfway on the seat and halfway on the floor, wet with the day's rain dripping off umbrellas and boots of passengers. Their dialogue was familiar, although the child spoke only with his body: "I heard what you said, but I don't feel like doing it. In fact, I usually don't do what you tell me to do, at least not right away, but I will sort of do it, and sort of not, which will probably annoy you enough that I may do it eventually." The mother repeated her directive out loud several times, in a low, resigned, and slightly annoyed voice, perhaps as much for the benefit of listening passengers as for her son. "I said, take a seat." Clearly already tired although the day had just begun, she not only had an oppositional son but an audience of seated and standing passengers. I had to get off the train before I could see whether the boy ever sat down. I suspect he did.

I can say with some certainty that you have been that parent and that your child has been that child, refusing a small sensible request or ambivalently carrying it out with his whole body. Through the experience of such interactions, which take place in the complex web of relationships that is your family, shaped by its values and beliefs, by the habitat you have created, and by your temperament and biological inheritance, you and your child develop not only a sense of self but also a habit of being with each other.

Interaction, Development, and Authority

Any book about human development written in the last decade will state that we are social beings.[153] Even the breath we take is coordinated with others.[154] Spending time with almost any infant or young child, even a timid one, is to encounter some degree of invitation to engage. Make me laugh! Surprise me! Make noise! Interaction helps shape not only her actions but her mental organization—not just of you but of her world.[155] Although you too will adjust and respond to the sounds she makes and the actions she takes, the young child has little control over the complex social situations in which her life takes place and in which her brain and understanding of the world develop. Where she spends her time and with whom she spends it are mostly consequences of your natural authority.

You are a partner in a lifelong relationship with each of your children. In day-to-day routines, you must coordinate your actions with each other to get dressed, prepare meals, get places, accomplish things. You do it without thinking, and yet it is a complex interpersonal process, one you notice most often when it doesn't go smoothly or when it is not working at all. Those moments of doing things together are not only living life but the moments that create your relationship and constitute the basis of your authority. How do we do it? How do we know how to do it?

In the last 40 years, developmental researchers have generated a great quantity of video recordings of interactions, particularly of mothers and babies. From these visual records, we now know that there is a minutely intimate dance between the two partners, not only at the readily apparent level of noises made back and forth, but also at the level of facial expressions, body language (such as the position of the head), and actual gestures. The interaction is evident even at intervals of $1/12$ of a second.[156] Unlike dancers on the ballroom floor, no one necessarily takes the lead in these minute, mostly unconscious interactions. In other words, despite the radical disparity in age, experience, power, and size, and despite his need for you to feed, carry, and diaper him, you respond as totally to your infant as your infant does to you.[157]

In early infancy, the apparent asymmetry of the dance is at its most extreme: The young infant cannot move independently, but the parent can move away or pick up the infant and move her, regardless of how she feels about it. Nor can the infant talk or understand the words the parent says. But she is still active in the dance: She can whimper and cry and squirm, and as the months and years go by, she can crawl, walk, and run away. Starting with "No!" she can push back, until she becomes like the little boy on the subway or the irritable adolescent on the other end of the phone.

This mutual responsiveness presents an often-difficult paradox for your natural authority across the span of childhood: Your child is dependent on you to make decisions about what happens next—what we might call an authority of care—but you are engaged in constant nonverbal communication and mutual influence. If her response to a direction is an eye roll, it can be hard to insist, because your natural inclination is to respond to the eye roll.

As the adults with the natural authority of age, responsibility, and experience, we may assume that it is only children learning from us; we tend to underestimate the degree to which we learn from each other. Each interaction you have, from cozy moments of saying good night to exasperated moments in the grocery store, registers in your child's brain and body and in yours, adding to your experience with each other. From thousands of exchanges with each other and with others, as you coordinate, co-regulate, and communicate with each other, each of you accumulates a history of experience, a history that also makes each of you *you* with each other. And in these exchanges, you learn about each other, adding another tidbit of meaning to how you think about your relationship, another small episode to your joint narrative. This is not learning in the sense you may think of it, i.e., school learning, cognitive learning, conscious learning. This is the learning that comes with the repeated experiences of being alive, having a brain and a body, and interacting with other people.

A Lifelong Game of Catch

Because you have a big head start on your child, you are somewhat more aware of what's going on in an interaction. But awareness is not required. Neuroscientists talk about different layers or systems of awareness. Neurologist Robert Burton's "hidden layer" is a way of understanding how the brain's processing of incoming information is affected by both experience (e.g., interactions, relationships) and biology (e.g., genes, temperament). The hidden layer is not a structure but rather a way of thinking about the web of neuronal connections that make each of us who we are. The hidden layer takes in all that goes on between a person and her environment—including, prominently, other people—and weighs and evaluates it before reacting. This happens rapidly and unconsciously.

Like any game of catch, all of human interaction is both joint and continuous. Where it begins or ends is arbitrary; it can be interrupted at any moment. With few exceptions, it is impossible at any point to say where one person's actions began and another's ended. If you watch a mother help an infant sit up, it looks from the outside as if she is simply pulling him up, but in fact her motions are calibrated to respond to his efforts to pull himself up, so they are actually doing it together. Perhaps the mother starts it by putting out her hands, but perhaps she is responding, in doing that, to a look on the baby's face or a noise he made. And perhaps he made that noise because, after looking at his mobile for a while, he noticed his mother come into view and "knew" she could help change his activity. And perhaps she came closer to him because she "knew" that it might be time for him to do something different.[158]

But what if the mother tries to pull the baby up—or, more likely, put a sweater over his head—and he doesn't cooperate? Everything changes. What happens then? Like the mother and her son on the subway, when two parties are at cross-purposes, the nature of the interaction becomes very different. What any one of us expects at any given moment depends on the complex mix of incoming data and what we—our committee, our hidden layer—make of it. Most of the interactions you will have with your child do not take place on the beach or anywhere like it, but in the kitchen or bedroom or family room or car. The stakes are higher than a sweater over an infant's head, but the essential model is the same. You and your child, whatever her age, whenever you are together—talking, playing a game on the computer, working on a school project together, riding the subway or bus, considering college choices or the weekend curfew—are interacting on life's beach, tossing a big virtual "ball" back and forth. You are two personalities, each driven by the imperatives of development and each coming to the interaction from a different perspective, with some degree of experience with each other and with others and the world at large.

The Power of Contagion

It is some version of this same effort to connect in which all of us engage whenever we are with another person. And our brains have tools to help us. When you are with another person, notice the position of your hands and legs, and then notice your companion's. Chances are you will find that you are each folding your hands under your chin, crossing your legs, or scratching your noses at the same time. What's going on?

This involuntary imitation is sometimes called resonance behavior or, more simply, mimicry, and is thought to be part of the system of mirror neurons, discovered in monkeys only in 1990.[159] The discovery came about by accident, when an Italian research team was studying the brains of macaque monkeys. When Monkey A reached for a peanut, his brain showed a certain pattern of neural activity. The same pattern of neural activity could be detected in Monkey B's brain even though he was doing nothing with his hands. If the researchers had seen only the brains, they would not have been able to say which monkey was moving his hands and which was still.

This discovery launched a cascade of research into the ways in which human beings watch and imitate each other. What has puzzled and fascinated researchers is not only the matching behavior but also the phenomenon of matching brains: What seemed remarkable was not only the apparent involuntary imitation inside the brain, but also the apparent detection by the watching monkey of the other monkey's intention to reach for the peanut. When Monkey A reached for a cup, for example, the neural patterns in both monkeys' brains were different from those seen when he reached for the peanut.[160] Why wouldn't it be enough to see what the other is doing, without showing the same neural activity?[161] Do matching brains mean that more than actions are matching? If my brain does what yours does, or if my body does what yours does, do I feel what you feel?

It can be useful to be aware of this phenomenon, sometimes called emotional contagion, defined by Hatfield and her coauthors as "the tendency to automatically mimic and synchronize expressions, vocalizations, postures, and movements with those of another person's and, consequently, to converge emotionally."[162] Although researchers disagree on whether or not such imitation implies empathy, it appears that when people mimic each other they also "catch" each other's emotions and then behave in ways that match the emotional expressions they have imitated.[163] Sitting across from my clients, I am so often aware of this resonance that when it's missing, it makes me work harder to connect. I might lower my voice, lean forward, look more directly at them.

Because these processes are so incredibly fast, they are virtually impossible to detect consciously. Nonetheless, many believe that they are highly influential in human life. This kind of unconscious attention to the behavior of others has been key to our survival in more dangerous situations than those in which most of us now live. And in contemporary clinical psychology, "hypervigilance" is a hallmark of children who have suffered physical abuse. It was once critical to their emotional or even physical survival that they detect the mood of their caretaker, lest they be physically hurt, and it is a hard habit to break. Emotional convergence motivates parents to mark an infant's or child's mood in words or behavior or facial expression: "I know what you're feeling."[164] When a parent does this more or less consistently, it builds the child's sense of security and trust.

Computers and mobile devices have dramatically changed this aspect of many human encounters. An earlier draft of this chapter, in which I talked about the awkwardness of being in an elevator with strangers because of the natural inclination to interact, has become obsolete. An elevator with five passengers is as likely as not to have five heads bent over mobile devices, short-circuiting both the awkwardness and the probability of interaction. In family life, if it is someone we love who seems distant or avoids eye contact, what happens? You probably feel cut off, and though you may or may not stop to consider it, that momentary experience is added to your relationship with that person. A dramatic demonstration of the pain of feeling cut off is the "still face" experiment, in which a mother holding an infant suddenly drains the expression from her face and keeps it still for a minute. The child gropes at her face and then gives up and crumples into tears.[165] It has of course become commonplace to see milder everyday versions of this, as the mobile devices of adults divert their attention from children or vice versa.

Interacting with Words and Bodies

Linguists and psychologists have mapped the way two or more speakers coordinate their conversation. Conversation has an underlying rhythmic organization that both parties sense; it is not unlike dancing with a partner, but the dance steps vary from culture to culture and family to family. Two mature speakers engage in precise timing of their conversational turn-taking. You either wait until the other is finished or until there is a natural opening. If you interrupt, you must speak loudly or insistently enough to take the floor. And almost certainly without your being conscious of it, you adjust the rhythm and volume of your speech to the other's voice.[166] Any pair of interlocutors who speak often will develop a systematic pattern, and disruptions can be part of the pattern.[167] It can feel uncomfortable to one person when someone speaks with a different rhythm or interrupts you before you are finished, while to another, it may feel as if not talking over someone else means you are not that involved in the conversation.

This kind of discomfort is often a sore subject between parents and children. "Don't interrupt me when I'm talking to you," you say, and your child responds, "You always interrupt me, Mom, I'm just trying to explain." The competitive nature of a relationship can be audible to all, which may bring in other family members until there is a free-for-all. At that point, your authority gives you the job of repairing the interaction or, if you believe your child is old enough to be capable of repair herself, noting that repair is necessary and perhaps helping her do it.

When I have a mother and a teenager sitting on the couch in my office, they may well get into a dueling match about who said what first, and whether the look was in response to a tone of voice, or the tone of voice in response to a look. In fact, conversation happens so fast and so unconsciously that it is a pretty hopeless task to get to the bottom of it. It is a continuous and mostly involuntary co-creation. And yet it is from these messy and confusing exchanges that both you as a parent and your children become who you are, that you build relationships, that you learn about life and other people, yourselves and each other. It is also in these exchanges that you negotiate the bounds of authority. For your child, whether he can rely on you to protect him, to limit him, to provide the emotional scaffolding he needs; for you, whether in this interaction you feel like the grownup, whether you have communicated in such a way that he will listen, that he will believe that you mean it.

It can be very useful to try to slow the process down to see if you can be more conscious of what's going on. Pay attention to what you find yourself doing: a smile, a quick exchange of eye contact, a touch on the shoulder, whether you seek contact more than once if you are rebuffed, and how it all feels. We will look at those signals in more detail in the next chapter. In an ordinary conversation, the task at hand is simply to understand each other, or perhaps to convince the other. In many other instances, especially between parent and child, you interact in order to accomplish a task or goal together. It can be as trivial as loading the dishwasher or as weighty as trying to discourage her from maintaining a friendship that has clearly hurt her. It can be as easy as giving a Band-Aid for a scraped knee or as challenging as staying calm in the face of adolescent rage.

Bridging Perspectives

In any interaction, you are inevitably somewhat bound by the limits of your own subjective experience—what you perceive from where you stand and how you feel. However, the nature of human interaction is to bridge your perspective and the perspective of one or more others enough to communicate, coordinate, and regulate. *(See also Chapter Nine.)* As the more mature, experienced, and responsible party in interactions of authority with a child, not only do you risk conflict and anxiety between the two of you, but the buck, for the most part, stops with you. In other words, you have no parent there looking out for your feelings, your needs, and your development. A major pitfall for parents at any stage, but especially as children grow into adolescence and young adulthood, is the very human but almost certainly unconscious need to be recognized as another human being with not only a mind but a vulnerable self. Not only does your need enter in, but implicitly and unconsciously your own history in other relationships. Many parents, especially those with less social support, may unwittingly expect empathy and support from a child. This is nothing to be ashamed of, but it does complicate matters to try to be both the authority and someone in need of sympathy.

Over time, each of us generates a store of familiar patterns—language, faces, how to get places, the way we like our coffee—and the greater the fit between previous patterns and the current pattern, the greater the degree of certainty you feel about the pattern and, in the case of interaction, about what happens next: what you will do, what the other person might do. When the responses are generally tuned in to your perspective, you both gain a feeling of trust and connection. A pattern of unavailability, lack of responsiveness, dismissiveness, or sarcasm may create mistrust and possibly a similar habit of ignoring your demands, or even oppositionality and defiance. What parents do matters. [168]

Authority in Action

Instances of authority are as variable as when a parent directs a child to start a chore or action or stop an annoying noise or a text exchange; they also include giving a child a consequence for a past forbidden action, rule violation, or unfinished obligation. In some instances, a parent is confronted, as Michael's parent was when calling him to dinner in Chapter Two, with interrupting the ongoing activity of the child and thus risking annoyance and an argument. Authority may mean restoring attunement when a child is upset. Other instances of authority might be ones in which you require a certain kind of behavior, like saying please and thank you, changing clothes, or brushing teeth.

Although I have focused primarily on the natural authority of parents, any adult, whether a visiting grandparent or an evening babysitter, can find it challenging to be in charge, to be confident in and able to communicate authority. They will co-create their own particular, even if temporary, relationship of authority with a child, emerging from what they do together over repeated occasions, and from an implicit agreement that they may have to work out misunderstandings and mistakes.[169] The more often the non-parental adult is in charge, the more the child will know what to expect.

Interaction requires implicit agreement among the parties about what they are doing, agreement generated not only by the demands of the situation at hand but also by the intimate affective history of a human pair and the culture of family and community.[170] The mother and the infant are working together so that he can do something he wouldn't be able to do alone: Each of these interactions has a purpose. If they didn't, the interaction might end or move into conflict. The mutual consent is not something anyone says out loud, although when conflict erupts, you or your child may allude to it: "But I thought I was going to get to stay up late, and I can tell by your voice that you're mad and you're not going to let me."

Interrupting someone's ongoing activity may not be a way to be a friend, but it is a way to be a parent, even if it risks an argument. If your daughter says, "I'll unload the dishwasher later" and you respond with "Stop being rude" because of her tone, stance, and expression, she is very likely to retort, "I am not being rude." What she *said* was perfectly straightforward: She will unload the dishwasher later. But you picked up on eye rolling, a sigh, a slump, and a reactive tone of voice, not to mention that you suspect she won't in fact do it later unless you nag her. You may both try to hold each other accountable for what the other said, but the nonverbal messages that expressed what she meant enter into your appraisal. In situations in which those nonverbal messages are unusual or excessive, like a really sour look or stomping out of the room, your instinct is probably to react. Whether or not you do is a matter of judgment: Was her rudeness over the line? How will she react if you call her on it?

The Teen and the Preschooler: Getting Out of the House

Anyone who has dressed a preschooler knows that it is one of the great underestimated challenges of parenthood, up there with getting a teenager out of bed. A 3 ½-year-old may be more flexible than he was at 2 ½, but there is no telling what obstacles might crop up. Maybe he wants to wear the pants that are in the washing machine and soaking wet, or the jacket that was left at daycare. I went through my share of "what to wear" discussions with my children, whether at 3 or at 13. From age 2 to age 7 one refused to wear pants with snaps or buttons and at 2 wanted his shoes tied "quadruple." Another always wore suspenders—even with pajamas, even with a bathing suit—until he was 5. With the first, I avoided the fights about getting dressed by using pants with elastic waistbands and agreeing to tie his shoes "triple." With the second, we simply moved the suspenders from outfit to outfit until he outgrew it.

Getting a young child dressed and out the door (indeed any child—each age presents its own particularities) pits the will of one small self against yours. Whether it's princess undies or torn jeans, children of all ages have amazingly strong ideas of what they want to wear out of the house. Getting dressed or getting homework done or getting to bed—the mundane interactions that take place in the course of a day—are full of potential conflict and frustration, which can make your job as coordinator-in-chief feel impossible.

To illustrate how interaction shapes authority in everyday family life, I will use two parallel examples of getting out of the house, one with a preschooler and another with a young teenager.

The scenarios that follow are hypothetical but very much inspired by my own real-life experience. Despite the enormous changes over the course of development, the essential dynamic between parent and child, teenager or preschooler, stays remarkably the same: You remain older, more experienced, and legally responsible, adjusting to developmental changes and uniquely attuned to the particulars of your family's life situation and to your children. I have imagined two hypothetical pairs, a grandmother and a 3-year-old girl, Abby, and a father and a 14-year-old boy, Charlie. Both ages can be particularly trying for parents. I ask you to imagine a grandmother in one story as a reminder that many adults can act with the natural authority of parenthood.[171] In their first frame, this seemingly chummy pair has agreed to go for a walk to a nearby playground. This is their understanding, their common goal. In the neighboring frame, Charlie and his father have talked about going to the mall to look at some electronics. They too have an understanding and a common goal.

Two Stories: Getting Started

Preschoolers and teenagers have a lot in common: Both have just enough ability to reason—and more than they had the year before!—to lull you into thinking you can engage them in rational negotiation. But in fact, both are also in the heady grip of a newfound sense of self, independence, and will. Developmental changes and corresponding demands can be stressful. Unlike an infant or young toddler, the preschooler can talk, can pick things up and throw them. She can say no in many different ways. She wants certain toys or food and insists on them with words; she remembers what you said yesterday. A teenager of 14, a high school freshman, is better at arguing than he was just a few months before. He can marshal examples from the outside world; he has more sense of alternatives and more ability to think logically and refute your reasoning. You don't need to be able to answer an essay question about child development any more than he needs to be able to put what he knows about adults into words; these are differences you sense and he feels and uses. But remember that even tough-talking adolescents are still immature and in need of your authority.[172]

In both cases, the child wants to go out but is involved in something else. If you have a teenager, thinking about getting the preschooler out the door may seem easy compared to what you're dealing with now. This is part of what I want you to consider, that is, how very limited each of us is within our own experience and perspective. When you see someone with a younger child struggling with authority, you may say to yourself, "If I knew then what I know now, it would be easy!" You may be right—or you may not.

What happens in a situation that requires a parent to get a child to stop one activity and begin another (in both cases an outing the child has agreed to)? At the beginning of our stories, the two children are in their pajamas and fully engaged in other projects. By the end of the dual story, Abby is not only asleep but stays asleep for two hours, and Charlie walks into the house with a spring in his step and a smile on his face. Each pair must go through a series of interactions. They will only be conscious of a fraction of what they communicate to each other. This is life; this is what we do all day, every day, whenever we interact with other people. And successful interpersonal negotiations, even regarding such a small slice of everyday life, take practice, which is why many developmental psychologists worry about children doing so much of their interacting with each other on screens.

A grandmother about to take a preschooler for a walk might be imagining fresh air, looking at birds, talking about what they see; perhaps, more practically, she sees the outing as a way to keep the child occupied while she makes a phone call or to get the child to sleep. The child, on the other hand, has a much more concrete and immediate notion of a walk and little sense of time. Maybe a sense of liking the motion, maybe a memory of things she saw or heard outside.

The father of the teenager could begrudge the obligation to drive his son somewhere since he has a list of tasks for the day. Or perhaps he's delighted that his child has consented to spend time with him, harboring a fantasy of a good talk about school, friends, maybe the worries he has about the boy's grades or the amount of time he spends on Fortnite. The teenager could want time to talk too, or he could be far more utilitarian. He wants to check out some new gear and can't get there by himself; he's supposed to have saved lawn-mowing money for his own spending, but he hasn't and hopes his father will feel generous or at least loan him money.

Maybe rather than expecting cooperation and ease in making things happen, we should marvel that we could ever bridge the gap with another person. Each comes to the moment with a physical presence and a psychological experience, including, first and foremost, the ongoing relationship with the other. Who the other is matters, which is why formulaic parenting strategies may fall short.

Two Stories: Getting Dressed

And all of that is just setting the context. Before you can go out, the child has to get dressed. The preschooler probably needs help; the teenager needs autonomy and privacy. Both may need a time frame, although the preschooler can't really understand time beyond long and short. In both cases, the adult is required for the outing, so the adult decides the terms. This is authority. Not "can we please go later, I'm talking to Sean" or "can we please go later, I'm watching *SpongeBob*." You may decide that it is in your interest to give the child more time: If you do, maybe the whole outing will go more smoothly. But you run the risk of seeming to give in. And you may not have the time. You *can* decide. You are the boss; this is a relationship that will continue tomorrow and next month and next year. But if the child is pleading and whining, do you want the child to learn that if she pleads or whines, you will give in? Probably not! Pleading and whining can mean many things: that he needs you to consider his perspective, that he is feeling stressed and vulnerable, or, most likely, that he has learned that when he pleads and whines, he gets what he wants. How you respond makes a difference; it affects the feelings and the response of the other.

As the adult in the relationship, you are in a better position to make judgments about safety and health; you're also in a position to teach and model values about both issues and the conversations about them. At the same time, you are a person with feelings and the capacity for action: Each time you decide whether or not to assert your authority you rapidly—and mostly unconsciously—consider what the likely response will be. The driving question for all of us as we go about our lives is "What happens next?" Whether you think about this explicitly or not, it is really your answer to that question that determines your behavior, because every action leads to another.

The Preschooler: I Don't Like That One

In some circumstances, you might ignore or override the resistance of a preschooler by presenting alternative approaches. If this grandmother were in a hurry, she might have simply grabbed a dress and insisted that Abby wear it, perhaps by the tone of her voice, perhaps by the incentive of a snack bag to bring along. If this were a routine departure, say, for school, there might be a familiar limit on the time spent negotiating the dress options in place. Some parents have more patience than others and choose to give a child the extra time she needs to make the transition or to make a game of it. Ultimately the parent or caregiving adult has to be willing to use authority to override or even oppose the child's will, something that is very hard for many parents to do, especially when they are new to the experience.

Perhaps the grandmother proposed that Abby choose one of two dresses, with some amount of negotiation required to settle on one ("I don't like that one"; "I wore that one yesterday"). Abby's grandmother could also choose one and insist on it or allow Abby to choose what to wear from among her entire wardrobe, but either of these alternatives has obvious pitfalls. With the former, she can refuse and throw a fit because she has no input; with the latter, she may be overwhelmed with too many choices and take all day to decide. A choice between a smaller number of outfits —or Popsicles, or stories—allows you to take your own perspective into consideration ("I don't have all day") and use your authority to frame the situation. The child gets to have some say but you have veto power. One way or another, possibly with intervening conflict, a dress is agreed on, but it is chilly outside, and she needs tights. Luckily the purple tights her mother just bought pass the test and she lets Grandma help her put them on. Shoes? Only two alternatives, thank goodness, and she likes her new pink cowboy boots with rhinestones.

The Teenager: The Subtext

For Charlie, the father dares to reject one shirt as too full of holes, and although Charlie rolls his eyes and groans, he goes upstairs again. I say "dares" because he knows that Charlie hates to be told what to wear. Charlie makes his own calculations, probably muttering to himself as he plods up the stairs, and comes down with a second shirt that looks as if it was just picked up off the floor. As he could have predicted, his father decides to ignore this: He rarely pushes Charlie past one reprimand. Charlie knows neither parent likes his pants worn low but decides to chance it and succeeds: He knows his dad hates to wait. Each of them has had to use what they know of each other and themselves to get through this phase of going out. The father does hate to wait, and the last thing he wants is a big scene with Charlie or an "I don't want to go anyway" response; Charlie wants to dress his own way but really wants to get that piece of equipment. He calibrates how much his father can tolerate.

At 3, dress begins to carry some meaning, often associated with an emerging and sometimes exaggerated consciousness of gender; think princesses and mermaids, knights and astronauts. By early adolescence, the meaning is more intense, connected to self-definition, peer acceptance, and sexuality; these forces affect all of us but are more acute for teens who are in the throes of working out who they are and who they want to be.

It sometimes feels impossible to understand the angst of the day for an adolescent, and yours is likely to remind you how little you "get" him. As one of my sons complained when, after he had an enjoyable camping trip with a friend, I gave him a birthday gift of a hiking backpack, "You're trying to make me something I'm not!" If Charlie has a girlfriend, he might hope to see her at the mall. Maybe he has made a plan to do so or is lingering upstairs to text her to make sure they are there at the same time. But he is not going to tell his dad that.

Such conflicts over dress may test your patience, but in a human society with choice, which ours certainly is, even in families of limited means, what we wear often represents a statement of identity, especially to our peers. When I submitted to one son's demands for shoelaces tied triple or another's for suspenders 24/7, I did so because it made the transitions easier than fighting and my concessions didn't matter that much to me. Does that mean the goal is to avoid fighting? No. The goal is to find a way that works for your household, your family, and your relationship. A teenager might take more time preparing for a quick outing than is truly necessary—but you never know whom you might meet!—or choose an outfit that you think sloppy or inappropriate. These can be tough moments.

Mutual Constraints: The Preschooler Whines but Grandma Wins

As our imaginary pairs get closer to actually setting out on their outings, each of the partners in these interactions has responded to or been constrained by the actions—verbal and nonverbal—of the other and by implicit anticipation of "what happens next?" If this were a video, you would be able to observe a great deal more; here you are limited by my sketchy account of the interaction. When you watch highly skilled dancing or skating partners, you are likely to notice the effect of what they create as a pair more than you are able to detect what each is doing and how the other is responding, even though you are aware that you are watching two separate bodies. Together such performers or athletes create *dance* through minute invisible interactions with each other. The more attuned they are to each other, the smoother and more "one" their dance will appear. The same goes for the most ordinary of human interactions.

In the grandmother's interaction with Abby, it takes some work to keep attuned to one another; unless the grandmother is the regular caretaker, they don't interact every day, or even every week, and they don't often interact in a situation that requires the grandmother to take a stand of authority. She may be right to be leery of using her authority with Abby; neither is used to it, and it might cause distress. This is because every relationship has its own history, its own style of interactions, its own co-regulation. Abby is used to her grandmother as a visitor, one who reads books to her and gives her treats, not as an authority. Charlie and his dad are a different story. Although they don't have one-on-one outings very often, Charlie is used to his dad being in charge. But he also knows that his dad doesn't care that much about what he wears. He may even suspect that his dad is applying his mom's standards and not his own, that for his dad it's not a hard-and-fast rule.

As all this maneuvering is going on, an adult may have to work hard to remain patient and calm. After all, in both instances the outing is optional; it doesn't really matter when they go out or even whether they go at all. In many of your interactions, you don't have that luxury; you have to get out of the house. But those are situations that are more amenable to the authority of routine, and you are likely to feel more certain and less hesitant about your demands. Each party has some stake in the outcome of the interaction; "the talks" could break down at any point if a wrong move is made. When the outing is less optional, there is more danger of negotiation because your stake in the outcome is greater (you can't go to work if she doesn't go to school); she knows it and may work harder to stall the departure. There is a similar dynamic at the concessions stand at the movies or the checkout counter at the grocery store. There is pressure from the line of customers behind you or from the need to get into the theater or to get home before a sibling is dropped off by the school bus.

This grandmother is tuned in enough to herself to know that her patience will run out at some point. She has started the process with full optimism and energy, goodwill, and patience, but now she has realized it is pretty cold outside and she is getting ready to pull rank, if need be, to get a jacket on Abby. On the other hand, she doesn't want to lose her temper or risk a major meltdown from her granddaughter.

"You need something warm. How about this red jacket?" she says as enthusiastically and emphatically as she can.

"No!" Abby says, with more emphasis.

"What about this?" she asks, holding up a big sweatshirt of her father's.

"No, it's not mine." Now Grandmother moves into authority mode, aware that she is starting to feel frustrated and short-tempered. The time invested in just getting ready is depleting her patience. She is going to up the ante. "Okay, we can stay home. You can take a nap upstairs, and I'll do some work downstairs."

"No! I don't want to take a nap," Abby says in a whine. So they review her choices: her jacket or Daddy's sweatshirt.

"Noooo! I don't want to wear *anything.*"

At this point Grandma reaches the end of her rope. She no longer feels calm, and she doesn't really feel in charge. She is physically and emotionally irritable, stressed by time passing, stressed by the misattunement, stressed by losing her sense of authority. You know the feeling.

Grandma keeps her cool, though, and makes her final offer, phrasing it as a forced choice rather than a threat. "Either we stay here, or you're going to put on your jacket." Something changes: Abby understands that Grandma is serious. In fact, she probably senses exactly what Grandma had sensed in herself, albeit without words to describe it: what might happen next (in this case, Grandma getting angry with her). She suddenly agrees to put on her jacket. She gets into the stroller without argument and they set off. Within minutes she is fast asleep. Ah! Maybe that was it, she was just tired! No wonder!

Mutual Constraints: The Teen Calculates His Odds and Concedes

Things are not going much better as Charlie and his father debate the same issue. Charlie thinks wearing a jacket isn't necessary; Dad starts to insist.

"Charlie, I'm not going to say this again: Get your jacket on." (Of course he probably will say it again.)

Charlie mutters something under his breath along the lines of "Yeah, you old people get cold easily." Dad, who just turned 45, bristles and is about to get into a secondary argument about Charlie's muttering. But he decides not to get into it. First, he starts to insist again, "I said, get your jacket." But something about the look on Charlie's face—a sort of recognition of the silliness of this argument—makes him say something different.

"Look, Charlie, you're 14, you can do what you like, but if I were you, I'd wear a jacket. And don't roll your eyes at me...." Here he acknowledges Charlie's growing autonomy but draws the line at his attitude, which, as Charlie knows, comes from a strict family value of respect. But he takes a chance and responds by rolling his eyes again as he moves ever so slowly toward the hall closet. "Charlie!" Dad says, this time harshly. And Charlie quickly says, sensing that he might lose this outing altogether, "I'm sorry. I didn't mean to. I'll get my jacket, okay?" And off they go. It could have gotten worse with Charlie if either of them had not caught themselves. Grandma and Abby have a harder time because Abby really doesn't yet have the self-control she needs to pull herself together.

Nevertheless, I think it is still useful to ask a different question: not what did Grandma or Dad do, but what did each pair do *together*?

Building a Relationship

Not only did Abby and Charlie bring their varying experience and development to these interactions, so did the grandmother and the father. What did they bring besides their ideas about an outing or an errand? Perhaps that they wanted to please the children in question; that they felt pretty good about their relationships and the offers they'd made, even that they thought of themselves as patient and somewhat easygoing. But they also may have brought other baggage. Grandma most likely did not want to end up yelling at her granddaughter; Dad didn't have all day for this trip to the mall. These kinds of insights into what makes you tick, and what might set you off, can be very useful at times when you find yourself engaged in a frustrating interaction that pushes your buttons.

The interactions you engage in moment by moment accumulate, not only within a given conversation or activity, but over the course of time, to create your relationship. You learn from the patterns of being with each other and with others in your world what to expect from this and other relationships, and you bring those learned expectations to each interaction. Each of you is also part of many other interacting pairs, and those pairs form a larger web of relationships, a reality that can hover over the moments you share with each other. If Charlie's other parent were within earshot, each might unconsciously be adjusting their responses for those ears as well. Your brains are not literally or physically connected to each other, but in fact they are in close communication, *even when you are not talking.* We communicate with others on at least two levels, what we say with words and what we say nonverbally, and much of that communication is easy to be unaware of until someone brings it to our attention. Maybe Charlie didn't realize he was rolling his eyes the second time until his dad noted it and he immediately brought himself around. Abby needed the scaffolding her grandmother could provide to be able to move from the fight about the jacket to getting outside.

Any situation can be analyzed in detail; this is the process I engage in with parents and children or couples who have developed a pattern of interaction that is causing distress or dysfunction. I'm not suggesting that you spend hours picking apart every interaction, but chances are that if you spend a little time thinking about it you will find reasonable, legitimate, and even obvious factors influencing you both. Every interaction gives messages to your child about whether you mean what you say, whether he could get away with flouting what you say, and so on. Key to this process is understanding more about what is going on between you nonverbally, both in response to your own internal emotional state and in response to what you hear and see and sense in your child's response. By seeing how interactions can be slowed down and by identifying some of the many elements of these moments together, you'll understand more of what can lead you to a voice of natural authority.

In infancy, the responsiveness of a primary caretaker and others in his intimate environment secures the infant's survival and early brain development. As childhood progresses, the responsiveness of other humans—especially those in intimate, daily interaction with a child—continues to be the core ingredient of development.

— Chapter Nine —

Human Thermostats:
One Body Regulates Another

Sunday morning. A father swears at his barely 2-year-old daughter as he tries to put her in the high chair. She arches her back and stiffens her legs. He raises his voice and grips her arm more tightly. The child looks startled by her father's reaction. She is too young to understand the obscenities. But she understands what he means. She couldn't tell us in words, but she knows *he* is mad as much as he knows *she* was: She knows it from the expression on his face, the tone and volume of his voice, the pressure of his hands on her arms. He knows it from her rigid body. Meanwhile, his spouse, who planned a special breakfast for cherished family time, is now also upset, which affects everyone. The attempt to coordinate two grownups and one toddler into a family breakfast has deteriorated into a big mess. Why?

Coordination and Regulation

When the father lost his temper, he lost his emotional regulation. Chances are that he came to the task annoyed or sleep-deprived or otherwise stressed. The child had been waiting for breakfast for too long. She was too hungry to cooperate. You may be embarrassed to admit it, but this scene, or something like it in intensity of feeling, probably happens in your house too, now and then, and not just with toddlers. It certainly happened in mine. From a simple request for help with homework to a complicated negotiation over curfew, every interaction between you and your child risks breaking down. And once it has, the breakdown is often contagious, turning any ordinary situation into a roiling cascade of emotion.

It is easy to forget that you and anyone with whom you interact are connecting and communicating with your bodies as much as with your words. As we saw in Chapter Six, your feelings, body, and expression are inextricably bound together. Your communication with your child comprises not only what you say but what you feel about what you say and the ways in which you communicate, nonverbally, how you feel about what you say.[173] For example, when you say "go to bed," do you just mean go to bed? Or do you mean, "You better go to bed easily because I cannot handle another night like last night"? Or, "Why does it have to be like this every night?" What does your child hear and understand beyond your words? How does what you communicate nonverbally bring your implicit authority to life?

Nonverbal behavior helps us communicate when words fail or are not fully communicative. You are likely to work especially hard to decode nonverbal behavior when something makes you less than trusting of the words ("I didn't draw on the wall," or "I didn't go to Jessica's house when her parents weren't home"). You use every sense at your disposal to get at the truth. You may often feel that you have a gut sense because of your history and relationship with this child about the truth of what she says but no real way to pin her down. Of course, that doesn't keep most parents and children from arguing vociferously about what they said with words even if what they said by other means was more compelling. This is why you need ultimately to believe in the legitimacy of your authority in order to communicate it to your children. If you don't show it, your child may not believe it, no matter what you say. Adaptation to the environment depends largely on how one understands behavior of others, not the least of which for your child is whether you mean what you say, a visceral feeling of clarity that you can communicate with your face, your eyes and your voice.[174]

In the interactions that coordinate the routines of daily life, nonverbal behavior is a crucial tool that helps you teach, model, and partner as your child develops his own capacity for managing moods and stress and communicating his emotions to others.[175] But when coordination breaks down, it often takes the emotional regulation of all parties with it, as it did for this family at breakfast. Your authority means keeping or recovering your equanimity so your child can keep or recover hers.

Day in, day out, children need to learn to recover from their anger, restrain their impulses, and work out their conflicts with others. Regulation brings with it its antithesis, *dysregulation,* those moments of irritation, hurt, and isolation that make up daily life, moments that you feel in your body but can't always put into words. Sometimes those moments come from inside—discouragement with a project, disappointment with a grade—but most often they come from relationships or, more specifically, from moments with other *people*—including, prominently, parents—and other *perspectives*.

When the toddler in the opening scenario refused the high chair with her body, her father saw her as a pain in the neck, rather than as hungry, irritable, and unable to cope. And their fragile attunement was broken. Every parent has said to a child, at one point or another, some version of "can't you just chill?" But chilling doesn't come easily to everyone, and learning to chill takes time. Sometimes the source of stress is unknown or hidden, as with the child with anxiety, and sometimes it is triggered by some apparently minor action like putting a toddler in a high chair.

Telling a child to do something she doesn't want to do is hard because your bodies involuntarily seek attunement, simply by being in each other's presence. And the particulars of your relationship history or something that happened yesterday or five minutes ago can interfere. Giving a command does not have to mean a lack of attunement, but it sometimes does. You are in effect saying to each other, "We don't want the same thing; we don't feel the same thing. Help!" When a relationship has a foundation and history of responsiveness and trust, commands are less likely to disrupt attunement.[176]

Despite the fact that interactions are essential to development and to life itself, breakdowns are inevitable. While your child must engage with others for survival, socialization, and the routines of daily living, the very nature of being a self, even a very immature self, means experiencing the constant pull of your subjective experience, i.e., the constant reality that is *being you*. That "you" doesn't always want to cooperate, that "you" doesn't always feel emotionally regulated and calm. The baby "you" could have his third dirty diaper of the evening, and the parent "you" could be trying to watch an episode of *Homeland*. Like your infant, child, or teenager, you are a *person with feelings*, but as the parent, you have more responsibility and less choice. The anticipation of conflict and the ensuing stress make many parents back off from insisting on behavior, even regarding well-established routines like staying at the table until dinner is done. The tendency to back off may be even more likely if the conflict has become chronic. But you can make a difference. Not only is it important for you to manage your own stress but also, as the grownup, to help your child manage his.[177]

The Body Speaks

The body is always in an emotional state of some kind. You communicate your emotional state to others either unconsciously through nonverbal behavior, like the upset baby and father, or more intentionally through words and actions. Any two interacting humans tune in to one another, in effect searching for cues about how the other is feeling, how the other is responding to their cues, how they should behave. The heat or cold in a room is completely invisible except as it affects what or who is in the room. People sweat or shiver, plants thrive or wilt. So too with emotional attunement, although it is not so invisible once you pay attention to it.[178]

If you have a fight with someone, even a momentary misunderstanding, what is it that tells you that you are out of sync with that person? Some absence of warmth, some slight avoidance of eye contact, some minuscule delay in responding to a question, some very physical sense, although it might be hard to put your finger on it. We are radios, emitting signals to the people around us. During my training in a children's hospital, for example, a mother brought in her child for testing for ADHD. The findings weren't clear; in my report I noted jittery, restless behavior that was also consistent with anxiety. I sensed something more than a deficit in attention. The mother was relieved. She confided that she hadn't wanted to "bias the results" by telling me that she had experienced domestic violence and that she was going to file for divorce. This 7-year-old's agitation was a sign of stress, communicated to him by the violence in his family and to me by his behavior. He couldn't cope and his mother knew it, although she was in no shape at that moment to help him.

This mother's worry was, in effect, a form of authority. If you have a teenager, you may have been asked more than once, "Why do you always worry about me? I can take care of myself." To which you probably answered, "Because I'm the grownup." Over the course of childhood, the infant's brain and nervous system develop in interaction with the environment, most prominently with you and other caretakers.[179] That interaction is effected through nonverbal behavior, i.e., *everything* we do to communicate, mostly unconsciously, besides using words. The toddler waiting for breakfast needed food, but she was too immature to know it or to put it into words. She was upset: "Feed me!" her body shouted. Instead, her show of emotion triggered rough handling and swearing by her father, shorthand for his emotional response: "I'm hungry too. I didn't get enough sleep. This pancake breakfast wasn't my idea. I'm mad."

In the film *Buck*, a dramatic documentary about Buck Brannaman, the inspiration for the horse whisperer in Nicholas Evans' novel of that name, the director Cindy Meehl shows how Brannaman uses the connection he makes with a horse, and what he calls "natural horsemanship" to bring a horse from his wild, untamed state to take bridle, saddle, and rider. His method is in stark contrast to "breaking a horse in," the traditional method, and grew in part from his childhood of abuse. Buck's natural horsemanship bears a lot of similarity to what I have called natural authority. Buck is always in charge, and has no doubt about it. Neither do the horses he works with. But they are not afraid of him. He neither shouts nor uses physical force. Instead he communicates both care and authority through his voice, his touch, and his movements.

What Parents Do

While co-regulation is common to all human interaction, it has a special function in the intimate interactions that build and maintain the relationship between parent and child. Regulation is part of what human relationships do: It works to keep our brains attuned to one another. Children need adults to help them regulate by both explicit teaching and implicit modeling. This is accomplished partly through the human tendency to mimic and converge emotionally, which can be explained in part by hypotheses about the function of the vagal nerve and the connections it makes between your nervous system and your face, eyes, and hands. Your body has mechanisms to communicate how you feel, in effect reaching out to others for co-regulation.

When a child is tiny and helpless, it is easier to visualize yourself and your child as parts of an interacting pair, a pair of communicating brains. It is considerably more difficult to realize how connected you are when you are furiously arguing with a teenager about the dishes that didn't get done. Still, it is just as true then. In both cases, you are engaged in mutual regulation and always at risk of disconnection.

In infancy, the parent lends her regulation to her child both explicitly through feeding, soothing, and putting the baby to sleep and more implicitly through mutual gaze, conversation, and touch. Some years ago, I visited a young neighbor with a newborn and found her frantically trying to soothe an agitated, screaming baby. Whether you know anything about babies or not, you would have known immediately that little calm was going to emerge in this scenario. I reached for the baby and held him tightly against my chest, patting his back vigorously and singing "Twinkle, Twinkle, Little Star." To the relief of all three of us, he quieted down quickly and went to sleep. All I had done was lend him the regulation of my nervous system through my body and my voice, free of the exhaustion, anxiety, and emotional involvement of the new mother.

When I was about 10, I used to try to sleep with my feet on my pillow and my head under the covers, like Pippi Longstocking.[180] That was about as far as I could go in imitating Astrid Lindgren's character's wildly unconventional life, a life without parents or school. With a chest full of gold pieces left by her seafaring pirate father, a mother in heaven, and a horse and a monkey for roommates, Pippi lived in happy eccentricity in her ramshackle house wearing a much-patched dress, striped stockings, and outlandishly big shoes. But Pippi is a fiction. Ten-year-old children don't live by themselves in big houses with horses and monkeys, although many may wish to at times.

Pippi shares characteristics with another rebellious, eccentric, and independent semi-orphan in literature, Huckleberry Finn. Huck exasperates and shocks his would-be guardians, Miss Watson and Widow Douglas, with his shabby clothes, his slang, and his irreverence. Woefully out of practice in following parents' rules or fitting into family life, Pippi and Huck are free spirits—and misfits. They do what they want to do when they want to do it. Neither has to interact with anyone on a regular basis, thus escaping the need to acknowledge and accommodate others' expectations about what to wear or how to behave. Sometimes sneaky, sometimes brash, sometimes even heroic, Huck and Pippi are masters at defying convention and adult authority.

Without the practice of commonplace moment-to-moment interactions, without the guidance, limits, and emotional support that the natural authority of parents provides, they live unsupervised, unmonitored, *unregulated* lives. Pippi has Tommy and Annika, the kids next door for whose sake she goes to school. But she so exasperates the teacher with her outrageous behavior and talk—and her rejection of authority—that she is sent home. Although Lindgren doesn't make much of Pippi's animal roommates beyond their antics, one can imagine her in moments of loneliness or sadness snuggled up with Mr. Nilsson, the monkey on her lap, or leaning against the horse's warm neck. For Huck, in Mark Twain's novel, emotional regulation comes from his relationship with Jim, the runaway slave with whom he travels down the Mississippi River. Through this relationship he begins, in his own inimitable, cockeyed way, to think about the value of all human life and to shape his own behavior in some interacting rhythm with another human being.

Pippi got into big trouble when she accepted an invitation to tea at Annika's house. And she anticipated it: She knew she didn't really understand social and cultural norms, what an anthropologist described almost a century ago as "patterns not necessarily discoverable by an observer, not so much known as felt" and to which we respond "with extreme alertness and, one might almost say, in accordance with an elaborate and secret code that is written nowhere, known by none, and understood by all."[181] This code is a significant part of what children learn from experience with the adults with whom they interact. It is a code shaped by your family and your culture, helping you work out the relationship between what you are feeling inside and what you perceive and experience coming from the outside as you interact with other humans. Temperament, experience, and the codes of culture and family are some of the many factors that influence people to respond differently to the same event. One of the ways cultures differ in their interaction with infants, for example, is in the degree of eye contact adults seek to maintain with them. Some cultures tend to face babies outward to the group of working and playing humans among whom they live, or even teach them to avoid eye contact.[182]

Never Too Late to Start

He won't take out the trash, and you keep doing it for him. She won't come in at her curfew, and your spouse thinks you worry too much. He tells you that you are way stricter than the parents of all his friends. She refuses to talk to you about birth control and can't sit still when you try to talk to her about anything serious. Maybe all of the above: You feel that you are losing—or have already lost—control. How can you regain your authority?

It begins with much of what we have talked about in previous chapters, looking for clarity about the ways in which you are still the authority, despite his growing independence, and clarity about the particular issues that seem to trigger conflict between you. But you need to communicate that clarity. Can body language help? There is no single answer: Every chapter in this book focuses on a different aspect of your relationship of authority. But central to the possibility of change is your own conviction, which can be communicated, at least in part, through nonverbal behavior. In any such interaction, you probably won't pay conscious attention to nonverbal signals as you each keep hold of your interactional bone and growl at each other. But you would most likely be quite able to recall exactly what you felt and could bring the feeling to life in your body. If there were a conflict between a parent and child in my office, I would not only ask them what they both were feeling but would also look closely at the direction of their gaze, their facial expressions, their gestures, the angle of their sitting positions. I would tune in to their voices, their pitch and volume, their rhythm and pauses—in short, I would pay close attention to their nonverbal behavior as they responded to each other.

One of the great lessons of parenthood is learning to read the nonverbal behavior of irritability in your child: Is he hungry? Tired? Anxious? Thirsty? As the parent, you have the natural authority of experience and a more mature nervous system, and your child needs you to recognize, empathize with, and reflect back to him what he has expressed, even if he can't put his feelings into words. The more of this kind of reflection he gets from you, the more likely he is to develop the ability to reflect on his feelings himself. Instead of guessing, it can be useful to use a child's own words and gestures in your response. "You didn't want me to turn off the computer" or "You didn't want to put away your toys. You stamped your foot you were so upset." You can be explicit about what you picked up nonverbally, too: "You sound really angry; you look angry." This is true even if the child is an infant to whom you might say, perhaps in response to his baby grumbles, "so you don't want your diaper changed, eh?" When you do that, you remind yourself that it is your job to figure out what he's trying to tell you, not to take it personally and react back. When you get connected again, it feels good, and even when you are most discouraged, it helps to remember that.

The Body's Balancing Act

Homeostasis is the state of equilibrium in your body's chemistry and its life-giving systems of heartbeat, respiration, digestion, and temperature: It is the origin of the same concept we saw applied to the family system. These processes are maintained by two branches of the autonomic nervous system, the sympathetic and the parasympathetic nervous systems (SNS and

PNS). The PNS promotes the growth and restoration of your organs, responding primarily to internal, visceral signals. We are more aware of the activities of the SNS, which is responsible for the arousal necessary to deal with external signals. If you see a stranger, hear a loud noise, or are otherwise startled or frightened, the SNS accelerates your metabolism and your heartbeat, and may also support movement away from the perceived danger. This response is what is usually called "fight or flight." If you are too hot, your face may feel flushed, and you begin to sweat. You do whatever you can, opening a window or dousing yourself with water, to relieve the uncomfortable sensations.

It has been known since the 19th century that the body seeks a balance of the activities of both systems for physical well-being. Scientists are now more aware of the effect of homeostasis on your emotional state as well.[183] When your body is in homeostasis, you feel safe; you feel "under control," regulated. When conditions are right, the sensory, motor, and affective circuits integrate to provide you with the experience of life working in an orderly fashion.[184] The opposite of the feeling of regulation is dysregulation or, more colloquially, stress. Your experience of the moment outstrips your ability to manage it. It is more like being hot without any way to find relief. But instead of sweating, you are too touchy, reactive, or preoccupied to read others' signals properly or at all. You have a hard time making your connections with others work well. When you interact with your child, your connection is shaped by how regulated or stressed you both are. This, of course, was the state of affairs with our breakfast group: Between hunger, possible marital stress, and likely overly high expectations, no one's system was in balance. And through the mysteries of nonverbal behavior, the imbalance cascaded from one to another.

There is strong evidence-based argument for the intimate relationship between your physiological and emotional well-being. This is something every parent knows but can forget in the heat of the moment: When you—or your toddler or teenager—are cranky, it is very possibly because of hunger or lack of sleep or some other underlying discomfort.

Social Engagement: The Power of Face and Voice

Years ago, when I was walking with two of my children in the park, one suddenly knocked the other one down. I quickly reprimanded the apparent aggressor, who turned to me and said, "But you don't know how he looked at me!" Even a quick glance can be filled with meaning. Not only was there much of this relationship that was taking place beyond my eyes and ears, I didn't know what it felt like, at that moment, for them to be in a relationship with each other. While I may have had ideas about the meaning of one knocking down the other, my son was right: There was much I didn't know.

We have come a long way from what are thought to be the earliest uses of facial expressions for communication: movements like baring teeth, opening eyes wide, or raising eyebrows. But like so much in evolution, we have added without taking away: The face remains the most important source of information for interacting humans. The combined activity of the eyes, eyebrows, nostrils, mouth, and other facial muscles produces an untold number of signals for feelings, intentions, and responses; they are a large part of how emotions and attitudes particular to you are expressed to others. Without knowing it, you are already an expert in the meaning of facial expressions.[185]

Families tend to have beliefs about the appropriateness of different types of expressiveness, practices learned and carried on by children.[186] When Charlie rolled his eyes at his father's comments about the need to wear a jacket, he actively used a facial expression to convey his feelings. But chances are there was a subtext. In other words, he was making a nonverbal comment not only about his clothing, he was but about other aspects of his life about which he had less control, as was his father. How?

The polyvagal theory proposes that even though the activity of the PNS is focused on the internal organs, this system has evolved to be crucial to both emotional and physiological homeostasis. Eighty percent of it is made up of a bundle of fibers called the vagus nerve or vagal system. True to its roots in an old word meaning to wander, like *vagrant*, it makes its way from your brain stem to your viscera (heart, lungs, kidneys, liver, stomach, etc.) and back again. Sensory neurons from the viscera carry information to the brain, and motor neurons from the brain help direct your body's response.[187] The theory proposes a special role for the vagus because of its connections to the muscles for facial expression, turning the head, speaking, and the detection and decoding of the meaning of the human voice.

This so-called social engagement system allows you to help your child put on a "vagal brake," that is, to find ways to restore emotional regulation without going into the defensive, aggressive, or avoidant mode of the SNS, the mode afflicting the father at breakfast.[188] The ability to communicate through facial expression and tone of voice gives both you and your child enormous flexibility of response before you stomp out of the room or lose your temper. If the father at breakfast had been able to remain calm when his daughter resisted getting into the high chair, speaking to her soothingly instead of with anger, she might have recovered her equanimity more quickly.

The Eyes: Look at Me When I Am Talking to You

The alertness of newborns and their ability to maintain eye contact often surprises new parents. When I asked my mother if my new little sister could see me, she told me that babies didn't really see until they were six weeks old. She was partly right. The eyes of newborns are working, but their brains are only just beginning to create the networks of connections that will help them make sense of what they see, including the people with whom they interact. Children who are congenitally blind struggle to develop normal social understanding without help because so many of our unconscious interpersonal signals depend on vision.[189]

Eye contact signals that the visual channel is open, an invisible arm reaching out to grab attention. It is nearly impossible not to join the gaze of another human.[190] I'm looking at you, what do you have to say to me? Eyes—and the muscles around them—communicate warmth or hostility, sadness or fear, arousal or intensity. Between parent and child, that makes eyes especially important: Eyes say, "You can trust me," or "You're on thin ice here, be careful."[191] This has to do with shared experience, of course, as well as eyes, but the eyes are somehow able to communicate that experience.

Along with the neck muscles, the eyes are how others know what you're looking at. Humans are the only primate whose sclera—the part of the eye around the iris—is white: The contrast between our somewhat smaller irises and the white sclera is crucial to human social communication because it allows others to see the eye's motion and gaze. What is that other human looking at? Uh oh! Mom sees the food I snuck into the family room! And then just as quickly, how is she reacting? Eye contact between you and your co-parent is important as well: You can literally have a silent conversation in which it sometimes feels as if you are reading each other's minds. Who should intervene this time? Shall we take this complaint seriously?

Eye contact is not only for getting attention: It helps sustain conversation. There is a rhythm to a gaze related to grammatical breaks and to interruption. Eye contact can communicate emphasis, dominance, even threat. Eyes, then, can enhance your persuasiveness. In other words, for parents, eyes are a way to say: I mean it.[192] There are unwritten rules that we know mostly by their violation, but the main factor to take into account is that eye contact matters. This means that being in the same room and facing each other matter too, especially in the communication of authority, when your child may want to do anything but meet your gaze. That means, of course, no screens!

The Voice: An Instrument of Emotion

Parents who wait until after their babies are asleep to have that fight over who was supposed to buy the milk on the way home from work may be dismayed to discover that fetuses in the womb react to different tones of voice, even when they are asleep.[193] If even the unborn can detect these differences of intonation, how much more sensitive are you and your child when you get involved in an exchange about chores or home-work undone or curfew violated? And what do these differences communicate anyway?

When I was around 8 or 9, I was a whiner. My mother used to tell me she would put on her "anti-whiners" so that she could only hear me if I used my "regular" (regulated!) voice. I com-pletely believed in the imaginary anti-whiners. By this subter-fuge, my mother could stay businesslike, seeming to ignore me but surely monitoring me as she folded the laundry until I was able to regulate my mood. It was painful, but I suspect it was effective. When I changed my voice, it probably felt better, and when I changed my voice, she listened to me, which definitely felt better. But what was I communicating when I whined all the time? That I wanted more attention? If that was true, why couldn't I just say so? Why can't any of us just say so?

No one likes the shrill accusations or whiny complaints of a child—or a parent—and for good reason. The tone of voice of one provokes a corresponding feeling in the other. Each of us is, in effect, an expert on tone of voice: Even if you were speaking a language that was completely foreign to me, I could almost certainly get a good idea of what you were feeling.[194]

Why is the voice so central? With the attachment system, evolution has given you and your child tools to help keep the child safe and, secondarily, to foster the development of his ability to keep his system emotionally regulated. Attachment is one evolutionary tool; the voice is another. Go back in human time, and picture yourself in the woods instead of in your home; you have been gathering berries and are ready to go back to your village. Your son and daughter have been helping you but know to keep quiet so as not to disturb or frighten animals that may also be in the woods. The brush is thick around you. How will you find them? Perhaps you have a special signal like a quiet click or a low whistle, or perhaps you just quietly say, "Time to go." Ears have developed not simply to hear voices but to distinguish voices from other background noise. Humans are more likely to use the nonverbal aspects of language—i.e., the voice itself—to keep socially and emotionally engaged and regulated with other humans than for physical safety.[195]

The young infant's communication is all voice and no words. But an infant's cry is a distress call to the caregiver: "Help me cope!" Research has shown synchrony between infants' and mothers' brains when the infant cries, motivating the mother, who herself feels distress, to soothe her infant. Her voice, her touch, her warmth, or her physically moving the infant all help release more oxytocin in the baby's brain.[196] Even in the earliest days, but increasingly as your child gets older, you may feel less sympathetic—even suspicious—of cries of distress. Part of your authority is to make frequent decisions about how to respond. As the parent, you use your knowledge of your relationship, the child's temperament, your values, and the current situation to make those decisions. You won't always feel that you have made the right choice. But you will get many more chances!

Research has shown that listeners will use the face for social and emotional information first if it is available, but the voice is said to give just as much information about affect.[197] There are four main channels for this information, which is known as prosody: pitch (high to low), volume (loud to soft), intonation (up to down), and intensity (full to slight). You might consciously use a quiet, whispery voice to talk a child down from a meltdown, but how conscious are you of the voice you use when you are annoyed or impatient or angry? And how often do you or your child complain about the other's voice? "Why are you so mad at me?" "I'm NOT mad!" "Yes, you are, I can tell by your voice." Emotional states such as stress, anger, or frustration are communicated in powerful, audible ways that many parents may not think about—even as they respond to them and use variations in their own voices that have been called "gestures of the larynx."[198]

The Hands Talk Too: The Authority of Gesture and Touch

It is human to want to be understood. Gestures help. When two people know each other, they can decode each other's gestures readily. Because any individual person tends to be consistent, we are very likely to pay close attention to breaks from what is expected.[199] Consider your eager 8-year-old, who so wants what she has asked for that she nods rapidly, bounces on her feet, maybe even shakes her hands in the air as you tell her what she needs to do first, as if to convince you beyond her "okay, I'll do it" that she means what she says. Or consider your angry teen, whose indignation is communicated in the finger she points at you, regardless of what she says.

Conflict sometimes erupts because the listener assumes that the speaker's gestures are within her control and explicitly add meaning to the verbal message, although the gestures are probably unconscious.[200] Charlie's eye roll is a classic for adolescents communicating something along the lines of "There's a lot I'd like to say here, but I know there is no point, so I'll do what you say and spare you the prose."[201] Not only do movements of the hands intensify words, but they also may be taken more intensely by interlocutors than words. "I can't remember what he said exactly," you might say, "but he was so excited he could hardly contain himself."

Face-touching in general and covering the eyes in particular occur more often when someone experiences a negative emotion such as shame. Touching oneself may be simply a spillover of emotion, or even a form of talking to oneself, and not intended as communication to others. And yet it is visible and therefore decodable, at least unconsciously, by others.[202] As one mother recounted to me, "My daughter says she knows what I really feel by my hands: If I touch my head I am feeling overwhelmed and not very assertive."

Do gestures enhance your authority? Gesture isn't standardized the way spoken language is, but gestures do carry meanings that in some cases override words. Say yes while you shake your head no; the gesture clearly overrides the words for you and for your listener. Interestingly, as ubiquitous as gesture is, it is not something that you can remember the way you remember and can easily describe speech. But if you do remember the feelings you had when speaking with someone, they may very well have come from nonverbal behavior. Even young children can make themselves understood with the help of gestures, and there usually is no mistaking when someone makes hostile gestures. You may not use the blaming gesture of a pointed finger, but chances are that you have a look and a set of movements that signal authority. Your gestures, the way you move, stand, or hold yourself, the direction of your attention or the look on your face, all prepare your listener for what you are about to say and supplement it as you speak.

The Authority of Proximity

Perhaps the most important takeaway from the importance of both eye contact and gesture is to be in the same room or physical space with your child when asserting authority. That extra few seconds may save you time and conflict in the long run: Not only can you communicate your attitude better, but you can "read" your child's body. Posture, or how one holds one's body, is an aspect of nonverbal behavior that you can decode in a nanosecond—that familiar slump that you recognize from behind when your son is at the computer, struggling with an English paper or immersed in posting on Instagram, or the way your daughter walks up the front walk after school. A few years ago, I made a plan to meet a college-aged nephew whom I hadn't seen since he was a young teen. I parked my car and started walking to our assigned meeting place, when more than a block ahead of me I "saw" my younger brother, the father of this nephew. But of course, it was my nephew with a body and gait that was totally familiar. Either because he shared height and build with my brother, or because he had grown up interacting with my brother, or both, their postural nonverbal behavior was eerily similar.

It was evolutionarily advantageous to humans to learn as much as possible about someone across the savannah long before a facial expression was visible or a voice audible. What can I expect from this person who is approaching me? What is his attitude toward me? Is he going to do me harm? Threaten me? Or do I threaten him? All these kinds of questions race through your system in the moments occurring in your own habitat between you and your child. Even your young child can threaten you, not so much with harm as with stress, fear of inadequacy, guilt, and so on. In situations of explicit authority, you may gird yourself for a defiant response from your child and feel tense as you prepare your retort, which may end up in a retreat or a compromise rather than insistence. Your body will tell this tale as much as or more than your words. *(See Chapter Ten for more about stance.)*

Nonverbal behavior helps bridge the gap between the two perspectives, and the two bodies, of you and your child. Moments in which authority is asserted are like all of the other daily moments in which both of you are asking yourselves, what am I going to do with my body now? Of the many ways one body bridges to another, perhaps the most powerful is touch. The skin has fast and slow systems of sensation. The fast ones send information about highly discriminated stimuli such as the prick of a pin to the spinal cord and the brain, including the insula (sometimes called the social brain), but implicated in all interoceptive awareness. *(See Chapter Six.)* But it is the slow fibers that process the caress-like gentle touch that is central to social connection. These signals also lead to the insula. One astonishing study demonstrated the ability of subjects to identify 11 emotions being communicated by the touch of another person, whose face and body they could not see.[203] Connection and trust are fundamental to a relationship of authority. And even a slight touch can communicate both. There is a touch of authority not in the belt or the spanking, but in reassurance.

Dare to Be the Authority

Helping your child stay regulated is an aspect of your authority that is physiological and often involuntary. But one's more conscious self can also take charge, including by making difficult decisions when a child is upset. This might mean being willing to take on the challenge of helping a child stay regulated rather than seeing his oppositionality as a fight you need to win or a behavior you need to punish. Instead of asking, "Why are you acting this way?" or generalizing ("You do this every night!"), you might take a step back to ask yourself what is happening between you in this moment, in your relationship, in the family system, in the habitat.

You can stop yourself from flying off the handle, or you can manage to recover quickly afterward and be curious: "You are so upset; what's going on?" You may not get an answer, either because he doesn't know or doesn't want to tell you. Still, the degree of trust your child has in your willingness and ability to respond to him in a way that acknowledges his perspective, the certainty he has that you are committed to keeping him safe and secure, will make him more likely to respond to your efforts, whether verbal or nonverbal, to help him calm down. What he learns from your interactions serves another purpose, to teach him what to expect not only from you, but also from others, from grownups, from men or from women, from people in authority.

Picture a child who refuses to stop texting to do what she is asked, whether to pick up her clothes, do her homework, go to sleep, or stop harassing her younger brother. You take the bait: You are sick and tired of her room being such a mess; she better bring up her math grade or else; she is sure to get a cold if she doesn't get more sleep, and don't expect any sympathy from you; she ought to know better than to be such a mean older sister. You could be right on any of these counts, but this isn't the time to talk about them. Because your child may have reasons completely unknown to you for whatever it is she's refusing to do, or for texting, your response to her refusal might trigger a meltdown. All the more so because what you are interrupting is her texting her friend, an activity that you know from your own experience is hard to stop.

Her refusal is challenging for you—but remember that such situations probably represent a greater challenge for her. She is dependent on you. She wants your approval. She wants things to feel okay again. Sometimes this is hard to believe because you have both gone down the rabbit hole of negativity. If you asked her, she would say that she doesn't believe that you want things to be okay. Before she loses it, or even after she has, it is possible that a slight touch on the shoulder matched by a calm, nonthreatening demeanor will break through her defenses to let her body know that you are in charge, things will be okay, she can lose face and agree to do what you say. Or at least be able to talk about it.[204]

Tantrums: You Both Have Them!

Let's end with a discussion of the dreaded tantrum, what every parent wants to avoid and what might have ensued from the breakfast scenario described above. A tantrum is a full-blown expression of stress; the child's whole body expresses stress from fatigue, frustration, confusion, the inability to say what he wants. Research has shown that tantrums are alike the world over, and occur both as a result of stress and a bid for help, thus the sometimes wild-seeming swings between anger and sadness. They tend to arise when a child feels thwarted, either by not getting a snack or a turn or wanted attention, or from not wanting to do what they're being asked to do.[205]

A tantrum lets you know that your ability to connect with each other has completely broken down. Sometimes a toddler in the midst of a tantrum doesn't seem much more manageable than a bucking bronco. Tantrums are the hallmark in popular culture of the terrible twos, and they are indeed common among young children because young children have less capacity for impulse control and self-regulation, less capacity for reasoning and verbal communication, and fewer inhibitions about making a scene. If a child perceives from the reaction of those around him that a tantrum brings attention and the satisfaction of demands, a tantrum can also become a learned behavior.

One of the main reasons tantrums are challenging is because as a co-regulating pair, it can be difficult to maintain your own mood regulation in the face of your toddler's frustration. Not only that, tantrums often happen in public places where it is harder to use some of your customary discipline strategies, such as time-outs, and where other people are watching your every move, easily triggering feelings of shame, despite the fact that it is the rare parent who hasn't had the same experience.

Preschoolers have no corner on tantrums. Every human is vulnerable to stress, and every human is vulnerable to a full-blown breakdown of regulation. In older children and adults, we call it a meltdown. Why can't a 2-year-old just say, "Mommy, I'm kind of hungry and tired. I'm not sure I want to go into the grocery store right now." Or, "But I really, really, really want to wear the blue shirt even though it's in the washing machine and it's time to go to school." Why can't he indeed? He may not know. Or he can't say it for the same reason that you have a hard time being reasonable when you walk into the house from work and everybody wants something, or when you have just settled yourself onto the couch to watch a show you've been looking forward to and your teenager calls from the mall and wants to be picked up—now!

But how does it help to know this when your toddler is screaming or your 10-year old is melting down about math homework? Think about the things you usually do. My guess is that you start by staying calm, making an effort to shift the balance of contagious mood in the other direction so that your child picks up your calm tone of voice—like your first-grade teacher used to do by whispering or turning out the light when everyone was noisy. This may do the trick, but if it doesn't, you are at risk of becoming stressed yourself. When you both are stressed, it will then be harder for either of you to calm down. At the other end of the continuum, you may be tempted to negotiate verbally, especially if the "reason" for the tantrum or meltdown is the frustration felt from a refusal to give in, but it is usually a losing battle, because your co-negotiator has been hijacked and has lost control.[206]

It Is Hard to Be the Grownup

Despite all the places that tantrums and meltdowns can happen, and all the reasons, and all the ages, it is your job, as the parent, to help your child get regulated or give him the opportunity to become self-regulated again. Repeated tantrums may be a red flag that trips to the grocery store on the way home from school are a bad idea: He's tired, he's hungry, and he's been holding it together all morning. Or that bedtime needs to be adjusted again: Now that she's in daycare all day, she can't make it to 8 p.m. anymore, even if that means you won't have as much time with her when you get home from work. When a parent reports that a 3-year-old throws a fit every time she has to put on a seat belt, it is time to slow everything down and think about the big picture. It is probably not just the seat belt. "But I can't make her do it!" The parent is as agitated in thinking about it as the child is in her refusal. What is she communicating? Intolerance of restraint? Fear of carsickness? Dislike of kindergarten? Habitual defiance brewed from repeated tantrums? This kind of thinking, these kinds of decisions, are part of parenthood: You regulate through interaction but you also regulate through more intentional, explicit decisions about activities and routines.

One of the hardest things for a parent to accept is not being able to help when a child of any age is unhappy or frustrated, whether mildly or acutely so. It can and does happen at any age—from the screaming of an infant who you know is exhausted and can't fall asleep to the panic of a 9-year old who hasn't started the book report due tomorrow or the overwhelmed college student who tells you everything is impossible but rejects all solutions. As the parent, you are the perfect target for venting: The child in question may need to fall apart somewhere and you represent safety, or she may be mad at you for thwarting her plans. It is hard to know how to intervene, because reasoning is not only unlikely to work but in fact may only exacerbate the dysregulation: "I don't care about that!" or "that will never work!" she might shriek when you try to suggest solutions. What she may need most is either time to cool down or simply a reflection of just how awful she feels.

The brain is always trying to figure out what is going to happen next, directing you to act accordingly. And it helps explain one function of your natural authority: If you can be calm in the face of your child's tantrum, so that he hears a calm voice or sees a calm expression on your face, then through mirroring and contagion he will be more likely to resonate with and imitate your behavior, to experience himself as more calm, and to behave more calmly himself. In other words, your more mature nervous system helps you put your own emotions in check and in turn helps your child keep his in check. Nevertheless, stress can trump control in any of us. Your daughter's tantrum over eating broccoli or your inability to tolerate her demands when you get home from work are times when the stress of external pressures forces your reactions to revert to their most primitive, like the father at the beginning of this chapter. Then your job is recovery.

Chapter Ten

Moments of Authority:
Where You Are and What You Say

Two young siblings play kitchen, gathering together plastic French fries, cooked carrots, and cans of refried beans for imaginary picnics. But now it is time to go out. You tell them once, and then twice. They make no sign of having heard you, and they have moved on to your iPad, which you had left on the kitchen table. At first you feel patient; you are delighted that they are playing so well together and relieved that you don't have to entertain them. You step over the toys and consider picking them up yourself. But then you remember doing it late the night before and you become exasperated. Still, making them do it not only requires you to interrupt their happy time on the iPad, but also will probably take longer than if you do it.

We have explored the presence and legitimacy of parental authority, much of it implicit, in your relationship with your child and in your family life. Our discussion turns now to those moments when your implicit authority is made explicit, when you, as the parent, seek to affect or change the behavior of others. These occasions have been called both "structures of control" and "directives."[207] These moments, which are really sequences of moments, occur when you can no longer rely exclusively on whatever routines or expectations are already in place. Something about the situation pushes you to make the implicit authority of your household, your values, and your relationships more explicit.

Authority Is Implicit and Explicit

I began Chapter One with a story of carrying a screaming toddler home from the playground. I knew I had to be the authority but didn't quite know how else to act on that knowledge. Parents' authority is natural, legitimate, and inherent to the role. But where *is* authority? We have talked about the relationship, the habitat, and the family; we have talked about moments of interaction between two bodies and selves; we have talked about voice and gaze and gesture. What else communicates the conviction and certainty that your child must pick up those plastic fries, do the dishes, or go to bed?

There must be authority in more than your words. Authority must infuse your relationship in all the aspects of family life we have talked about in this book: your connection to and experience with each other, the household routines, parent teamwork and good boundaries of your habitat, your body language, facial expression, and tone of voice. But even if all of that is true, you have to be sure you have your child's attention, and you have to choose the words you use. How is authority conveyed when you must interrupt a video game, or when your child defies you? How is it conveyed when he is bigger than you?

I have four sons. Somewhere between 14 and 17, each of them grew to be taller than I am. I found myself looking up at them as I told them to clear the table, practice piano, or do whatever the task at hand might be. I felt pretty confident doing that, but I also often marveled that I did, knowing that any one of them could easily overpower me. There *was* something marvelous about the fact that they stayed to listen to me. I am tempted to say that I was not using physical force to keep their attention, but in a way I was. I was using the force of the implicit authority built up in our relationship from the time they were tiny tots, the force that was my particular version of natural authority with each of them. When they were small, I could and did pick them up. At that time, it was often the only way to communicate authority, because I was inexperienced as a parent, they were inexperienced in life, and our relationship was in its early days.

Explicit authority begins when you decide whether or not to intervene in the first place. Should I make the kids pick up those toys? My mother-in-law, also the mother of four sons, used to quote *her* mother-in-law, mother of nine sons: "Don't sweat the small stuff" (or some early 20th-century version of that). And there is something to be said for that. You are human, and your household is a family, not a factory or an army. There will be times when your mood or your energy or your judgment about the situation provokes a moment of indulgence. For some parents, it is hard to let a rude remark go, while for others it is hard to assert authority. At the same time, be aware that each time you give in, you have lost another opportunity to practice authority, and you risk their reliance on your giving in. This is what psychologists call intermittent reinforcement, which is the most powerful form of reinforcement. In other words, your child's repeated requests or defiance are like playing a slot machine. Another try is worth it to him because maybe this time you *will* get him water when he's in bed or ignore the minor curfew violation.

The Importance of Attention

Bodies take up space; bodies demand attention; bodies make noise. Conversation analysis broadened our comprehension of spoken language by showing how it could be understood in reference to the physical context surrounding ongoing conversation. In other words, what is happening *besides the words themselves?* Linguistic anthropologist Marjorie Harness Goodwin and her colleagues at UCLA studied sequences of parents' directives and children's responses in everyday routines like brushing teeth, leaving the house, or family dinnertime by extending the model of conversation analysis to the actions and gestures of the bodies involved and to the relation of these actions to physical spaces.[208] This model can be applied to almost any sequence in which a parent asserts authority.

To be effective, a sequence of authority requires physical gestures, even touch, what Goodwin and her coauthor Eve Tulbert call the "'embodied' choreography of attention." This phrase aptly suggests a complicated dance of interaction, requiring of you, as the more experienced dance partner, "sustained parental work." In other words, authority may be natural, but the means to achieve it are complex. It is no mean feat to sustain "children's active engagement" in today's digitized and distracting world.[209]

Human beings are acutely, if unconsciously, aware of the need to maintain connection. How you try to command attention and sustain your connection involves many things, including, prominently, your language and your behavior. Researchers into nonverbal behavior emphasize the way participants in an interaction arrange themselves physically to express or display their agreement with or commitment to a common perspective. How and where you and your child stand give each of you clues to your attitudes toward the interaction, what is sometimes called your "stance." In the terms we have used, your stance either does or does not communicate authority to her, and her stance does or does not communicate respect and intended compliance to you. Remember the boy sprawled on the subway.

The basic position that signals readiness and openness to the interaction has been called the facing or "F" formation.[210] If your child turns toward you when you speak to him, he has taken a step toward giving you not only his attention but his willingness to listen—a word that many parents even use as a stand-in for respect or obedience, as in, "Now, you listen to me!" When we first got our mongrel Bobi, we learned that every command should begin with the dog's name to ensure his attention. So perhaps with children. The effectiveness of any directive begins with your ability to engage and sustain your child's attention and in his degree of reliance on your attention and responsiveness to him, including, as we will note below, eye contact and touch. What parents do involves attention, movement, and even the spaces in which families function, in addition to words themselves, as they work to get their children's attention and ultimate compliance.[211] Remember that the brain, and therefore the self, is always in a body, always linked to the environment, always alert to what happens next.

But more important than any particular position is the social nature of your embodied choreography. In the complicated but everyday process of interaction, your bodies are trained in an unconscious dance of communication: what you do with your body when you scold, what he does when he ignores you. Often a conflict sequence itself becomes the routine. You walk into the room and say, "Get ready for school." He has his back to you, hunched over a screen, and says, "Just a minute." He is in the middle of something, but it is something that is prohibited, even if you don't always enforce it. You become tense, realize you're getting trapped, and ask again; his voice rises with exasperation, and you detect a slight shake of the head when he answers, "I said just a minute, Mom! Jeez!" This happens several mornings a week.

Children have notoriously short attention spans (although all of ours seem to be decaying with the omnipresence of screens). Attention gets a bad rap with parents. To describe a kid as "just wanting attention" suggests some fault with him. He wants it, but he also needs it. Not only is looking for attention from adults as natural as breathing, your child's wants and needs have developed in relationship with you and from cues communicated by your family environment. A child may look for attention inappropriately or rudely or in the middle of the night, but the looking isn't bad per se. It is a means of connection as well as a means of authority.

Attention and Authority

The importance of attention in the assertion of authority cannot be overemphasized. The nature of consciousness is such that despite all of our efforts to the contrary, no one is truly capable of attending to more than one thing at once. Long before the lure of social media and texting, William James talked about the limits of attention; he referred to "dispersed" versus "focused" attention and the common instances in which you find yourself in a reverie, with no idea what has been said to you. I am someone who is easily distracted, and it is not uncommon for me to find myself at the end of a paragraph with no idea of what I have just read because while I was "reading" my attention was focused elsewhere—maybe on dinner, or my next client, or the pain in my little toe. It is easy to forget that your child may sometimes have the same experience. But James also talked about "voluntary attention" and the need for any of us to actively bring our attention back from its wanderings.[212]

We all grow up hearing mothers and fathers and teachers asking or telling us to "pay" attention. Perhaps the monetary metaphor is apt; attention might just be the most valuable asset we have as conscious human beings. Stop paying attention and you may be eaten! Researchers into consciousness make the obvious but fundamental point that being conscious is not the same as paying attention. Once you engage your attention, you are ready for more interaction with your environment; attention is a sense of readiness.[213]

Take an interaction recounted by two of the UCLA researchers, between an 8-year-old boy and his mother, who wants him to clear his dishes from the table. The boy is in another room, and it takes several shouts for his mother to even get his attention and a response. When he responds, it is by shouting back at her, not coming into the kitchen, so she goes to where he is. The mother intersperses her directives with affectionate physical gestures and some joking around, delivering quite a different message, i.e., that her request is not that serious. In the end, the boy runs away laughing. A little later, she resorts to escorting him after her words and gestures have failed. She doesn't have to physically carry him, as I did my toddler from the playground, but she does have to physically shepherd him. Attention, then, not only has to be achieved, but maintained, and maintained in some cases from one place to another. A perfectly ordinary moment, but one full of resonance for any parent.[214]

And *both* of you must pay attention. In a dramatic *New York Times* photo from several years ago, a family was depicted sitting together on the couch, each staring at his or her own mobile device. It has become completely ordinary for one parent to have a deadline for work and the other to not yet be home. There you are, on your computer or mobile device, and you call to the kids to come to dinner. Despite repeated shouts, they don't come, and you never actually stop working; perhaps you don't even look up. But it is you who gets frustrated at their disobedience, without even noticing your own inattention. Extreme? I think we can all see ourselves in this kind of inconsistency.

In order to get your child to do something she is supposed to do, you must first create alignment, i.e., make sure she is on board with you, which almost certainly involves what Goodwin aptly calls "dislodging" her from a competing activity. You must build, in effect, at least a psychic and perhaps a physical boundary of attention, reinforced by your body and its position in space, say, in front of the nearest exit or in the way you stand or hold your head. When the child ignores, defies, or only halfheartedly responds, when she tries to avoid answering, pleads, or negotiates—or as linguists call it, baldly refuses your directive—your job is not finished, and it in fact gets much harder. This is when many parents give up: those all too common times when you and a child get tangled in a many-turned back-and-forth, "recycling" the same arguments or excuses. I'm texting now; it's Michael's turn; I'm tired. Or bargaining positions: I'll do it after I finish this; I'll do it if you help me. (Recycling in this case is not such a positive thing!)[215]

Reprimands

Sequences of explicit authority, those interactions in which you are trying to get your kid to do what he's supposed to do—or what you want him to do—vary in form and intensity. In Chapter Eight, we saw a grandmother and a father interact in sequences with, respectively, a 3-year-old and a 14-year-old. A common assertion of authority is a reprimand or scolding: You tell your son you heard from his teacher about a poor test grade or tell your daughter that you are sick and tired of finding her belongings everywhere but in her room. These moments of authority may be assertions of values, reminders that as a family you have standards and rules that have not been followed. Or they may be expressions of disappointment about what you perceive to be failures to live up to a promise, a project, or a plan. You use your authority to bring the violation to your child's attention and to communicate to the child what will happen next.

It is usually unproductive to ask a child (or anyone, for that matter) why they did what they did. First of all, even a teenager probably doesn't know, any more than you know your motivation for every behavior; the reason might be convoluted and illogical. And secondly, what good does it do? What you really mean is that you are upset at what he has done, that it is not what you wanted him to do or what he knew he was supposed to do. Being clear with yourself about what your reprimand hopes to communicate will help you think twice about useless outbursts.

Reprimands often become or include threats, and threats are often not carried out—partly because they can be wildly out of scale. I'm sure you have said things like, "I am sick and tired of this mess. If you don't clean your room you are never going to have another friend over!" Or maybe you've threatened, "That's it, I'm taking away your phone for the next month" when the infraction was not so bad in itself but, rather, came at the end of a long string of small violations, or happened when you were already at the end of your rope for something entirely different.

Maybe the violation included a roll of the eyes, a rude remark, or a stamp of the foot. You mean the threat when you say it, in an effort to show that you are serious or to instill at least a little anxiety in the culprit. But because children, like the rest of us, rely on what they have learned will happen next, a threat not carried out may actually undercut your authority.

Prohibitions and Permissions

One of the most common directives from parent to child is "Stop it!" The "it" to be stopped might be annoying noises or inappropriate or unsafe behavior: loud music, being rough with a pet or a household object. Another common kind of intervention occurs when there is conflict between two of your children or a child and another playmate. Parents have a wide range of attitudes toward conflict, noise, and physical activity. Some tolerate it, but not in their presence; others invoke gender or age, as in "Don't hit your sister again!" because of some unstated reason: "She's a girl" or "She's younger than you." Whatever behavior it is you want to stop, the point is that this expression of explicit authority is neither premeditated nor part of a routine, but rather your reaction to something happening in your presence or at least within earshot. You may be driven to intervene because you can hear or see or feel emotion in the interaction, or you may feel you need to come to the rescue of the apparent victim. But be careful: Remember that when you intervene, you put your power at the disposal of one person when you are not necessarily privy to the whole exchange.

Interventions in conflict are one sort of prohibition, but the list of things children must learn that they aren't allowed to do is long, and it changes as they get older. For a young child, there are above all safety prohibitions: Don't put that in your mouth. Don't touch that outlet. Don't go down the stairs or outside alone. Don't hit the dog. Many that start when a child is young survive toddlerhood: Don't throw your clothes on the floor.

Don't play with your food. Don't wear that out of the house. For young children, many if not most of these will be learned by the "stop it" kind of authority we just discussed, accompanied by physical intervention in cases where it would be dangerous to wait to see if they respond.

On the morning I write this, I saw a father attempt to cross a Manhattan avenue with three children, one in a stroller, one holding his hand, and one walking free. He started once the walk sign had switched to a blinking warning, and the son walking alone started to run ahead as a taxi came around the corner. The father shouted and was able to grab him in time. It was a vivid example of the risks of letting kids try out independence without adequate preparation. Many prohibitions must be well-learned in advance, particularly those having to do with safety. And as the parent, you must make the call about whether your child is ready. This boy apparently was not.

Not all prohibitions are as dramatic: "No, of course you can't have a sleepover on a school night," or "No, you can't go to the concert without a parent along." For a child of any age, how much you need these or indeed other structures of control will depend on how many other structures you have in place—whether, for example, you have gates at the top of the stairs, the kind of clothes your child has in her closet, rules and expectations to fall back on so that explicit assertions of authority are less necessary.

Closely related to prohibitions are permissions and denial of permissions. Asking to be taken places, signing up for camp, wanting to spend money on something, bringing a friend home for dinner, and so on. These are perhaps the moments of authority in which values are most at play in what you decide. How much input does your child get to have and which factors do you bring to bear—siblings, safety, other obligations? Sometimes parents who disagree must hash out their values on the spot, even at the risk of triangulation. You're at the mall and your daughter sees a friend, who invites her over: Your spouse says sure, forgetting that your mother is coming over. Something has to be decided.

There are of course some areas of permission and denial with very high stakes: "Yes, I will make an appointment for you to get birth control" is a sentence you may not be able to imagine yourself saying until you are confronted with a daughter who announces her intention to engage in sexual activity. "I can't believe you are going to call Dave's mother about whether they're going to be home when he has his party. That is so embarrassing." "Well," you answer, "if I don't make the call, you don't go."

There are less inflammatory occasions for authority in decision-making and advising that can still be tough because you must consider your values regarding your child's ability to make decisions. Questions like, "Should I invite Joe to my birthday party?" "Should I join the soccer team?" "Should I use my allowance to go to the movies, or should I add it to my savings?" How much say does a child get in picking a middle school? Can you bear it if she makes a mistake that you could see coming?

Interruptions

Often it is necessary to interrupt an activity your kids are engaged in to get them out of the house or to get them to do something they must do. Michael was playing a video game; Samantha was with a friend. These are the moments with which parents sometimes have the most difficulty. "I'll do it in a minute." "I'll do it when I finish this." "I'm in the middle of my math homework." This is not a question of discipline ("Go to your room because you knocked your brother down"), but rather a question of authority ("It's time to go, now"). But whether the activity is homework or texting, your interrupting it with your request or admonition or command, however legitimate, is still an interruption. Why is interrupting your child—or anyone, for that matter—difficult?

Interruption comes from "rumpere," the Latin word for break. It means to break or stop the continuity of a line, or the continuous progress of an activity. For human brains, having forward movement stopped is frustrating. Your child is not like the ant crossing the picnic table who simply turns the corner if you put something in his way.

To be interrupted, then, is no small thing—and I suspect we don't think about it enough. Some people find it more difficult than others, and children often find it more difficult than adults. Some children, of course, find it all too easy to interrupt what they're doing and need help sticking to it, but not generally when it comes to things you want them to do. Since their brains are less developed and their experience more limited, children have the luxury that meditators aspire to, of being in the moment, whether it be in play or at a meal or on the computer. Your parental perspective represents the voice of a demand, which, given the child's dependence and your inherent responsibility, is a legitimate one.

But how parents communicate this is as variable as personality. One common style is counting to three; another, especially with small children, is a race or a challenge ("I bet you can't get your shoes on by yourself!"). Some parents use what I think of as the expansive, patient approach: They ask, they wait, they show some interest in what the child is doing or how he feels and ask again. Such an approach requires allowing enough time, as well as patience. But it is just as authoritative and can be just as effective.

The tension in interruptions comes from the fact that there are in even the most trivial and momentary interaction two selves, two perspectives with expectations, needs, wants, and experience expressed in words and actions. Each moment of authority springs from your ongoing relationship and the potential momentary clash of two perspectives. But you, as the responsible adult, must take the lead when it comes to tasks or activities that benefit the household. There are many times when *you* are interrupted to consider a child's request. And you may well express your frustration at the interruption. This is the stuff of a parent's everyday life, completely ordinary and largely unconscious, another piece of the pattern of interactions that is your relationship with this child, another lesson in what it means to live in this habitat and this family, and what it means to be the authority.

When a parent interrupts a child's activity to direct her to another activity, unless it is an announcement that you're going out for ice cream, there is likely to be some resistance, if not outright defiance. When you interrupt to ask for a favor, you must, of course, be sensitive to what the other person is doing; it is easy to take advantage of your child's dependent status. If she is, like Charlie and Abby, engaged in something else, I suspect that you don't always stop to think about what she is doing. You might experience any delay or resistance as orneriness or rudeness or lack of respect or inattention—any of which could be true. But it could also be true that she is truly engaged in what she is doing, whether a Facebook post, a book, a text, homework, a movie.

As we saw in Chapter Seven, children vary in their ability to break away from an activity, and as they grow older, they have to learn what is expected of them in your habitat and in your relationship. Your chances of communicating your authority effectively will depend in part on your ability to balance your request (whether your needs or a family routine) with her situation in that moment, perhaps by giving her five or 10 minutes' notice. Such respect for her perspective also makes yours the voice of authority; authority is not only a bold insistence on your demand. When a child is being what we used to call "fresh," i.e., impudent or disrespectful, such behavior is often the assertion of his need or desire over the family need. But even if you represent the family, whether the family's schedule or the family's values, you come in the form of a body, a bigger body (until they outgrow you), a voice, an interruption. And your authority will be more effective if you take his perspective—how it feels to be him in that moment when you interrupt—into consideration.

Expectations: One Thing Leads to Another

When you interact with your child, say, to get out of the house to go to school in the morning, you engage in behavior that is both somewhat routine (he needs to be dressed appropriately, have shoes on, and bring a backpack or lunch) and particular to the situation (if it's winter, he needs to wear a coat and hat and gloves). But there are almost certainly what we might call subroutines that are particular to your relationship when you engage in this interaction. They change over time because of your child's age and increasing ability to take care of himself, and they probably retain a quality particular to the ways you and he typically engage: Perhaps he is easygoing or even proactive about getting ready, and things go off smoothly. But perhaps he refuses to come to the door, and you respond with a ritual complaint that he is never ready, that he should be ready by now.

The human brain loves patterns. We learn by recognition of patterns outside of us, from letters forming patterns that create words to what someone close to us habitually does. We learn by the linking together of neural patterns in our brains, associating things one with another, whether behavior or sounds or visual images. The sponge that is your child's brain absorbs it all. Are you surprised that your child remembers not just what you asked her to do last time but the fact that you didn't hold her accountable when she didn't do it, or that you said it was her last chance and then you gave her another chance? And yet you are likely to expect her to behave differently in a repeating situation even though you are behaving in the same way.

The idea that we remember things, and therefore learn, through association is at least as old as the ancient Greeks: In the fourth century BC, Aristotle and others wrote, for example, about "the art of memory," i.e., techniques of recall based on association. William James described habits as "pathways through the nerve-centers." What he calls "currents," or the forces activating brain activity, "can only deepen old pathways or create new ones." In another metaphor, he describes the folds in paper: Once a fold exists, it will be easiest to fold the paper there the next time. It is notable that James saw learning as anchored in the nervous system.[216]

The brain's tendency to make associations was also key to 20th-century thinking in both psychology and neuroscience. Ivan Pavlov noticed that dogs salivated not only at their food but also even at the sight of the technician who fed them. In other words, they associated the technician with the arrival of food. Later, they were trained to salivate at the sound of a bell, even though the bell had nothing directly to do with their food but had been associated with it only experimentally. Neuroscientist Donald Hebb was the first to propose that learning might take place through the associations that occur at the level of neural synapses. He proposed that if two cells are active at the same time and cause a third cell to "fire," or to be activated, the next time, because both of the cells are now associated with the firing of the third, either of the first two cells can make the third cell fire in the future. This idea is expressed by a phrase frequently quoted by popularizers of neuroscience: "Cells that fire together, wire together."[217]

Like the Greeks, contemporary neuroscientists take this concept a step further to emphasize *contextual learning.* If, like Pavlov's dogs, he explains, a rat receives a shock while in a certain box, then, when he is returned to that box, he will react with fear because thanks to the seahorse-shaped brain structure, the hippocampus, he associates the box with the shock.[218]

Why do parents underestimate the power of learning? You know how fast your child learns new words and bad habits! Why, then, you might ask, can't my kid "learn" to get ready on time? Why do I have to bribe him with stickers? That is because he is not only learning what you intend for him to learn, but whatever else he knows or can pick up on. For example, if you and your child have a negative routine about leaving the house, in which you yell at least three times before he comes downstairs, chances are that such a routine will perpetuate itself unless you actively seek to change it. It is habit. This is why rewarding kids, even with stickers, is effective. You build up a different set of associations. If a child gets a sticker when she gets ready to go out without complaining, gradually the new behavior is associated with the going-out routine, without need of stickers.

Consistency matters for children of all ages. Even if you and your co-parent have agreed on and communicated a clear and appropriate consequence to your child, unless you actually follow through with it, it won't be as clear the next time. Instead of learning that violating curfew brings an evening or weekend at home, or a docking of his allowance, he will learn that the violation brings annoyance, an unpleasant interaction, but no reason not to stay out late again.

Rules and Routines of Conversation

Your experiences form pathways in the brain, habits of behavior, for better or worse. Routines and sequences are enormously helpful to parents and children in moments of authority: Parents need a structure to fall back on ("Remember what we do when we go to bed?"), and children learn by practicing routines over and over. Creating a sleep routine that fits your family and your infant, for example, is a crucial task for parents' authority and family well-being when a baby is born, but *maintaining* your chosen routine may be a bigger challenge for your authority because of the unwritten subroutines, which are usually only acknowledged in exasperated outbursts: "I can't believe we have to go through this every night!" There is nothing like a whining child asking for water when you yourself are about to collapse to trigger an escalation. You get stern; she whines more; you shout; she cries; you slam doors; your spouse criticizes you; you give in; peace returns. But it happens the next night too. What has your child learned? Keep whining and you might get what you want.

In conversation analysis, which brought an interactional framework to the study of language, the unit of study is the flow of utterances, not just full sentences but attempts by one or another to speak, breaks in the conversation, who has the floor and for how long, and so on. There are rules about how one turn of conversation leads to another. This is a different kind of path or linking of associations than we discussed above. In this case, the linking of one kind of utterance with another has to do with the form. A question requires an answer: "Are you going out?" "No, not till later." A command requires agreement or disagreement: "Close the door, please." "Okay, just a minute, let me put these things down." An accusation requires an explanation or, more often, a defense: "You are so mean to me!" "No, I'm not, I'm just telling you what to do."

I train couples and families to start sentences with "I" for this reason: You are more likely to get a response that also begins with "I." For example, you tell your child, "You never do what I say," after you have, for the third time, reminded her to set the table. Her response may be something like: "You're always telling me what to do," which is likely to lead to an escalation from you. If you instead say, "I have reminded you to set the table three times," you are likely to get a protest like "I'm going to!" which shifts the conversation to *when* not *if* and helps avoid an exchange of accusations.

How Many Ways Do I Have to Ask You to Clean Your Room?

Conversation analysis is not only what couples and family therapists do, but it is also what all of us do implicitly in ordinary life: "But I thought you said X, that's why I said Y!" In other words, we expect certain kinds of utterances to lead to certain others. This can be far subtler than "a question requires an answer." For example, there are at least three common ways of communicating to your child that it is time to clean her room. When you say, "You have to clean up your room now," it is different from "Will you please clean up your room?" or "I'm going to ask you to clean up your room this afternoon, okay?" The syntactical structure of each demands a different response.

To the first, "You have to clean up your room," or the slightly less personal "It's time to clean up your room," your child might say, "Do I have to?" She gets that you are giving her a command, even if she is hoping that she can weasel out of it. If her response is to stall, rather than not doing what you say, she is nevertheless implying by her question that she knows the answer is up to you, not up to her. In a more combative mood, she might say, "I don't have to clean up my room just because you say so. It's *my* room," even though she knows full well that cleaning her room is a family rule. From a conversation analysis point of view, you are collaborating, as her phrase "have to clean up my room" incorporates your command, so it may be a clue that she is listening closely.[219]

You may think that your child is the only one in your relationship who pleads. But look closely at my second example: "Will you please clean up your room?" If you have asked in a tone without any particular emphasis, she might say, "Sure, Mom, I'd be glad to" (albeit on another planet than the one we all seem to live on!). I remember as a fifth or sixth grader being in awe of the readiness with which a playmate agreed to her mother's request to set the table, without the whining I was prone to do. Children frequently ignore, resist, or refuse to do what their parents have asked them; no wonder parents plead. Children's resistance can also lead to sarcasm, as in this exchange between a father and his 7-year-old daughter: "I'll tie your shoes. When are you going to learn to do this? When you're 15?"[220] This father's message is mixed; he's trying to make a joke, but it's at the child's expense when, in fact, her acquisition of this skill is his job. Such exchanges show the power of talk and the importance of taking charge of both the overall expectations and the tone of the particular exchange.

There are other more likely possibilities, still polite, but incorporating delay: "I can't do it now, Mom, I'm working on a project, but I'll try to do it later," or the less agreeable (but still compliant), whiny "Okaaaaay, I will!" You then must decide how important it is to you that it be done now and how willing you are to impose your schedule on hers. You may have begun the exchange in a frustrated state of mind, perhaps because you had the same conversation yesterday. Right at the start you said, "Will you *please* clean up your room?" implying that you are repeating a request or that you are pleading. You may come across like the woman on the subway at the beginning of the last chapter: pessimistic about your chances of success, leaving you at risk for a different response than the one you want. Pleading, which can easily become a habit, is communicated not only through your words and syntax but also through the tone of your voice.

In the third version of the clean-your-room directive—"I'm going to ask you to clean up your room this afternoon, okay?"— you have added at least three forms of "mitigation," or softening of what you have asked. You have given notice that there *will* be a request, you have said that it will be a *request,* and therefore not a command, and at the end you have said, "okay?" The directive becomes a question, suggesting that your child has as much input into the outcome as you do. When you do this, you may mean "are you listening?" or "do you hear me?" an after-the-fact effort to be sure you have your child's attention. If you are conscious that your "okay" is checking for attention, then you would do better to make sure you have your child's attention and eye contact before giving the directive. But you may indeed be uneasy with power: "It's not negotiable, okay?"[221] Children have been found to be less compliant when a directive is mitigated by a tentative tone of voice.[222]

With "okay" you may also be striving for politeness, not wanting to impose your will on your child. There is ordinary politeness, and then there is the theory of politeness that grew out of the sociologist Erving Goffman's classic analysis of human social interaction and his theory of "face." Face is the management of one's identity in relation to a social context, e.g., "saving face." Each member of an interacting pair manages "face" in the tension between the often-conflicting desires for connection and autonomy. Such tension is perhaps more basic to the parent-child relationship than to any other, and one that must be elastic enough to change as the child's autonomy increases with age and experience.

Politeness Theory: Not Just Manners

These same parent-child interactions could be analyzed according to politeness theory.[223] Politeness in this sense refers to the ways, often culturally determined, in which people adjust their messages to one another in order to avoid threats to their connection to each other or to the autonomy of either of them, sometimes all at once. You feel like yelling at your 3-year-old who has just spilled milk all over the floor, but you know it was an accident, and you know that she will cry if you do. So you keep your cool and say, albeit more brightly than you feel it, "No use crying over spilled milk!" a phrase that most likely has its origin in millennia of such accidents. It's harder to hold onto your own equanimity when your child is older and you know he could have used more care in how he put his glass down. But even so, you decide that given his sensitivity about being clumsy, being on good terms is more important than blurting out, "Again?" You help him save face.

There are different rules for families than for society at large. There is frequently a built-in tension between parents' need to be direct and their frequent desire to mitigate or soften that directness, as in the examples above. The higher status of a speaker pushes others to defer to him verbally and allows him to "make control moves." This is one reason it is important for you to maintain a sense of your status as the parent. You are the big object![224]

Unlike most social situations, family conversation allows for a much greater degree of directness, particularly from parent to child, because of the parent's status—what I am calling natural authority, although the directness is often softened by mitigation, like the ubiquitous "okay." It is easy to see how politeness theory applies to families, especially to parents whose ambivalence about having power over their children and their concern about losing connection conflicts with their responsibility as parents.[225] If you push too hard, maybe you will hurt feelings, or maybe you will be a bad parent. Directness—whether from you or your child—is a way of communicating power, which is why you startle when a child is too direct, and why it is important for you to feel comfortable using it.

With these excuses, your child avoids accountability. Your response may take many forms: You may refuse to yield, even if you have to repeat yourself, or you may yield just enough to undermine your own directive.[226] You know these moments well: Each of you strives for legitimacy in your back-and-forth. The dad who couldn't get his kids to eat dinner could plead that he had work to do, that they, despite being only 2 and 8 years old, should have been able to recognize that and do as they were told without his repeated input. But you are the parent! Even if you are a parent whose values include a democratic approach to family life, there are instances in which you must be willing to say, in effect, "I am the captain of this ship."

Like your initial decision to intervene or not, you will have to decide, moment by moment, how to proceed. Will you, for example, expect them to come to you? Or will you sometimes be willing to go to them? Do you want your child to be in the habit of being able to look for—and find—things herself? Are you nervous about her being in her room alone and perhaps climbing on something and falling? Do you consider it your job to be available?

Can you change this pattern? Can you find or get back a voice of authority you have lost? The answer is yes, but don't expect to do it all at once. By thinking about the implicit factors discussed in previous chapters, you can increase your certainty about the legitimacy of your authority. Ordinary routines give you the best opportunity. Any exchange is made up of components of voice and words, stance and expression. A change in your own level of certainty will be conveyed nonverbally; if you add the self-discipline to enforce whatever directive you have given, it will help you avoid the inevitable recycling of the argument.

Collaboration

You are pretty familiar by now with the idea that you and your child are engaged in ongoing moment-to-moment interactions, and about the ways you adapt to and make predictions about each other. What I have described is, in effect, "collaborative action," what you hope will happen once you have grabbed your child's attention. Humans are built to cooperate; we wouldn't survive as a species if we didn't.[227] I can hear your guffaw: "Yeah, right. Doesn't happen in my house." But, in fact, it is true, even in your house. Your implicit and explicit authority can work to make it truer. Your children may appear to be able to survive without cooperating with you, but consider cooperation simply the effort two parties—in this case, parent and child—make to communicate to each other their ongoing acceptance of the common orientation to the task at hand. It could be going to the mall or getting ice cream, brushing teeth or getting ready to go to school. As an adult, you are more conscious of time and more able to plan and anticipate; whether you mean to or not, you expect your children to do these things as well. Particularly with children who may have been interrupted in the middle of another activity, or who may be hard put to stand still, both participants must continue to affirm their commitment to collaboration, and part of parental authority is the ability to persistently seek compliance.[228]

Cooperation is not unlike fishing: The fish may take the bait, but it can take a lot of skill to reel it in, net it, and get it into the boat. Each step of the way, the hook of your authority extends itself, through your body, what you say, and how you say it, to maintain its hold on your child's attention. This requires you to simultaneously pay close attention to the responses you get, responses in his gestures and movement, as well as his use of language and more subtle forms of nonverbal behavior. The fish may have some fight, expressed verbally or with the body, as if you needed a name for what you know all too well.

Think about what a parent's role is here from the beginning. What are your expectations? How do you treat refusals? How much do you affirm what your kids do right? As the parent you have a variety of arrows in your quiver, to change our metaphor, that you may leave unused. Accountability can be socialized with the active and persistent use of a facing formation, eye contact, and a no-nonsense stance. If you stand, "arms akimbo" with your hands on your hips, you are standing in a challenge position. If you ask, "Did you take out the garbage?" chances are you will get the response you are looking for.

What the no-nonsense stance involves in your house is the big question. I am sure that you regularly make the effort to show that you mean business, but there are lots of things that can get in the way: other family members jumping into the conversation, feeling stressed and tired and not having the energy to fight the fight of authority, a habit of threatening punishments that you don't usually carry out, reading nonverbal signals in your child that make you guiltily back off the assertion of authority and try a different tack, of empathy and discussion. Moments of authority come in all shapes and sizes, chores and separations, rudeness and fights, screaming and stonewalling. The final chapter looks at a mundane but ubiquitous example, one wet towel on the bathroom floor.

Chapter Eleven

Wet Towels:
Being the Grownup

Your 15-year-old son with ADHD does not seem to be able to get out of bed in the morning; he has missed the school bus on several occasions, and you have driven him to school, afraid that being marked late will tip the balance of his record in an irreversible way. A close friend recommends a parenting website which promotes a "foolproof four-step strategy to get your ADHD teenager out of bed." *

1) Let him know that you are sick of waking him up;
2) Buy him his own alarm clock;
3) Review the morning schedule and routine together in a calm moment;
4) Agree on a consequence of some import, perhaps a fine or being grounded after school, if he is late.

This seems a reasonable formula with a clear road map, but just to be sure, when you have the discussion with him, you add that you will *under no circumstances* drive him to school if he oversleeps, so he will also have the natural consequence of an absence, even if he has an important deadline or test or event. You are not so sure about this last part, and you suspect your

---

* This is hypothetical, not from a real website.

spouse will be less so, but you go ahead.

Your son keeps to the schedule for a couple of weeks. You breathe a sigh of relief, but too soon. On a morning already stressed by a work deadline and a younger sick child, he forgets to set the alarm clock. Twenty minutes before the bus's arrival, you suddenly realize that he has not appeared. You know he has a big test. Should you go upstairs and wake him? Should you drive him to school? Should you write him a late note? Or should you remain firm and let the consequences of the missed test take effect, along with his being grounded? You call your spouse, already at work, who suggests other worrisome possibilities that get to you: Maybe he's getting sick too; maybe being nervous about the test made him forget to set the alarm. A familiar fight ensues: You should have reminded him! As if on cue, the other child vomits. You lose it. Your spouse hangs up on you. And your son sleeps on.

The Feeling of Authority

Real life is so full of unanticipated complications and unique family moments that the effectiveness of a formula is always limited when you attempt to apply it to your own household. It's as if you get a toy online that requires putting together, but the directions don't say what to do if a screw is missing or the metal is a tiny bit bent. Maybe you can find something on YouTube. Not so for my oversleeping scenario. But wait! There *are* many good parenting resources all over the Web. Still, whatever advice you find, in the end it is *you* who must make a choice and *you* who must follow through—with a living, breathing, feeling human being and probably with one or more other human beings putting in their two cents.

There is a foundation of natural authority implicit in your relationship with your child and the wide scope of responsibility, care, and decision-making required of you as a parent. But as we have reviewed from many angles, explicit authority happens in the random moments of daily life, triggered into action by the needs at hand. Such moments unfold in tandem with your conscious and unconscious values and beliefs; they are the stuff of your relationship with each other as you move forward, day to day, in the context of your household, your family system, and the wider culture. We have looked closely at the way the relationship develops over time, how it takes on layers of personality and history and emerges and develops from your bodily and emotional selves through the interactions between you. Aided by lenses from different disciplines, we have looked from many angles at the patterns of experience that accumulate between you and your child to create that relationship and, integral to it, your natural authority. In fact, any moment can be looked at from any and all of the angles we have used in the last ten chapters.

My argument for parents' natural authority has been a lesson in its legitimacy. If you are confident that you have natural and legitimate authority, you are more likely to communicate that confidence to your child, verbally and nonverbally, and he will respond accordingly. It doesn't always work that way, of course, so I have also sought to highlight some of the roadblocks and risks that may hinder you from having the confidence you need to act with authority.

We return now to clarity, that feeling of certainty that both fuels and is fueled by confidence and authority. Clarity is necessary for both implicit and explicit authority. You need a foundation of ongoing implicit authority in your relationship to make your explicit authority convincing. Moments of explicit authority both test and reinforce the authority already implicit in your relationship. If you are confident about your authority, it will help give you a feeling of clarity about what to do in a given moment. But even if you lack confidence at times, as everyone does, feeling clear about a given moment can bolster your confidence.

At Ease with Your Natural Authority

Some parents might find it easier to be in charge with an infant or toddler and shrink a bit when the child begins to talk back; for others the reverse is true. In earlier chapters I used hypothetical scenarios to illustrate each chapter's concepts, keeping my focus on a single aspect of the interaction. But any of those moments, from Michael not coming to dinner to Charlie resisting wearing a jacket, could be expanded to illustrate many other aspects of authority. When you are learning to speak a foreign language, each lesson focuses on one or two things, such as the vocabulary to use in the grocery store or the past tense. As you grow in proficiency, you practice many aspects all at once.

Fluency in authority is a cumulative process as well. We have looked at concepts one by one, but in your daily experience you are confronted with many things at once and a feeling of authority may be hard to come by. I have given you a number of different ways to think about and deconstruct those moments before, during, and after an incident: "I am (or was) feeling this, I wonder what he is (or was) feeling?" "If I do this, then maybe that...." Both your clarity and your effectiveness also depend on the support of the family system, that is, whether or not you expect to be backed up, challenged, or undermined by your co-parent or others. With apologies to Robert Frost, good boundaries make good parents—good boundaries and the willingness to face and resolve conflict when it flares up. Many elements of authority come together in even the most mundane of situations to help you decide whether to act and, if so, how. How does clarity translate to authority in action?

Patterns of Interaction

It is the big picture that matters most for your authority, that is, how your family behaves with each other and what family life feels like in your house. But the big picture is made up of run-of-the-mill interactions and miniature daily dramas between mothers and fathers, parents and children, brothers and sisters. Authority is broad in scope and grounded both in the way you organize your household and in what goes on in it, whether in regard to unfinished homework or undone chores, mean friends, sleepless children, or sick grandparents. Still, however broad the definition of authority and however complicated by all the influences we have talked about here, authority is in your relationship with your child, tested over and over in each moment of interaction, with endless chances for renewal.

As a clinician, I look closely at such moments. When I work with a couple or with a parent and child, I zoom in and out, probing into just what goes on between them, especially what each was feeling in that moment, and then back to a wider focus on their history together, the personality of their relationship, their family system, and habitat. Every moment is important, but with literally endless moments in a relationship, it is the pattern of interactions that shapes its personality.

Even when you have clarity, it is not necessarily obvious what to do next. You may ask yourself "What would so-and-so advise?" (Fill in your favorite parenting expert here.) But you still need a way to get from the particulars of your presenting problem to a workable solution for you, your child, your relationship, and your household. You need to be able to think on the spot about what to do when things take an unexpected practical or emotional turn, for any of a million reasons. If there are things to learn about being a parent, such problem-solving is surely near the top of the list.

In an instance like the scenario with which I opened this chapter, as the parent you would have to navigate your way through interactions with your spouse, your sick child, and your oversleeping child to find a solution. Each interaction would depend on your relationship history, your own feeling of clarity about the situation, and the feelings and actions of the others in response. You might decide to persist in the fight with your spouse by saying, "Look, I'm the one at home; don't try to make me feel guilty. I'm going to stick to the deal we made. It's not the end of the world. He'll learn from it and so will we." Then mop up the vomit and reassure the sick child, check your watch, and make an assessment of the situation.

Is there time for your son to get himself up and ready for the bus even if you do wake him? Are you willing to drive him? Why would you drive him, given the agreement? Is that test more important than getting his getting-to-school behavior back on track? If you do drive him, what are the implications? What will your co-parent say? What will happen next time? Will you be able to hold the line then, or will you drive him again? No parenting expert or therapist can tell you the answers to these questions. In the pages that follow, using some of the many concepts we have discussed in previous chapters, we will retrace our steps from problem to action for an even more mundane situation, wet towels on the bathroom floor.

Daily Drama in the Bathroom

There is a soggy red towel on the floor of the family bathroom. A grinning, naked toddler stands next to it, fresh out of the bathtub. Perhaps you pick her up in a rush of affection and leave the towel there until she's in bed and you have time to pick it up, or perhaps you say, "Now pick up the towel and hang it on the hook." She may know at 18 months that towels need to be hung up but couldn't really understand, at that age, that someone has to clean the bathroom and do the laundry. Even if you have a pile of email waiting for you, the awareness of her babyhood allows you to enjoy the moment and move on, if necessary hanging up the towel yourself before scooping her up to get on her pajamas and read stories. Even this brief vignette triggers your awareness of child development, household organization and responsibility, bedtime, the different perspectives you each bring to the moment, and the short history of your relationship with this child.

Now picture the soggy red towel on the floor of the bathroom again. The light is on, and there is a path of puddles on the hallway floor leading to your 12-year-old son's room, where, when you peek in, you see him in boxers with earphones on, tapping his fingers on the desk as he bends over a textbook. You could hug him with a rush of affection too, perhaps along with a private roll of the eyes at the familiarity of the situation, or you could say with rising irritation, "Jason, why is there a wet towel on the floor of the bathroom and puddles down the hall?" Your waiting email presses on you and you become more irritated. "Do you think I have time to clean up after you? You are 12 years old! I have work to do too. Now get in there and clean up after yourself." And you walk away.

This is quite a different picture: a child old enough to know better than to leave a towel on the floor, a child with his own life of music and homework and habits, a relationship of 12 years in which you both have had plenty of time to get to know each other, with the backdrop of household organization and the urgency of your work and exasperation pitted against his obligations and habits.

In order to think about authority in family life, we can stop the action anywhere and zoom in. Focusing on something so sloppy, smelly, annoying, and seemingly trivial as wet towels helps illustrate that *every* moment is part of your relationship and that there are countless times in which you are, and must be, the one in charge. What happens around wet towels, as in any of the other moments, both tests and shapes your authority and by extension the relationship with your child.

Family Life in Just One Towel

Change, habitat, values and beliefs, the self, your two bodies, and finally the relationship with not only one child but with everyone else who lives in the house: All are implicit in the two imagined encounters, triggered by the trivial fact of a towel left on the floor. If you live, or have lived, in a house with children, you won't be surprised to hear that there hasn't been a family in my office for whom a wet towel—or something close to it, say, dirty dishes—has not come up as a chronic household issue. If you are reading this before having children, you'll know what I'm talking about too, since you grew up somewhere and presumably had to do something with wet towels and dirty dishes along the way. A wet towel may be something that simply annoys the parents, or one of the parents, or it may be a chronic cause of sibling or marital conflict. I've had more than one family for whom it seemed to represent a breakdown in family life.

When I mentioned to one of my sons that I was writing about wet towels, he commented, "That was one of Dad's most common scolds. You guys didn't care much about whether our rooms were clean, but Dad cared about the towels." He was right, and my husband still does, and I don't, really. It wasn't that I thought they belonged on the floor; it was more that I didn't mind picking them up, along with dirty socks in the hallway, perhaps a legacy of growing up with eight siblings and a certain degree of chaos. On a recent overnight visit to our apartment, another son, this one married and with his own family, emerged from the bathroom dressed spiffily in a suit and tie for a business meeting. A couple of minutes later I went into the bathroom and discovered that he too had left his wet towel on the floor. I called him on it with a smile, after I put it in the washer, and told him too that I had been writing about this very topic. He was surprised at himself: "I'd never leave a wet towel on the floor at home!" he said, grinning sheepishly. Apparently my kids did learn that I didn't really care that much.

Most families share bathrooms. Unlike other rooms in the house, you are usually in the bathroom alone (except when you have young children). And yet, while a bathroom is a private place when you're in it and a private place for the next person, it is a place where private paths cross. Because the next person in it usually knows who was there before, a bathroom is a fertile field for blame. But there is a lot more going on with wet towels than blame. In fact, much of what is important—and difficult—about becoming and being a parent can be represented by wet towels on the floor.

Because all the threads we have been following are so entangled, where we start is somewhat arbitrary, but how you go about solving a problem begins with how you define it. What is the problem with a wet towel on the floor? If the towel is on the floor and no one sees it, does it matter? Is your concern one of appearances, hygiene, laziness, not following rules, or all of the above?

Assumptions Meet Reality

We have to make some assumptions even to have a discussion, so I am going to assume that whatever your primary concern, you won't argue that wet towels *belong* on the floor. In the average household, where everyone is scrambling to get to school and work, wet towels have been used once, maybe twice, maybe more. They may smell. They may block the path to the toilet or sink or tub. They may be so wet as to leave a puddle on the bathroom floor or a stain elsewhere. If you don't hang them up, they will never dry out. They may even be on the floor of the bedroom of the offender. So the first problem is, there is a wet towel on the floor. Who cares? What happens next?

Another assumption: You, the parent, do care, if not fanatically, then at least somewhat. No one likes a mess, though some can tolerate mess more than others. But what happens next? If the towels need to get from the floor to the rack or the hamper, whose responsibility is it? Warning: This is a trick question! What is "it"? Is it putting the towels away or in the wash, or is it making sure someone else does it? It may seem obvious to you that it is the responsibility of whoever left the towel there to take care of it, but that still begs the question, how do you know who left it there? Not that there are too many candidates, but still, if the perpetrator is at school or a friend's house, do you hang the towel up and follow up later, or do you wait until he comes home? Or will you chase him down? Really, you're wondering, for a wet towel? And you suspect that he will wonder the same thing, with a spicy edge of sarcasm: You're texting me about a wet towel? OMG. LOL. But if, like the hypothetical father of the oversleeper, you have drawn a line in the sand, your authority could be undermined by even such a small concession. If there is a rule about hanging up towels after a shower, is there a consequence beyond just getting them hung up? What are the rules, and what are the consequences? Towels are complicated! You need clarity to cope with them.

Most parents have both an ideal of what family life should be, along with the conviction that other families are living that ideal or at least coming a lot closer than they are. You and your co-parent (if there is one) have a probably mostly unspoken philosophy of family life, a set of principles or beliefs that guides you. These values probably by and large stay unconscious until things go wrong, or at least not as smoothly as you imagined they would, or until they go enough against those values that you have to make a decision. Even about wet towels. For some parents, cleanliness and hygiene are paramount; wet towels to them (and perhaps to you) are disgusting sources of bacteria. For these parents, the value is a value rooted in health and safety. For others, it is order they crave more than cleanliness; the towels don't need to be washed that often, but for goodness' sake, keep them off the floor: They look sloppy. The value might have to do with appearances or from an inherent sense of order you have and need to maintain. It may even surprise you that there is any other way to think about it than the way you think.

Your gut values or your mood or both make you pause as you catch a glimpse of the towel on your way past the bathroom door; your beliefs about what a 3- or 8- or 12-year-old can do start your wheels turning. There are implicit habitat and systems questions as well, such as whether or not he or she shares the bathroom with anyone else, who is expected to pick the towels up, who is responsible for the cleanliness of the bathroom. In real life, all of these factors are present at once, but let's look first at your relationship with the assumed perpetrator.

You Are the Grownup

We keep coming back to being the grownup. A big part of clarity is the realization that in making both humdrum and major decisions relating to your child, you are simply acting out your clear responsibility. You have answered the questions, "Is this my job? Is my authority legitimate in this situation?" You know that it is your responsibility, along with your co-parent, to decide what is supposed to happen, which includes ensuring that those in your household know the rules about wet towels. And it is your responsibility either to compel someone else to pick them up or to take care of it yourself and then decide whether to hold someone accountable. That someone will be a person who learns from you in a relationship with a changing degree of dependence. Picking up towels is not innate; it has to be learned, whether by modeling and teaching or by assigning responsibility and consequences. You are the big object, or one of them. You have led the way, whether you realize it or not, as surely as the goose leads her goslings to water or away from danger.

As you stand there (and this is all happening at lightning speed), you take in the stimulus of the wet red towel in the context of your relationship to the child who left it there, assuming you know who did: We've been getting along well lately, and he's been a little under the weather. I don't think I'll bother him about it. Or, I cannot believe that I am seeing that towel on the floor again; we just talked about picking up after yourself yesterday! This is unacceptable; I am not going to let this one go. Picking the towel up yourself is also an act of authority, but let's assume here that you decide to hold someone responsible.

How your child learns from you and how he responds when challenged about his transgression or his responsibility depends in large part on the trust that he has developed in you as a reliable and responsive "big object" and on the history of rupture and repair you have together. Even wet towels bring us back to attachment and to your relationship; your relationship is founded on the elemental attachment system, not so much for safety and mobility here, but for emotional regulation. Every moment together adds to your history together, and your relationship's history influences how you act in each moment.

One of the most important aspects of your relationship is how constantly it changes, influenced by what happens every day of your lives and by ongoing developmental change. As your child changes, so does the nature and scope of your authority, but not the fact of your authority. At first the infant is helpless and needs you for survival; no wet towels, just wet diapers. But soon enough, she walks and talks and is able to imitate and gradually understand the behavior around her, including what to do with towels. She looks to you not only for security, but also for what to expect—from you and, in the long run, from other people.

Once you take the next step about that red towel, that moment joins the flow of moments that is your relationship. Because no one moment makes the difference, if you hang up the towel this time for your 12-year-old but demand that he do it the next, that's okay. What matters more is whether in general you stick to the habitat policy so that he knows what to expect from you. You might frame your decision to do it for him as a favor and remind him to do it next time, which creates some scaffolding.

Crucial to your relationship as you engage in each momentary interaction, including one over a wet towel, is your willingness or ability to be sensitive and responsive to your child. This entails the risk of separation or rupture always implicit in relationships, and especially in the assertion of authority. In other words, is there room in your relationship for him to be forgetful or stressed or apologetic? Many parents consciously or unconsciously come down on one extreme or another. On the one hand, if I leave room for him to be forgetful or stressed, I'll never be able to get him to listen; on the other, I better be careful as he is feeling so stressed, if I demand anything he'll fall apart. But being authoritative *means* being sensitive to the other's perspective! In fact, this is your job as a parent; it helps him, and you and your household, stay regulated.

Habitat

The moment over towels does not take place in a vacuum but in the very particular habitat of your household, the ecological niche in which your child is growing up. As the co-creator and co-sustainer of this habitat, you are at least partly responsible for the habits and practices with which your children will go out into the world, including myriad trivia about routines of daily life, including the wet towels in their future. I say partly responsible not because you are only one parent but because there are so many influences on children, from the other parent, siblings, and additional caretakers in your house or elsewhere to the other households where they spend time, television, and the great wide world, both material and digital. Understanding those influences doesn't excuse behavior but puts it in a context that may decrease blame. Habitat is first and foremost the organization of your living space and the practices around taking care of it, including learning what's expected and how to do it, through explicit teaching, modeling, and guided participation. In the UCLA study mentioned earlier, the important role of "stuff" in family life was noted, both the acquisition of it and the management of it. Wet towels fit right in.

Your child learns all sorts of things without being told, but not everything. He may be able to read your emotions from your face but not the list of household chores. It is easy to fall into the trap of thinking your children must know that towels are meant to be hung up, that of course one has to have consideration for the person who follows, that you have your hands full with work and meals and laundry. The more children learn explicitly the better: It gives you both a common frame of reference to refer back to. Such training may seem self-evident, but it relies on both a sense of values—that kids should learn to pick up after themselves—and beliefs about what kids can do and when.

If you do have explicit rules, chores, or guidelines, your biggest challenge, as in my opening oversleeping anecdote, is whether your child can rely on your enforcing them. Why would your child want you to enforce the rules? Because reliable enforcement of family rules is not only part of authority but part of security: Remember the anecdote about curfew in which a teenager said, "Doesn't anybody care where I am?" How your authority is asserted and received, however desirable it is, has as much to do with the expectations and routines of your family habitat around order, laundry, chores, and so on, as it does with what you say and how you look in the moment. But even with a strong infrastructure of routines, if you don't hold up the rules, you undermine your own authority.

Who Did It?

Depending on when and where you encounter the wet towel, you may barely pause a moment before you shout, scream, or just mutter to yourself in disgust and exhaustion, "Who left this towel here?" You have a relationship not only with the person who left the towel there but also with anyone else who might use the bathroom and be annoyed by it. We have already considered some of the implications of the system in which the towel, like you both, is embedded, but within this system are a number of someones.

Having decided not to pick up the towel yourself, you march to your son's room: There he is, sprawled on his stomach on his bed, headphones in, feet tapping, idly examining a magazine on top of his homework. Who is this, this other someone who, like you, brings "baggage" to that moment? Your baggage, like the proverbial grandmother's trunk, is quite full, albeit not alphabetically organized: Your history with towels and parents, your expectations of yourself as a parent, how you feel right then, your general experience with that child and with that or other household tasks fuels and shapes how you feel, how you react, how you act, and what you do next.

What does he bring? His bag is lighter, his history is shorter and, around towels, probably exclusively with you and your co-parent. In this scenario, he is old enough to have had some experience in other family habitats. He has a gender, a temperament, an age, and a birth order, all of which shape his perspective and your interaction. He has grown up in your habitat, experiencing the interactions in your family system. Because you are still a "big object" in his life, his experience at that moment is very sensitive to your behavior. He senses you come in and turns around. Each of you is in a body, eyeing each other carefully, if unconsciously, and gauging the emotion of the other.

Since you are in his room because of a wet towel, your body has already begun to feel and react in some way, and how you react will affect, and be affected by, a great many things. In the moment itself, and in you, there is your mood, your level of fatigue, hunger, and stress, the time of day, what else you have left to do, whether work or chores. You grew up in a household with its own rules (or lack of them) about wet towels and with a parent or parents who had certain ways of reacting to wet towels (and other things). You might also be affected by the other relationships in your life: Maybe you just talked to your mother or mother-in-law and heard someone in the family is ill, or that she is depressed or angry with you about something. Maybe you just had a fight with your spouse or a close friend. Maybe you just argued about something else with him and you either can't face another fight or, conversely, are on the warpath.

If you lose your temper, he may have an outburst too, which may draw the attention of and bring in other family members, causing a big family upset. Or he may withdraw. His reaction will be familiar to you. Your relationship has a pattern. His feelings, and yours—of anger, frustration, and exasperation—are important, but they have less to do with the towel on the floor and more to do with who each of you are and with your relationship. Can you catch yourself? Is this the moment to just be the authority, cut through the emotion, and sternly tell him to pick up the towel? Sometimes talking about feelings takes us further from needed action; it takes too much time, and still the towel is on the floor. Instead of assuming that it's important for everyone to air their feelings, let's instead try to solve the problem. Then, if there are still feelings to work out, we'll do that later.

Or is this the moment to wonder, when he blows up, if there is something else going on? Have the two of you had one too many fights this week? Is it time to slow down and learn more about what is going on with him? Does he need you to provide some emotional scaffolding and coaching to bring him back not only to a feeling of well-being but also to the ability to remember to pick up his towel? This too is authority. And finally, if you are willing to slow things down, you can interact on both levels at the same time, i.e., put aside picking up the wet towel for a few minutes and think about the wet towel in the context of the way you two work things out, whether there is blame, favoritism, other stresses, and so on.

Relevant to your reaction to the wet towel and your belief about what should happen, of course, is the age of your child, as my brief vignettes suggested. Parents can err from one extreme to the other: expecting too much of a young child and not enough of an older one. How do you know when a child can be expected to learn to pick up a towel? Child development is a gradual process whose stages have no set beginnings or ends. Children are always learning, and you are always modeling. If you approach picking up towels or any other kind of cleaning up as the responsibility that follows taking a bath or shower, and if you do it together when the child is young, in theory he will learn what to do and do it when he is alone. But anything, wet towels included, can be subject to feelings, defiance, and forgetfulness. You or your co-parent might leave a mess in the bathroom after giving a toddler a bath. She may learn one way of doing things from you, another from the other parent, and, by the way, learn what happens when people in your family disagree.

Temperament and other individual differences among children and parents play a role too: You might expect more of a quiet or helpful child and less of a more difficult one, just to avoid conflict. But remember that you are building a relationship with each moment and that your child is learning from you about that relationship, including what happens when she leaves a wet towel on the floor. Chances are you are not thinking that way when you see the wet towel, but it is implicit in what you do next. If you know that your toddler already likes trying to hang things up, or tends to be oppositional, that will affect whether you engage with her in learning about hanging up towels. If you have just been to visit your sister, whose kids are older, and you notice her picking up after them, you may register, "Oh, so that's normal," or "Jeez, she is babying them! I'm going to do it differently."

Being Parents Together

Wet towels are pretty universal, like dirty clothes, but crucially, they exist in a shared space. Whatever age your children are, questions arise from those towels: What is supposed to happen in this house and why didn't it happen? Does everybody know what's supposed to happen? Whose problem is it? Do people care in different ways? If that's true, how do they talk about it? Do the towels stand in for some other problem? Do the parents, if there are two, agree that this is a problem? What do they do about it if they disagree? Here is where habitat overlaps with the family system.

If you live with a spouse or partner or any other adult with whom you share the responsibility for your household and children, then in addition to the decisions you make about the towels and the children (if indeed it is a child who has left the wet towel on the floor!), you must also grapple as a couple or as co-parents with the towel issue. Your list of possible actions, then, includes, "Will I talk to my spouse (partner, co-parent) about the towels (again)?" To make things more complicated, it is very possible that you and the other parent have different ideas about wet towels: Either one of you may not notice or care, and the other cares a lot, or you don't agree on what to do about it. If there are other differences between you, as there certainly must be, those differences or abiding tensions will undoubtedly spill over, at least sometimes, to the trivia of wet towels and other household chores.

It no longer surprises me when couples come to blows over household minutia: Who left the wet towels in the washer so they got smelly and had to be washed again? Who left the dry towels in the dryer, too lazy or forgetful to fold them, so that when I went to put my laundry in the dryer, there was no room? Why do I bother expecting anyone else to follow through? I might as well do it all myself—and then be a martyr to the laziness of others. Again, the ghost of what other families do, what you think is normal, can be painfully haunting, because you want to do it right.

And then there are the disagreements about how the other parent handles her encounter with the wet towel. Let me reiterate what I wrote about in Chapter Five, that perhaps the hardest, and most important, part of being parents together is being able to let the other have a relationship with your child or children. You are in a system, so you will inevitably affect each other, but both your joint and individual authority will be supported or undercut by the way you treat the authority of the other. It is terribly easy to make fun of the other parent, to roll your eyes, to express frustration—and if, as with my husband and me, one of you cares about something and the other doesn't, you can easily run into trouble.

Parents Don't Have to Agree, Redux

It is not so much about needing to agree but about how you handle your disagreement. The old saw about not fighting in front of the children is wiser than you might think: not because conflict is bad, per se, but if the conflict is about the children or the handling of discipline, then there is a real risk of the authority of one parent or the other being undermined. There is nothing wrong with acknowledging your differences. One of you can take the lead on towels, and the other can say, "You know how your father feels about wet towels on the floor; you'd better pick that up before he comes to read to you." This is preferable to "You know that your father gets upset about wet towels on the floor; I'm going to pick it up so you don't get into trouble. I don't feel like hearing you two fight tonight." You might, though, just go ahead and pick up the towel and not say a word. Or, if you are the one who cares, decide whether you care more about whether it gets picked up or about who does the picking up—as those are two different problems. If you are divorced or separated from a parent whose house constitutes another habitat for your children, then each of you must acknowledge the possibility of a different set of expectations and make clear that in your house, your rules prevail.

Although the relationship between each parent and each child has a different history and a different personality, for your children's sake, authority must be clear, consistent, and persuasive to be effective, even if your styles of being the authority are different. If either of the following is said in front of a child, it is worlds away from saying it privately after the child goes to bed. "I can't believe you didn't get him to pick up the towel. You're always babying him!" Or "Why did you get into a fight with him about the towel? He's tired; he had a big game this afternoon."

It may seem minor, on the face of it, to have a difference about towels, but given the frequency of showers and baths, and the likelihood of families sharing bathrooms, it is no surprise that it can be a loaded issue. If the issue comes up repeatedly, it would be worthwhile to make an effort to come to some agreement about the family policy and the consequences. One of you will probably end up dissatisfied with the result, and you won't eliminate every fight, but you will have a rubric for all of you to refer to. If the rubric makes clear that the kids have to pick up the towels and you confront one of them about it, don't then pick it up if he doesn't. That would be an affront to the other parent, a gesture of solidarity with the child that flies in the face of the family policy, and a weakening of your authority in future moments. But there is always whimsy: You walk past the bathroom and notice a towel on the floor, and you decide to pick it up and let it go at that. Being a consistent authority doesn't mean you need to be consistent 100 percent of the time, but it does mean that you should not break family policy unilaterally.

Another common corollary to wet towels is a fight between two consecutive bathroom users: "He left his wet towel in the middle of the floor!" says your daughter, to which your son responds, "Don't yell at me, she did it—and she left her dirty clothes there too." Whom to believe? Whom to punish? Should you get involved at all?

Where are we in our deconstructed wet towel moment? The towel has been spotted by a responsible adult; it needs to be picked up. The parent in question decides not to do it herself but to confront the likely perpetrator, since *she* knows *he* knows it is part of their household routine. Her co-parent isn't involved at the moment, but she is confident he will support her as this is something they have recently discussed. What happens next?

In the Moment

The Austrian philosopher Ludwig Wittgenstein made the memorable paradoxical statement that "the depths are on the surface."[229] So too, in a sense, with the natural authority of parents. It is in everyday moments that you express your authority, but it is always there, in the depths, ready to come to the surface. When I began work on this book, I knew that what was most important to communicate was that authority is in your relationships, not in your strategies. I knew too that every relationship is built up moment by moment and that every moment is influenced and shaped by the people in it, their history, their context, their other relationships. What I hadn't yet spelled out, even for myself, was the incredible depths and richness of every moment. In the journey I've taken with you over these 11 chapters, I have come to understand not just how much surrounds, underlies, and impinges on a given moment, but how much happens in that split second of life.

As I have attempted to weave together the strands of interaction around a wet towel, I have already alluded to the interactions you and your child might have once you have encountered the wet towel and decided what action you will take. Because every experience with another person registers and informs future experiences you will have with each other, the moment following that first encounter of authority with your child is extremely important. What is the nature of your "consensual frame," that is, what is the answer to the question, "What are we doing here?" Are we talking about the towel? Are we talking about the household rules and whether they were clear, whether they were forgotten or ignored? What the consequence is going to be, if any? Fights we have had in the past? About this or other moments? Am I paying enough attention to how you feel? How do *I* feel? What is going on here now between us? Every moment matters and doesn't matter at the same time. It matters because moments build up into the patterns and habits of a relationship, but it doesn't matter for the same reason. It is the patterns and habits that matter, not any particular deal-breaking moment.

Over time, you have generated both customary ways of interacting with each other and expectations of the other. What will happen next? How do you throw that beach ball? The most important question for your child is whether he can rely on your being responsive to him, whether you will make an effort to empathize with what he is feeling. This is true whether he is 2 or 12 or even 20.

If you slow the process down, you will both be better able to consider what the other is saying, but even at the lightning speed at which you tune in to each other, you take in the other's facial expressions, gestures, body, and voice. Part of responsiveness is making accommodations to what you sense in the other. You may interrupt what attunement you usually have; you may avoid interrupting it; you may struggle to restore it. What shows in each of your faces may be as much from what you bring from other aspects of your day as from the "wet towel moment," but it is still there, still perceived, still responded to unconsciously. The possibilities are too endless for me to even begin to suggest them; I will sketch a generic scenario.

Wet Towels and Natural Authority

First, the need to interrupt the child on an electronic device: You must get his attention enough for him to turn to look at you. If he doesn't hear you at first, you might touch him on the shoulder. He looks at you distractedly, or guiltily, or sullenly—and you tell him to pause or turn off the device or take off his headphones. He hesitates and pleads, "Just a few more seconds, Mom!" You give them or you don't, but eventually your face-to-face interaction begins, an interaction in which you use those age-old biological mechanisms to grab and hold his attention and to communicate: your voice, your face, your hands. Your words are reprimanding: "You left the towel on the floor again." You haven't raised your voice or even used a scolding tone, just stated the facts, but the facts speak plenty, as this is a familiar topic between you. In fact, you have chosen to keep your tone restrained on purpose, in order to keep things from escalating if you can. You are engaged in regulation even as you reprimand. You know each other deeply, which may even mean that he "knows," on some level, that you are very annoyed but are being restrained. Will he react to the annoyance he infers or the restraint you offer?

This is why his trust in you and in your authority becomes so important, and why your own confidence in your authority matters. If he responds to your restraint, the outcome of the interaction might be different than if he responds to his guess about how annoyed you really are. And you have to be able to not lose track of the wet towel, even as you navigate this potentially emotional exchange. Because you are the big object, you must try to stay aware of his feelings and needs, not only because it is your responsibility but because it will, in the end, increase the effectiveness of your authority. So even as you state the reprimanding facts, you are taking in his gaze or avoidance of gaze, whether or not he seems anxious, perhaps revealed by a slight, fake smile.

You and he have your ways together, your subroutines, that are different from the routines you might have with another child or your spouse, or even with this child when he was younger. Perhaps he used to have a lot of tantrums, so that it always behooved you to tread lightly, but perhaps you and he have talked over the years about his tendency to explode and you have been trying to help him learn more self-control. That is your authority as much as is getting that wet towel picked up. Your approach embodies your authority too, in your physical stance and in your tone of voice. Sarcasm or a tendency to provoke shame and guilt trips up many a parent, especially with an adolescent, as their language and interactive skills grow rapidly. If other family members are present or overhear this exchange, they may contaminate whatever valiant efforts you make to keep things calm and businesslike; if someone throws in her two cents, the pressure on you increases.

And, in fact, the pressures on you are already great in this and in any moment of authority. Not only do you have your own life's demands to cope with, the exigencies of the household, and one or more children's complicated arrangements, idiosyncrasies, and crises to manage, you also have the emotional pressures of being a parent, the demands of the relationship and your own self-assessment of how you're doing. All of this can affect the confidence with which you use your natural authority. From this moment, both of you will make associations that will be threads in the brain's pattern-making around your relationship, your habitat, your relationships with the others in your family, and your authority.

So there you both are, and there I leave you. I hope that he decides to get up out of his chair and lumber, however resignedly, down the hall to the bathroom to hang up the towel. I hope that you, however provoked by the loud sigh he lets out as he gets up, can breathe your own sigh of relief that you have brought the depths to the surface and found your own particular voice of natural authority.

Acknowledgments

There is no one to whom I owe more than my husband, comrade in parenthood, best friend, and the love of my life since age 19, Tom Gerety. Our life together for more than 50 years has been full, above all, of conversation, especially about families and relationships. He has read this book over and over again, in pieces and as a whole; he has listened patiently and weighed in on everything from commas to Wittgenstein; he has shared his wisdom as father, teacher, writer, lawyer, and philosopher. But most of all, he has loved me and believed in me as a parent and as someone who could counsel other parents.

Frequent total immersion in the families of my sons Finn and Amias, along with conversations about family life with them and with my daughters-in-law, Amy Lou Stein and Margaret Gerety, have helped me understand 21st-century parenthood. Their embrace of natural authority, albeit with different family cultures, has affirmed my belief in the importance of clarity and confidence over strategy or technique. Visits with and babysitting stints for my grandchildren, Addie, Cosmo, Susie, Pierce, and Jenny, has not only been full of stories, hugs, and making things, but has given me ample opportunity to feel again the challenges of being the grownup and the many forms of love and limits.

It was my son Rowan who asked me, "Why haven't you ever written a book?" He then suggested that I write about parenthood. He has been ready ever since with a sympathetic ear, a writer's sensibility, and editorial help. My son Carrick, ever the artist, has helped me keep perspective during the long process of making something, and has urged me not to be shy in self-promotion. Not yet parents, both nevertheless read and made valuable edits to the book. Rowan's wife, Lena Jackson, and Carrick's fiancée, Jesy Odio, have given me both technical and social media help.

I came to parenthood from the rich family life created by my parents, Jenny McKean and Paul Moore, and learned much of what I know about love and limits from them. My husband's parents, Helen Martin and Pierce Gerety, who were wonderful grandparents to our boys, embraced me as a daughter. I am also grateful to my eight siblings, Honor, Paul, Rosemary, George, Marian, Danny, Susanna, and Patience, and to many in-laws, nieces, and nephews. They have given me love and support, and have shown me some of the variety of family life. Four of my sisters have been closely involved with the evolution of this book. Rosemary, also a writer, has been a wise, sympathetic, and creative advisor; Susanna delved into both the writing process and the challenge of using natural authority, especially during a cherished few days in Mendocino. Patience was one of the earliest to say, "You can do it," and always checks in. Marian is consistently supportive, and gave me confidence during her childrearing years by her frequent mantra, "What would Adelia do?"

My deepest thanks go to the clients from whom I have learned just how many different ways there are to be parents—and the kinds of conversations that can help. I owe a huge debt to the expansive network of friends and relatives with whom I have shared the experience of parenthood for 45 years. Some may recognize bits of their families' stories in the pages that follow, although I have disguised or made composites of them in order to protect their privacy.

In countless breakfasts years ago, Nancy Rankin recognized my longing to write and encouraged me to go for it. Weekly conversations with Nancy Hechinger during the last fifteen years have been and continue to be stimulating, crucial to my wellbeing, and fundamental to the book's conceptualization and writing. I am enormously grateful to have such devoted and faithful confidantes as Ebe Emmons and Elizabeth Seamans. Ebe and I have maintained a mighty and sustaining friendship since freshman year in college, as fellow mothers, artists, and therapists; I met Elizabeth as a young mother, and we have been soulmates in motherhood and creativity ever since. For their great friendship, I also thank Elaine Fink, Karen Will, Mary Sherwin, Helen Burton, and Ruth Abram.

For the important decisions about the book's title and final cover I reached out to a list I call "children of my friends and friends of my children." Thanks to all of them. Thanks also to countless other friends, relatives, and colleagues for conversations about parenthood and writing, as well as unflagging interest and encouragement. These include David Rudenstine, Marie de la Soudière, Debra Busta, Wendell and Dessa Goddard, Tod Houghtlin, Lee Burnham, Lindsay Wright, Tricia and Jeff Rosen, Joe Seamans, Larry Aber, Lindsay Butters, Barbara Kass, Mary Willis, Mary LaPorte, Fran Ludwig, Deanna Leikin, Maggie Hand-Miller, Gwenn Mayers, Karen Halverson, and Elly Vozzola, colleague, friend, and mentor. A number of people I have listed here read a chapter or more at different stages. Their comments and edits were invaluable. Thanks to my nieces Bridget Small, Maeve Caffrey, and Faye and Violet Shneider for enthusiasm and advice.

Writing workshops with Anne Greene, at Wesleyan University, and Evan Imber-Black, at the Ackerman Institute for the Family, jump-started my writing. Much of this book was written at the Paragraph Writers' Studio in Manhattan. My agent, Jim Levine, has been unfailingly affirmative and generous in his support from our first correspondence. Ginger Campbell's Brainscience Podcast introduced me to current work in neuroscience. Academics who were helpful in conversation or email include Robert Burton, Thomas Weisner, Harriet Smith, Elaine Hatfield, Diane Ehrensaft, Tami Kremer-Sadlik, Bambi Schieffelin, Daniel Hill, Elinor Ochs, Joseph LeDoux, and Carlin Wing. I was especially influenced and inspired by the work of anthropologist Marjorie Harness Goodwin and the Center for the Lives of Families at UCLA. Psychologists (and friends) Richard Bock, Melissa Gordon, and Zina Steinberg gave me invaluable feedback and wise comments on the entire manuscript, along with encouragement from the perspective of their own lives and work. Many other colleagues have strengthened my clinical work over the course of my career, especially Liz Buckner, Robin Goodman, Mary Courtney, Barb Rosen, Peter Hunt, and Michael Kern.

A far-flung group of people helped me produce the book. Nan Newell not only shared early childrearing days and has remained a friend, but also helped me realize that I was writing about authority and continued to advise me as the book took its final shape. Janet Steen was instrumental in helping me craft the book, and Barbara Spindel did the final copyedit with great care. Valerie Sauers designed the book's interior and dealt with many last-minute changes with unfailing patience, efficiency, confidence, and style. Rosie Wood brought well-honed skills to the index from across the Atlantic, and Jennifer Caven did the exacting work of final proofreading. Oliver Munday's cover design skillfully captured the book's message. Thanks to Ben Fink-Shapiro for my cover photo. Louise Crawford of Brooklyn Social Media has been variously cheerleader, book-therapist, and sometimes editor, as well as a wise advisor about all things to do with PR and social media: Thanks to her whole team. Others who helped me navigate the world of publishing include Maria Goldverg, Steve Axelrod, Kathleen Cook, Ilene Smith, Lindsay Farmer, Laurel Davis Huber, Tom Costello, Eric Sullivan, and Cindy Engalla, among many others.

This book emerged from my life as a parent and as a psychologist, a life that has encompassed many places and many people. I cannot possibly acknowledge them all. I am grateful to everyone whose lives have intersected with and enriched mine in both experience and conversation. To those I haven't mentioned individually, please know that you too have contributed to this story.

Endnotes

Before We Begin

1   E.g., Sax, *Collapse of Parenting;* Sommer, *A Childhood Psychology;* Ochs and Kremer-Sadlik, "How Post-Industrial Families Talk," 90; Doepke and Zilibotti, *Love, Money and Parenting.*

2   There are many rich sources regarding cross-cultural differences in development and attitudes to babies including LeVine and LeVine, *Do Parents Matter?*; Lancy, *The Anthropology of Childhood*, especially Chapter Four; Schieffelin, *Give and Take,* 79; and Otto and Keller, *Different Faces.*

Chapter One

3   See, for example, Christakis, *The Importance of Being Little;* Stern, *The Interpersonal World of the Infant;* Siegel, *The Developing Mind,* and Gopnik, *The Gardener and The Carpenter.*

4   Brazelton and Sparrow, *Discipline,* xxi; Siegel and Bryson, *No Drama Discipline.*

5   Porges and Carter, "The Neurobiology and Evolution of Mammalian Social Behavior."

6   Sapolsky, *Behave,* 358.

7   Baumrind, "Effects of Authoritative Parental Control on Child Behavior,"; "Current Patterns of Parental Authority"; "Authoritative Parenting Revisited."

8   Damon, *The Moral Child,* 25.

Chapter Two

9   Sommer, *A Childhood Psychology,* 11–38; Fogel, *Developing Through Relationships.*

10   Winnicott, *The Child and the Family* and "The Theory of the Parent-Infant Relationship."

11   Maestropieri, *Primate Psychology,* 135.

12   Hrdy, *Mothers and Others,*175–208; Meehan and Hawks, "Maternal and Allomaternal Responsiveness," 113–135.

13   Bowlby, *Attachment;* Karen, *Becoming Attached;* Cozolino, *The Neuroscience of Human Relationships.*

14   Bowlby, *Attachment;* Cozolino; Siegel; Hrdy, *Mothers and Others,* 113.

15   Karen: Bowlby's theory was highly controversial at first, especially among his fellow psychoanalysts, but the existence of an evolutionarily adaptive attachment system is now widely considered part of normal development. There are, however, many caveats regarding the need for more research: E.g., Lamb et al., *Infant-Mother Attachment;* Otto and Keller, eds., *Different Faces of Attachment.*

16   Bowlby, *Attachment,* Chapter 12, especially 210–216.

17   See Siegel, *Developing Mind.*

18   "Mistreats her:" e.g., Reiss et al., *Children and Violence,* 102–106; Konner, *The Evolution of Childhood,* 231.

19   Multiple caretakers and hierarchy: Bowlby, *Attachment,* 303–309, and Karen, 99; Otto and Keller; Lancy, *Anthropology of Childhood;* Konner, 233; Pruett, "Role of the Father." Although Bowlby coined the term "monotropy" to describe the infant's preference for one attachment figure in his early writing, in *Attachment* he insisted that he had always believed that multiple attachment figures were not only possible, but common.

20 Western Europe: Druckerman, *Raising Bébé*, and Laske, *Achtung Baby*.

21 "Provide for them:" Konner, 383ff, Chapter 13. An amusing take on imprinting: www.thegoosesmother.com/id6.html.

22 Warmth and safety: Bowlby, *Attachment*, 208, 235-264; mother animals: Allport, *Natural History of Parenting*; secure base: Mahler, Pine, and Bergman, *Psychobiological Birth of the Human Infant*.

23 Bowlby, *Attachment*, 235–264.

24 See note 16.

25 Hrdy, *ibid.*, 209–231; Hrdy, *Mother Nature*, Chapters 7 and 19; senses: Hobson, *Cradle of Thought*, Kagan, *Human Spark*, Siegel, *Developing Mind*, and Stern, *Interpersonal World*; spatial sensitivity: Kagan, *Human Spark*.

26 Overlap between the brain circuits implicated in attachment and addiction: Cozolino, 120–126; epigenetics: Meaney, "Epigenetics," 99–131; Siegel, 20. Genes and the environment can be considered in "dialogue," making genes more a template for, rather than being absolute determinants of, gene expression.

27 Two good sources for cultural variation are LeVine and LeVine's *Do Parents Matter?* especially Chapter 4, "Face to Face or Skin to Skin," and Lancy.

28 Why do we attach when we do? Kagan, 46ff., 59: Jerome Kagan is one of the foremost critics of attachment theory, arguing that brain maturation taking place at the end of the first year, especially improvement in working memory, may be sufficient to explain the phenomenon of attachment behavior. He also argues that differences in cultural and family context as well as temperament could explain individual differences in attachment style. Wander off alone: Belsky; different exposure to strangers: Otto and Keller. A comparative study of attachment behaviors showed Israeli infants to be more reactive than American infants when exposed to strangers, presumably because they saw few adults who did not live in the kibbutz, while American infants see strangers on playgrounds, grocery stores, and so on.

29 Separation anxiety and stranger danger: Allport; Bowlby, *Attachment*, 321–330; Bowlby discusses the differences and similarities between these two concepts at some length.

30 Mahler, Pine, and Bergman, *Psychological Birth*, 65ff.

31 Hewlett and Lamb, *Hunter Gatherer Childhood* and Hiltrud and Keller, *Different Faces*, Chapter 1.

32 Howe et al., *Attachment Theory, Child Maltreatment and Family Support*.

33 Kagan and Snidman, *The Long Shadow of Temperament*.

34 Recent trends for young adults to remain in or return to their parents' home exacerbate this dilemma: Lewin, "More Young Women Waiting to Leave Home."

35 Throughout the brain: See Chapter Two, note 10; Right brain and long-lasting attachment: Siegel; Cozolino, Schore, *Affect Regulation*; attachment effects: Ainsworth et al., *Patterns*; Belsky, "Modern Evolutionary Theory," 141–161. In order to classify the quality and degree of attachment of infants and mothers, Mary Ainsworth designed the "strange situation" experiment in the 70s, based on her work in Uganda and Baltimore. Although there is much evidence to suggest that there are indeed individual differences among children's attachment behaviors, there remains a fair amount of controversy as to the reason for the differences: Do they arise from the history of the relationship, or reflect its current status? Do they have anything to do with the past behavior of the primary caretaker, or might they be attributable to other variables, including especially temperament, contextual demands, or cultural expectations?

36 You can read about the classic Ainsworth test in many places, including her own work, e.g., Ainsworth et al., *Patterns of Attachment*, or in a reference like Lamb et al., *Infant-Mother Attachment*.

37 See note 20, above. For a look at Japan: Behrens, "Reconsidering Attachment."

38 Crying: Panksepp, *Affective Neuroscience*, 265ff; Bowlby, *Attachment*, especially Ch 12 and 13.

39 Beebe and Lachmann, *Infant Research and Adult Treatment*.

40 Rat pups: "Licking Rat Pups;" in The Nerve Blog; Romanian orphans: Weir, "The Lasting Impact of Neglect."

41 Stimuli: Field, *Touch*, 75–89, and Linden, *Touch*, 33–75; outcomes: Linden, 26–27; Field, 59–74; NICU: Personal communication, Debra Busta, Pediatric Nurse practitioner and lactation consultant, Berkeley, California. This practice was originally inspired after studies by Marshall Klaus and John H. Kennell who were instrumental in the natural childbirth movement of the 70s, and the development of the "rooming in," option, birthing centers, etc.: e.g., Klaus and Kennell, "Labor, Birth, and Bonding," 22–98, although later studies reduced claims of long-term effects, e.g., Hertenstein et al., "Touch."

42 Importance of touch: Linden; Field; Montague, *Touching*; Cozolino, *Human Relationships*; Craig, *How Do You Feel?*; premature babies: Rosenberg, "The Human Incubator."

43 Being held: Montague; Cozolino: well-being: Cozolino, 60–61, 103.

44 Hewlett and Lamb, *Hunter-Gatherer Childhoods*.

45 Panksepp, 280ff; Pruett.

46 Also see Taffel and Israeloff, *When Parents Disagree*.

Chapter Three

47 McCloskey, *Make Way for Ducklings*.

48 Bronfenbrenner, *Ecological Psychology*; Winnicott, "Contemporary Concepts," 138–151.

49 It is hard to keep pace with the numbers of children with phones or tablets, and it varies by country and class. One good source is Common Sense Media. In their 2017 report on children from zero to eight, 95 percent of their families owned a smartphone; 78 percent owned a tablet; and 42 percent of the children had their own tablet. A 2018 report on teens in the UK found that 46 percent of parents of teens felt addicted to *their* phones, while 44 percent of teens did.

50 Super and Harkness, "The Developmental Niche: A Conceptualization at the Interface of Development and Culture;" Lancy; LeVine and LeVine.

51 Lareau, *Unequal Childhoods*.

52 Weisner, "Ecocultural Niches;" Schieffelin, *The Give and Take of Everyday Life*.

53 Evolution: 636–650; indulgence, 566–67; carrying, 628; physical proximity, 576–77; exceptions, 641, all in Konner. Chores: Klein and Goodwin, "Chores," in *Fast Forward Family*, edited by Ochs and Kremer-Sadlik, 111–129; early childhood: Christakis, *Importance of Being Little*, 138–166.

54 Weisner, "Culture."

55 E.g., Turkle, *Alone Together*; Steyer, *Talking Back to Facebook*; Hoffman, *iRules*.

56 Schieffelin.

57 Whiting and Edwards, *Children of Different Worlds*.

58 Wergins, "The Case for Free-Range Parenting."

59 Ochs and Kremer-Sadlik, *Fast Forward Family*, 67–93.

60 Ehrensaft, *Spoiling Childhood*; Lareau.

61 Vygotsky, *Mind in Society*.

62 Coppens, et al., "Learning by Observing," 69–81.

63 How you're supposed to do it: Tomasello, *Why We Cooperate*; cooperation evolved: Hrdy, *Mothers and Others*.

64 UCLA study: Klein and Goodwin.

65 What everyone knows: Sapir, "The Unconscious Patterning of Behavoir in Society;" learn from adults: Rogoff, *Apprenticeship in Thinking*; Rogoff et al., "Guided Participation."

66 Rogoff et al.

67 Ehrensaft, *Spoiling Childhood*.

68 In *Achtung Baby*, the author describes the German value of developing independence at a much earlier age, both inside and outside the house.

69 E.g., Brooks, *Small Animals*; Skenazy, *Free-Range Kids*; and see "Let Grow," letgrow.org/blog/.

70 Porges and Carter discuss the evolution of both social attachments and mammalian reactivity to stress: surely experienced by human parents.

71 Orenstein, *Girls and Sex*.

Chapter Four

72 In his encyclopedic analysis of human behavior, *Behave*, Robert Sapolsky, a primatologist, shows that for any instance of human behavior there are telescoping levels of explanation, from the microchemical to evolution and culture.

73 Rogoff, *Cultural Nature of Development*; Panksepp, *Affective Neuroscience*; and the Brain Science Podcast, Episode 106. Function of emotion: Moll, Oliveira-Souza, and Zahn, "Neuroscience and Morality;" complex rewards and relationships: Vozzola, *Moral Development*; stages: 26–34, and relationships: 41–48.

74 Sigel et al., *Parental Belief Systems*; Goodnow and Collins; *Development According to Parents*; Bornstein, *Cultural Approaches to Parenting*; Harkness and Super, *Anthropological Perspectives*; Center for Parenting Education, "Values Matter."

75 Rogoff, *Cultural Nature of Human Development*: list of standards; Sax, *Collapse of Parenting*, and Thompson, "Early Foundations."

76 Ochs and Izquierdo, "Responsibility in Childhood," 391–413.

77 Hoban, *Bread and Jam*.

78 Churchland, *Brain Trust*.

79 Damon.

80 Temperament: Manfredi et al. "Temperament and Parental Styles;" fear and anxiety: LeDoux.

81 Oxytocin: Porges and Carter.

82 Separation: Panksepp, 274–275.

83 Sapolsky, *Behave* 42–43, 56–58.

84 Ochs and Kremer-Sadlik, *Fast-Forward Families;* quote, 9.

85 *Ibid*.

86 Goodnow and Collins, *Development According to Parents*, Rogoff, *Cultural Nature of Development*, e.g., Chapter Six, "Interdependence and Autonomy," and Sommer.

87 Hoban, *Best Friends*.

88 Parent differences: e.g., Pruett; Harris, Jenkins, and Glaser, "Gender Differences," 48–63; Harris and Jenkins, " 'My Son's a Bit Dizzy.' "

89 Weisner, "American Dependency Conflict."

90 Girl or boy: e.g., Eliot, *Pink Brain, Blue Brain*; effect of gender: Klass, Gender in the Toy Box;" Miller, "A Disadvantaged Start Hurts Boys More than Girls."

91 Taffel and Israeloff, *When Parents Disagree.*

92 Lieber, *Opposite of Spoiled.*

Chapter Five

93 Bemelmans, *Madeline.*

94 Livingston, "More than Half of Kids Today Live in a Traditional Family."

95 Idealist vs. pragmatist: Taffel and Israeloff; Hochschild, *The Second Shift.* Both books grapple with the tough reality that women continue to be the primary caretaking parent in most families.

96 Gág, *Gone is Gone.*

97 Taffel and Israeloff, *When Parents Disagree.*

98 Hinde, *Ethology,* especially Part III, 201–272.

99 See Siegel and Hartzell, *Parenting from the Inside Out.*

100 Minuchin, *Families and Family Therapy,* e.g., 51.

101 Minuchin and Fishman, *Family Therapy Techniques,* 58.

102 Grolnick, *The Psychology of Parental Control,* 33.

103 Bowen, *Family Therapy in Clinical Practice.*

104 Seyfarth and Cheney, *Baboon Metaphysics.*

105 Security: See Cummings and Davies, *Marital Conflict and Children,* 59ff; conflict not always harmful: *ibid.,* 114; canary in the coal mine, i.e., children's behavior brings attention to parents, *ibid.,* 118.

106 *Ibid.,* 133.

107 Detectable changes: ibid., 53–96.

108 Carter and McGoldrick, *The Family Life Cycle.*

109 Bronfenbrenner, *Ecology,* 46, 288.

110 Hans Selye, a Hungarian endocrinologist is said to be the first to identify stress as a biological phenomenon. See Wikipedia Contributors, "Hans Selye," and Selye, *The Stress of Life.*

Chapter Six

111 James, *Principles of Psychology, Vol. 1,* "The Stream of Thought," 224–290, and "The Consciousness of Self, 291–401; Cooper, "William James's Theory," 504; Pomerleau, "William James."

112 Each have a will: Fogel, 48; guesses about the other: Fogel; acted out: Fogel, 76.

113 Ready for action: Llinás, *I of the Vortex,* Panksepp, *Affective Neuroscience;* sensation of the moment and homeostasis: Craig, *How Do You Feel?* Body image and motor activity: Panksepp, *Affective Neuroscience* and Panksepp, "Primary-Process Emotional Systems," 74–94; "I feel, therefore I am." After writing this, I found this phrase used as the title for an article about Spinoza and Damasio: Eakin, "I Feel, Therefore I Am."

114 Although the first experience of most babies is being held and supported, there is an intriguing movement among breastfeeding advocates to allow babies to be placed between the mother's breast and allowed to "crawl" to the mother's nipple and start nursing without help from adults. See Klaus, "Mother and Infant." For a video of a baby actually doing this, see www.breastcrawl.org/.

115 Craig, *How Do You Feel?,* 222.

116 Happening now: Llinás, Thompson, *Mind in Life;* Burton, *Skeptic's Guide.* Quash my memories: Stockton, "Your Brain Doesn't Contain Memories. It *Is* Memories."

117 Bonobos: Savage Rumbaugh, Shanker, and Taylor, *Apes, Language and the Human Mind;* share feelings: Among developmental psychologists, this is often called "interpretation," e.g., Kagan, *Human Spark,* 199. Among clinicians and clinical theorists, it is called "mentalization" and thought to be crucial to secure attachment in adulthood. See Fonagy, Gergely, Jurist, and Main, *Affect Regulation* and Hill, *Affect Regulation Theory.*

118 Make meaning of what you are sensing: Feldman-Barrett, *How Emotions Are Made;* "actions expressive of certain states of mind:" LeDoux, *Anxious,* 114.

119 Alarm system: Sunderland, *The Science of Parenting;* experience of emotion: Damasio, The *Feeling of What Happens,* especially Chapter 2; Panksepp, *Affective Neuroscience;* LeDoux, *Emotional Brain.*

120 What is going on at that moment: In LeDoux's words, "when information about the external world is integrated with sensations arising from within the body, we have feelings," *Emotional Brain,* 102; also, Feldman-Barrett, *ibid.*

121 Discussion of brain and emotion relies heavily on Feldman Barrett, Sapolsky, Panksepp, and LeDoux.

122 Panksepp, *Affective Neuroscience,* 301ff; Feldman-Barrett, *ibid.,* 78.

123 See Schore, *Affect Regulation;* Siegel, *Developing Mind;* Cozolino, *Neuroscience of Relationships;* and Hill, *Affect Regulation Theory.*

124 Definitions: *New Oxford American Dictionary* Apple Dictionary application.

125 Interpersonal function: Barrett, "Shame and Guilt," 39; visual, prohibition: Schore, *Affect Regulation,* 134.

126 Schore, *Affect Regulation,* 245–247; Cozolino, 234.

127 Schore, *ibid.*: Prohibition, 200, rage, 241–242.

128 *Ibid.,* 200.

129 This conceptualization from Brain Science podcast, Episode 123, with Chemero.

Chapter Seven

130 Brazelton, *Infants and Mothers.*

131 Zentner and Bates, "Child Temperament," 7–37.

132 Dunn and Plomin, *Separate Lives.*

133 Young mother: Brazelton; biological measures: Kagan and Snidman; Zentner and Bates.

134 Dimensions: Zentner and Bates.

135 Agreement: Zentner and Bates; filter: Rothbart, *Becoming Who We Are,* 30. Neurobiological profile: A discussion of neural correlates to temperament is beyond the scope of this book, but it is the new frontier of research, e.g., www.ncbi.nlm.nih.gov/pubmed/23142157.

136 Two types: Kagan and Snidman, especially Chapters 4 and 5; uncertainty: *ibid.,* 86ff; anxiety: LeDoux, *Anxious.*

137 Rothbart.

138 *Ibid.,* 55.

139 Dunn and Plomin, *Separate Lives;* Plomin and Daniels, "Children in Same Family."

140 Mischel and Berkowitz, "Delay of Self-gratification," and Mischel, "The Marshmallow Test."

141 Different mechanisms, latency, etc.: Zentner and Bates, "Child Temperament."

142 There are many good resources for parents with children for whom every day can feel like a battlefield, including the following books and related websites: Greene, *Explosive Child*; Turecki, *Difficult Child*; Aron, *Highly Sensitive Child*, and *Highly Sensitive Person*, and Glasser and Easley, *Transforming the Difficult Child*.

143 Touch: Turecki; Zina Steinberg, NICU psychologist, personal communication: In the NICU, parents tend to use a delicate touch with their fingers with a preemie, but are taught instead to hold the head, for example, with firm pressure.

144 Kagan and Snidman.

145 Rothbart, 235–237; also Kagan and Snidman, 199–202; Eliot, *Pink Brain, Blue Brain*; Miller, "Disadvantaged Start Hurts Boys."

146 E.g., Ehrensaft, *Gender Born, Gender Made* and *Gender Creative Child*; Tabuchi, "Gender-Specific Toys."

147 Darwinist approach to birth order: Sulloway, *Born to Rebel*; large study: Rohrer et al., "Effects of Birth Order."

148 Dunn and Plomin, *Separate Lives*; Plomin and Daniels, "Children in Same Family;" Moore, *Sibling Conflict and Parent Intervention*.

149 Dunn and Plomin; mother with different ages, *ibid.*, 78–79; Plomin and Daniels, "Why Are Siblings So Different?"

150 Siegel, *Developing Mind*, 21ff.

151 Domains: Nucci et al., "Parental Control of the Personal;" Smetana et al., "Changing Conceptions;" tattoos: Wikipedia Contributors, "Legal Status of tattooing in the United States."

152 Galinsky, Six Stages, 119–177.

Chapter Eight

153 Fogel; Konner.

154 Sapir.

155 Fogel, 6.

156 Beebe and Lachmann. Infants can imitate within as little as 20 milliseconds: See oft-cited experiment with neonates: Meltzoff and Moore, "Imitations of Facial and Manual Gestures by Human Neonates," in *Science, 198*, 75–78.

157 Fogel, *Developing Through Relationships*, 27.

158 Fogel, 18–20.

159 Iacoboni, *Mirroring People*; Hatfield, Cacioppo and Rapson, *Emotional Contagion*, Rizzolatti et al., "Resonance Behavior and Mirror Neurons," 85–100; www.ncbi.nlm.nih.gov/pubmed/10349488.

160 Blakeslee, *Mind of Its Own*, 164–166; Gallese, "Shared Manifold Hypothesis." Researchers believe that intention has been detected because different neurons were activated for different actions, e.g., picking up a peanut as opposed to grasping a cup.

161 Why would brains match? Gallese, "The Shared Manifold Hypothesis," 33–50; Batson, *These Things Called Empathy*, 1–15. Also see: Marsh, "Mirror Neurons."

162 Hatfield et al., *Emotional Contagion*, 4.

163 Emotional contagion: see Hatfield et al., *ibid.*, and Nelson, "Neurobiological Basis of Empathy." For skepticism, see Burton, 121–131. Do mirror neurons cause mimicry or vice versa? See Hatfield, Rapson and Le, "Emotional Contagion and Empathy."

164 "Feel themselves into others' lives": Hatfield et al., *Contagion*; marking by parents: Fonagy et al., *Affect Regulation*; hypervigilance: Reiss et al., eds., *Children and Violence*, 106–107.

165 The original still face experiment was developed by Ed Tronick in 1975 (Tronick et al., "Infant Emotions"), but there are many articles and videos that describe and demonstrate it readily available on the Web. See Tronick, *Neurobehavioral and Social-Emotional Development.*

166 Fogel.

167 Interlocutors: Couper-Kuhlen, *Prosody,* 164, disruptions: *ibid.,* 170.

168 Hidden layer: Burton, *On Being Certain* and *A Skeptic's Guide;* parents matter: Schore, chapters on mother-infant interaction, 71–211.

169 Fogel notes in *Developing Through Relationships,* that in infancy, "Parenting can be done by almost anyone because in the company of an infant, if one is willing to enter into a co-regulated communication, parenting behavior will emerge over repeated encounters," (97).

170 Fogel, 26–42.

171 For primate differences and reference to human differences, see Bard et al., "Group Differences," 616–624; Ochs and Schieffelin, *Language Socialization;* Schieffelin, *Give and Take.*

172 Winnicott, "Contemporary Concepts," 138–151; Neufeld and Mate, *Hold On to Your Kids;* Sax, *Collapse of Parenting.*

Chapter Nine

173 Margaret Wetherell describes this as "affective practices," in *Affect and Emotion;* see also Feldman-Barrett, *How Emotion Is Made,* especially Chapter 6.

174 Gallese, "The Roots of Empathy," 171–180.

175 Cozolino, 86–87.

176 Involuntarily: Hill; "We don't feel": Wallin, *Attachment in Psychotherapy,* 56.

177 E.g., Sunderland, *The Science of Parenting,* especially 258–269; Siegel and Hartzell, *Parenting from the Inside Out,* 154-184; Markham, *Peaceful Parent, Happy Kids;* Runkel, *Scream-free Parenting.*

178 See Craig, *How Do You Feel?* e.g., Chapters One and Two, and many sources already cited, including Cozolino; Hill; Damasio, *Descartes' Error* and *The Feeling of What Happens;* Siegel.

179 E.g., Cozolino; Siegel, and many others.

180 Lindgren, *Pippi Longstocking.*

181 Sapir, 32–46.

182 LeVine and LeVine, Chapter Four, esp p 74.

183 Cozolino; Porges, *Polyvagal Theory.*

184 Interrelated: Porges, *ibid.,* 81; "Safe inner world," Cozolino, 65.

185 Argyle, *Bodily Communication,* noted 60 possible facial signals like "shifty eyes" or "set jaw," and cited Ray Birdwhistell's estimate of 20,000 possible expressions, (211–228).

186 Argyle.

187 Porges, *ibid.,* 134, 138–150.

188 "Vagal brake," see Porges, *ibid.,* 102–117 and "neural substrate," 11–19; also Porges, "The "Polyvagal Theory," 504.

189 Hobson.

190 Kendon, *Conducting Interaction.*

191 Schore, 75.

192 Goodwin, "Participation, Affect," 519; Kendon, *ibid.;* Argyle, 233 ff.

193 According to a recent study: Holohan, "Unborn babies."

194 Foreign language; understand what you were feeling; voice qualities into words: Wennerstrom, *Music of Everyday Speech.*

195 Social engagement: Carter and Porges, "Neurophysiology and Evolution;" sense of the other: Craig, *How Do You Feel?*

196 Synchrony: Cozolino, 106; help me cope: Sunderland, 37; for emotional cues in voice see Wennerstrom; Kappas, Hess and Scherer, "Voice and Emotion."

197 Kappas, Hess and Scherer, 218.

198 Couper-Kuhlen, "Prosody," 175.

199 Understood: Kendon, *ibid.*; rapport: Bernieri and Rosenthal, "Interpersonal Coordination," 413, 420; expected: Kendon, *Gesture,* 13; display rules: Haberstadt, "Ecology of Expressiveness," 110ff.

200 Kendon, 7ff; As they interact: Argyle, *Bodily Communication,* 270.

201 Damour, "Why Teenage Girls Roll Their Eyes."

202 Argyle, 265.

203 Social brain": Cozolino, *Neuroscience of Human Relationships,* 84; fibers: Craig, *How Do You Feel?* Insula: Critchley et al., "Neural Systems Supporting Interoceptive Awareness;" Craig, "How Do You Feel – Now"? 102–103; Bechara and Naqvi, "Listening to Your Heart," 189–195.

204 Linden, *Touch,* 86.

205 Krisch, "All Kids Throw the Same Tantrum."

206 Goleman, *Emotional Intelligence.*

Chapter Ten

207 Ervin-Tripp, O'Connor, and Rosenberg, "Language and Power in the Family;" Ervin-Tripp, "Structures of Control."

208 Paugh and Izquierdo, "Why Is This a Battle?"

209 Tulbert and Goodwin, "Choreographies of Attention," 79–92. See also Pehlan, *1,2,3 Magic,* who distinguishes between start and stop behavior.

210 Kendon, *Conducting Interaction.*

211 Dog training: The Monks of New Skete, *Raising a Puppy;* children's attention: Tulbert and Goodwin.

212 James, *The Principles of Psychology, Volume One,* 402–458, esp 416.

213 Damasio, *Feeling,* 183.

214 Tulbert and Goodwin, "Choreographies of Attention," 79–92.

215 "Recycling positions:" Goodwin, "Participation, Affect and Trajectory," 513–542, esp. 522–530.

216 William James begins *Psychology, the Briefer Course,* published in 1892, one of the founding works of the field, with a chapter called "Habit," which is essentially a chapter on learning.

217 Synapses: LeDoux, *The Emotional Brain,* 213–220; Hebb quote, LeDoux, 214.

218 LeDoux, *ibid.*, 165 ff.

219 Goodwin. "The Cooperative, Transformative Organization of Human Action."

220 Ochs and Izquierdo, "Responsibility in Childhood"; Ochs, and Kremer-Sadlik, "How Postindustrial Families Talk."

221 Goodwin, "Participation, Affect, and Trajectory," 527.

222 Ervin-Tripp, "Request Retries."

223 Brown and Levinson, *Politeness*.

224 Ervin-Tripp et al., "Language and Power," 118.

225 Ochs and Sadlik, "Talk."

226 Adapted from Ochs and Sadlik.

227 "Pursue compliance:" Ochs and Sadlik; "collaborative action," Tomasello.

228 Goodwin, "Participation, Affect, and Trajectory."

Chapter Eleven

229 Wittgenstein, *Zettel*, 77.

References

....

Ainsworth, Mary D. Salter, M.C. Blehar, E. Waters, and S. Wall. *Patterns of Attachment: A Psychological Study of the Strange Situation*. Hillsdale, NJ: Lawrence Erlbaum Associates, 1978.

Allport, Susan. *A Natural History of Parenting: A Naturalist Looks at Parenting in the Animal World and Ours*. Lincoln, NE: Universe, 2003.

Argyle, Michael. *Bodily Communication*. London: Routledge, 1975.

Aron, Elaine. *The Highly Sensitive Child: Helping Our Children Thrive When the World Overwhelms Them*. New York: Random House, 2002.

Aron, Elaine. *The Highly Sensitive Person: How to Thrive When the World Overwhelms You*. New York: Kensington Publishing Corp., 2013.

Bard, K.A., M. Myowa-Yamakoshi, M. Tomonaga, M. Tanaka, A. Costall, and T. Matsuzawa. "Group Differences in the Mutual Gaze of Chimpanzees (Pan Troglodytes)." *Developmental Psychology*, vol. 41, no. 4 (June 2005): 616–624.

Barrett, Karen Caplovitz. "A Functionalist Approach to Shame and Guilt." *The Psychology of Self-Conscious Emotions: Shame, Guilt, Embarrassment, and Pride*, edited by June Tangney and Kurt Fischer. New York: Guilford, 1995, 25–63.

Batson, C.D. "These Things Called Empathy: Eight Related but Distinct Phenomena." *Social Neuroscience. The Social Neuroscience of Empathy*, edited by J. Decety & W. Ickes. Cambridge: MIT Press, 2009, 3–15. dx.doi.org/10.7551/mitpress/9780262012973.003.0002.

Baumrind, Diana. "Effects of Authoritative Parental Control on Child Behavior." *Child Development*, vol. 37, no. 4 (1966): 887-907.

Baumrind, Diana. "Current Patterns of Parental Authority." *Developmental Psychology*, vol. 4, no. 1, pt. 2 (1971): 1–103.

Baumrind, Diana. "Authoritative Parenting: Revisited: History and Current Status." *Authoritative Parenting: Synthesizing Nurturance and Discipline*, edited by Robert E. Larzelere, Amanda Sheffield Morris, and Amanda W. Harrist. Washington, DC: American Psychological Association, 2012, 11–34.

Bechara, Antoine and Nasir Naqvi. "Listening to Your Heart: Interoceptive Awareness as a Gateway to Feeling." *Nature Neuroscience*, vol. 7 (2004): 189–195, doi:10.1038/nn1176.

Beebe, Beatrice and Frank Lachmann. *Infant Research and Adult Treatment*. Hillsdale, NJ: Analytic Press, 2002.

Behrens, Kazuko. "Reconsidering Attachment in Context of Culture: Review of Attachment Studies in Japan." (2016). Online Readings in Psychology and Culture. 6. 10.9707/2307-0919.1140.

Belsky, Jay. "Modern Evolutionary Theory and Patterns of Attachment." *Handbook on Attachment*, edited by Jude Cassidy and Phillip R. Shaver. New York: Guilford, 2008, 141–161.

Bemelmans, Ludwig. *Madeline*. New York: Viking, 1967.

Bernieri, Frank J. and Robert Rosenthal. "Interpersonal Coordination: Behavior Matching and Interactional Synchrony." *Fundamentals of Nonverbal Behavior*, edited by Robert S. Feldman and Bernard Rimé. Cambridge: Cambridge University Press, 1991, 401–432.

Blakeslee, Sandra and Matthew Blakeslee. *Mind of Its Own: How Body Maps in Your Brain Help You Do (Almost) Everything Better*. New York: Random House Trade Paperbacks, 2008.

Bloom, Paul. "The Moral Life of Babies." *New York Times Magazine*, 5 May 2010. www.nytimes. com/2010/05/09/magazine/09babies-t.html. (Accessed: January 30, 2019.)

Bowen, Murray. *Family Therapy in Clinical Practice.* New York: Jason Aronson Inc., 1978.

Bowlby, John. *Attachment and Loss, Volume I: Attachment.* New York: Basic Books, 1969.

Bowlby, John. *Attachment and Loss, Volume II: Separation: Anxiety and Anger.* New York: Basic Books, 1973.

Bowlby, John. *Maternal Care and Mental Health: A Report Prepared on Behalf of the World Health Organization as a Contribution to the United Nations Programme for the Welfare of Homeless Children.* Geneva: World Health Organization, 1951.

Brazelton, T. Berry. *Infants and Mothers: Differences in Development.* New York: Dell, 1969.

Brazelton, T. Berry and Joshua Sparrow. *Discipline, The Brazelton Way.* Boston: Da Capo Lifelong Books, 2003.

Breastcrawl website, www.breastcrawl.org/. (Accessed January 30, 2019.)

Bronfenbrenner, Urie. *Ecological Psychology: Experiments by Nature and Design.* Cambridge: Harvard University Press, 1979.

Brooks, Kim. *Small Animals: Parenthood in the Age of Fear.* New York: Flatiron Books, 2018.

Buck. Directed by Cindy Meehl. Cedar Creek Productions, 2011.

Brown, Penelope and Stephen Levinson, editors. *Politeness: Some Universals in Language Usage.* Cambridge: Cambridge University Press, 1978.

Burton, Robert. *On Being Certain: Believing You Are Right Even When You Are Not.* New York: St. Martin's Griffin, 2008.

Burton, Robert. *A Skeptic's Guide to the Mind: What Neuroscience Can and Cannot Tell Us About Ourselves.* New York: St. Martin's Press, 2013.

Busta, Debra, APRN. Personal Communication. (September, 2015.)

Campbell, Ginger. "Andy Clark on Prediction, Action, and the Embodied Mind." *Brain Science*, Episode 126, 28 January 2016. brainsciencepodcast.com/bsp/2016/126-andyclark?rq=Andy%20Clark.

Campbell, Ginger. "Miguel Nicolelis, M.D., Ph.D." *Brain Science*, Episode 79, 3 December 2011. brainsciencepodcast.com/bsp/miguel-nicolelis-md-phd-bsp-79.html?rq=Nicolelis.

Campbell, Ginger. "Phenomenology and Embodied Cognition, An Interview with Michael Chemero." *Brain Science*, Episode 123, 28 October 2015. brainsciencepodcast.com/bsp/2015/123-phenomenology?rq=Chemero.

Carter, Elizabeth A. and Monica McGoldrick, editors. *The Family Life Cycle: A Framework for Family Therapy.* New York: Gardner Press, 1980.

Carter, Sue C. and Stephen Porges. "Neurobiology and the Evolution of Mammalian Social Behavior." *Evolution, Early Experience, and Human Development: From Research to Practice and Policy,* edited by Darcia Narvaez, Jaak Panksepp, Allan N. Schore, and Tracy R. Gleason. Oxford: Oxford University Press, 2013, 132–151.

Cassidy, Jude and Phillip R. Shaver, editors. *Handbook on Attachment.* New York: Guilford, 2008.

Center for Parenting Education. "Values Matter: Using Your Values to Raise Caring, Responsible, Resilient Children." Retrieved from centerforparentingeducation.org/library-of-articles/indulgence-values/values-matter-using-your-values-to-raise-caring-responsible-resilient-children-what-are-values/. (Accessed January 30, 2019.)

Chance, M.R.A. "Attention Structure as the Basis of Primate Rank Orders." *The Social Structure of Attention*, edited by M.R.A. Chance and R.R. Larsen. New York: Wiley, 1976, 11–28.

Chemero, Anthony. *Radical Embodied Cognitive Science*. Cambridge: MIT Press, 2009.

Christakis, Erika. *The Importance of Being Little*. New York: Penguin Books, 2016.

Chua, Amy. *Battle Hymn of the Tiger Mother*. New York: Penguin, 2011.

Churchland, Patricia S. *Brain Trust: What Neuroscience Tells Us About Morality*. Princeton and New York: Princeton University Press, 2011.

Circle of Security website, circleofsecurity.net/ (Accessed 26 July 2013.)

Colin, Virginia L. *Human Attachment*. New York: McGraw-Hill, 1996.

Commonsensemedia. "The New Normal: Parents, Teens and Devices Around the World," October 1, 2018. www.commonsensemedia.org/research/The-New-Normal-Parents-Teens-and-Devices-Around-the-World. (Accessed February 5, 2019.)

Cooper, W.E. "William James's Theory of the Self." *Monist*, vol. 75, no. 4 (1992), 504–520.

Coppens, A.D., K.G. Silva, O. Ruvalcaba, L. Alcalá, A. López, and B. Rogoff. "Learning by Observing and Pitching In to Family and Community Endeavors: An Orientation." *Human Development*, vol. 57, no. 2–3 (June 2014): 69-81 doi:10.1159/000356757.

Couper-Kuhlen, Elizabeth. *English Speech Rhythm: Form and Function in Everyday Interaction*. Amsterdam: John Benjamins, 1993.

Couper-Kuhlen, Elizabeth. "Prosody." *The Pragmatics of Interaction*, edited by Sigurd D'hondt, Jan-Ola Östman, and Jef Verschueren. Amsterdam; Philadelphia: John Benjamins, 2009. 174–189.

Cozolino, Louis. *The Neuroscience of Human Relationships: Attachment and the Developing Social Brain*. New York: Norton, 2006.

Craig, A.D. *How Do You Feel? An Interoceptive Moment with Your Neurobiological Self*. Princeton: University of Princeton Press, 2015.

Craig, A.D. "How Do You Feel--Now? The Anterior Insula and Human Awareness." *Nature Reviews Neuroscience* 7 (2004):102–103. doi:10.1038/nn0204–102.

Critchley, Hugo, Stefan Wiens, Pia Rothstein, Arne Öhman, and Raymond J. Dolan. "Neural Systems Supporting Interoceptive Awareness." *Nature Reviews Neuroscience* 10 (January 2009): 59–70. doi:10.1038/nrn2555.

Cummings, E. Mark and Patrick Davies. *Marital Conflict and Children*. New York: Guilford, 2010.

Damasio, Antonio. *The Feeling of What Happens: Body and Emotion in the Making of Consciousness*. New York: Harcourt Brace, 1999.

Damon, William. *The Moral Child*. New York: The Free Press, 1988.

Damour, Lisa. "Why Teenage Girls Roll Their Eyes." *New York Times*, 17 February 2016. parenting.blogs.nytimes.com/2016/02/17/why-teenage-girls-roll-their-eyes/. (Accessed January 30, 2019.)

Darwin, Charles. *The Expression of the Emotions in Man and Animals*. Oxford: Oxford University Press, 1998.

Dell'Antonia, K.J. "Why Couldn't My Kids Clean the Kitchen? They Didn't Have To." *New York Times*, 20 May 2014. parenting.blogs.nytimes.com/2014/05/30/why-couldnt-my-kids-clean-the-kitchen-they-didnt-have-to/. (Accessed January 30, 2019.)

Dennison, George. *The Lives of Children: The Story of the First Street School.* New York: Vintage Books, 1969.

Doepke, Matthias, and Fabrizo Zilibotti. *Love, Money and How Economics Explains the Way We Raise Our Kids.* Princeton: Princeton University Press, 2019.

"Dr. Spock." Wikipedia. en.wikipedia.org/wiki/Benjamin_Spock. (Accessed January 30, 2019.)

Druckerman, Pamela. *Bringing up Bébé: One Woman Discovers the Wisdom of French Parenting.* New York: Penguin, 2012.

Dunn, Judy and Robert Plomin. *Separate Lives: Why Siblings Are So Different.* New York: Basic Books, 1990.

Eakin, Emily. "I Feel, Therefore I Am." *New York Times,* 19 April 2003. www.nytimes.com/2003/04/19/books/i-feel-therefore-i-am.html. (Accessed January 30, 2019.)

Ehrensaft, Diane. *Gender Born, Gender Made: Raising Healthy Gender-Nonconforming Children.* New York: The Experiment, 2011.

Ehrensaft, Diane. *The Gender Creative Child: Pathways for Supporting Children Who Live Outside of Gender Boxes.* New York: The Experiment, 2016.

Ehrensaft, Diane. *Spoiling Childhood: How Well-Meaning Parents Are Giving Children Too Much—But Not What They Need.* New York: Guilford, 1997.

Eliot, Lise. *Pink Brain, Blue Brain.* New York: Mariner Books, 2009.

Ervin-Tripp, Susan. "Structures of Control." *Communicating in the Classroom,* edited by L.C. Wilkinson. New York: Academic Press, 1982, 27–47.

Ervin-Tripp, Susan. "Request Retries." *Lenguas Modernas, Universidad de Chile* 15 (1985): 25–34.

Ervin-Tripp, Susan, M.C. O'Connor, and J. Rosenberg. "Language and Power in the Family." *Language and Power,* edited by C. Kramarae, M. Shultz, and W. O'Barr. Beverly Hills: Sage Publications, 1984, 116–135.

Evans, Nicholas. *The Horse Whisperer.* New York: Delacorte Press, 1995.

Feldman-Barrett, Lisa. *How Emotions Are Made: The Secret Life of the Brain.* New York: Houghton Mifflin Harcourt, 2017.

Feldman Barrett, Lisa. "Solving the Emotion Paradox: Categorization and the Experience of Emotion." *Personality and Social Psychology Review* 10 (February 2006): 20–46.

Field, Tiffany. *Touch.* Cambridge: MIT Press, 2003.

Fogel, Alan. *Developing Through Relationships.* Chicago: University of Chicago Press, 1993.

Fonagy, P., G. Gergely, J. Jurist, and M. Main. *Affect Regulation, Mentalization, and the Development of the Self.* New York: Other Press, 2002.

Gág, Wanda. *Gone Is Gone.* Minneapolis: University of Minnesota Press, 2003.

Galinsky, Ellen. "The Authority Stage." *The Six Stages of Parenthood.* Reading, MA: Addison-Wesley, 1987, 119–177.

Gallese, Vittorio. "The Roots of Empathy: The Shared Manifold Hypothesis and the Neural Basis of Intersubjectivity." *Psychopathology* 36 (2003): 171–180. www.ncbi.nlm.nih.gov/pubmed/14504450. (Accessed February 7, 2019.)

Gallese, Vittorio. "The Shared Manifold Hypothesis: From Mirror Neurons to Empathy." *Journal of Consciousness Studies* vol. 8, no. 5–7 (2001), 33–50.

Glasser, Howard and Jennifer Easley. *Transforming the Difficult Child; The Nurtured Heart Approach: Shifting the Intense Child to New Patterns of Success.* Tucson: Nurtured Heart Publications, 2016. http://difficultchild.com/. (Accessed February 7, 2019.)

Goleman, Daniel. *Emotional Intelligence: Why It Can Matter More Than IQ.* New York: Bloomsbury Mass Market Paperback, 1996.

Goodnow, Jacqueline J. and W. Andrew Collins. *Development According to Parents: The Nature, Sources, and Consequences of Parents' Ideas.* Hillsdale: Lawrence Erlbaum Associates, 1990.

Goodwin, Charles. "The Co-Operative, Transformative Organization of Human Action." Spring Colloquium Lecture, New York University Anthropology Department, 28 March 2013.

Goodwin, Marjorie Harness. "Participation Affect and Trajectory in Family Directive-Response Sequences." *Text & Talk,* vol. 26, no. 4/5 (2006): 513–542.

Goodwin, Marjorie Harness, Asta Cekaite, and Charles Goodwin. "Emotion as Stance." *Emotion in Interaction,* edited by Anssi Peräkylä and Marja-Leena Sorjonen. Oxford: Oxford University Press, 2012, 16–41.

The Goose's Mother and Father website. www.thegoosesmother.com/id6.html. (Accessed January 30, 2019.)

Greene, Ross W. *The Explosive Child.* New York: Harper Paperbacks, 2014.

Grolnick, Wendy. *The Psychology of Parental Control: How Well-Meant Parenting Backfires.* New York: Penguin, 2003.

"Hans Selye." Wikipedia. en.wikipedia.org/wiki/Hans_Selye. (Accessed January 30, 2019.)

Harkness, Sara and Charles Super. *New Directions for Child Development, 8: Anthropological Perspectives on Child Development.* San Francisco: Jossey-Bass, 1980.

Harris, Christine R. and Michael Jenkins, " 'My Son's a Bit Dizzy,' 'My Wife's a Bit Soft': Gender, Children, and Cultures of Parenting." *Gender, Place & Culture: A Journal of Feminist Geography,* vol. 4, no. 1 (1997): 37–62.

Harris, Christine R., Michael Jenkins, and Dale Glaser. "Gender Differences in Risk Assessment: Why do Women Take Fewer Risks than Men?" *Judgment and Decision Making,* vol. 1, no. 1 (July 2006), 48–63.

Hatfield, Elaine, Richard Rapson, and Yen-Chi L. Le. "Emotional Contagion and Empathy." *The Social Neuroscience of Empathy,* edited by J. Decety and W. Ickes. Cambridge: MIT Press, 2011, 17–28.

Hatfield, Elaine, John T. Cacioppo, and Richard L. Rapson. *Emotional Contagion.* Cambridge: Cambridge University Press, 1994.

Hertenstein, Matthew J., Julie M. Verkamp, Alyssa M. Kerestes, and Rachel M. Holmes. "The Communicative Function of Touch in Humans, Nonhuman Primates, and Rats: A Review of the Empirical Research." *Genetic, Social, and General Psychology Monographs,* vol. 132, no. 1 (2006): 5–94.

Hewlett, Barry S. and Michael E. Lamb, editors. *Hunter Gatherer Childhoods: Evolutionary, Developmental, and Cultural Perspectives.* New Brunswick: Transaction, 2005.

Hill, Daniel J. *Affect Regulation Theory: A Clinical Model.* New York: Norton, 2015.

Hinde, Robert A. *Ethology: Its Nature and Relations with the Other Sciences.* New York: Oxford University Press, 1982.

Hoban, Russell. *Best Friends for Frances.* New York: Scholastic, 1969.

Hoban, Russell. *Bread and Jam for Frances.* New York: HarperTrophy, 1992.

Hobson, Peter. *The Cradle of Thought: Exploring the Origins of Thinking.* New York: Macmillan, 2002.

Hochschild, Arlie. *The Second Shift: Working Families and the Revolution at Home.* New York: Penguin, 2012.

Holohan, Meghan. Interview on the *Today Show.* www.today.com/parents/unborn-babies-are-hearing-you-loud-clear-8C11005474, October 14, 2016. Last accessed February 5, 2019.

Howe, David, Marian Brandon, Diana Hinnings and Gillian Schofield. *Attachment Theory, Child Maltreatment and Family Support: A Practice and Assessment Model.* Mahwah, N.J.: Lawrence Erlbaum Associates, 1999.

Hrdy, Sarah Blaffer. *Mothers and Others: The Evolutionary Origins of Mutual Understanding.* Cambridge: Harvard University Press, 2009.

Hrdy, Sarah Blaffer. *Mother Nature: Maternal Instincts and How They Shape the Human Species.* New York: Ballantine Books, 1999.

Iacoboni, Marco. *Mirroring People: The Science of Empathy and How We Connect with Others.* New York: Picador, 2009.

Ingraham, Christopher. "Less than Half of Kids Now Have a Traditional Family." *Washington Post,* 23 December 2014. www.washingtonpost.com/news/wonk/wp/2014/12/23/less-than-half-of-u-s-kids-now-have-a-traditional-family/?utm_term=.a9faeb8e33ae. (Accessed January 24, 2019.)

James, William. *The Principles of Psychology, Volumes I and II.* New York: Dover.

James, William. *Psychology: The Briefer Course,* edited by Gordon Allport. Notre Dame, Indiana: University of Notre Dame Press, 1985.

Kagan, Jerome. *The Human Spark.* New York: Basic Books, 2013.

Kagan, Jerome and Nancy Snidman. *The Long Shadow of Temperament.* Cambridge: Belknap Press, 2004.

Kappas, Arvid, Ursula Hess, and Klaus Scherer. "Voice and Emotion." *Fundamentals of Nonverbal Behavior,* edited by Robert S. Feldman and Bernard Rimé. Cambridge: Cambridge University Press, 1991, 200-238.

Karen, Robert. *Becoming Attached: First Relationships and How They Shape Our Capacity to Love.* Oxford: Oxford University Press, 1998.

Kendon, Adam. *Conducting Interaction: Patterns of Behavior in Focused Encounters.* Cambridge: Cambridge University Press, 1990.

Kendon, Adam. *Gesture: Visible Action as Utterance.* Cambridge: Cambridge University Press, 2004.

Klass, Perri, "Gender in the Toy Box." *New York Times,* February 5, 2018. www.nytimes.com/2018/02/05/well/family/gender-stereotypes-children-toys.html.

Klaus, Marshall H. "Mother and Infant: Early Emotional Ties." *Pediatrics,* vol. 102, supplement E1 (November 1998). pediatrics.aappublications.org/content/102/Supplement_E1/1244.

Klaus, Marshall H. and John H. Kennell. "Labor, Birth and Bonding." *Parent-Infant Bonding,* 2nd ed., edited by Marshall H. Klaus and John H. Kennell. St. Louis: C.V. Mosby, 1982, 22-98.

Klein, Wendy and Marjorie Harness Goodwin. "Chores." *Fast-Forward Family: Home, Work, and Relationships in Middle-Class America,* edited by Elinor Ochs and Tami Kremer-Sadlik. Oakland: University of California Press, 2013, 111–129.

Konner, Melvin. *The Evolution of Childhood: Relationships, Emotion, Mind.* Cambridge: Harvard University Press, 2010.

Krisch, Joshua A. "All Kids Throw the Same Tantrum." Fatherly Blog, November 6, 2017.

www.fatherly.com/health-science/science-all-kids-throw-the-same-tantrums/ (Accessed February 5, 2019.)

Lamb, Michael, Ross A. Thompson, William Gardner, Eric L. Charnov, and James P. Connell. *Infant-Mother Attachment: The Origins and Developmental Significance of Individual Differences in Strange Situation Behavior.* Hillsdale: Lawrence Erlbaum Associate, 1985.

Lancy, David. *The Anthropology of Childhood: Cherubs, Chattels, and Changelings.* Cambridge: Cambridge University Press, 2015.

Lareau, Annette. *Unequal Childhoods: Class, Race, and Family Life.* Berkeley: University of California Press, 2011.

Larzelere, Robert E., Amanda Sheffield Morris, and Amanda W. Harrist, editors. *Authoritative Parenting: Synthesizing Nurturance and Discipline.* Washington, DC: American Psychological Association, 2012.

Laske, Sara. *Achtung Baby: An American Mom on the German Art of Raising Self-Reliant Children.* New York: Picador, 2018.

LeDoux, Joseph. *Anxious: Using the Brain to Understand Fear and Anxiety.* New York: Viking, 2015.

LeDoux, Joseph. *The Emotional Brain: The Mysterious Underpinnings of Emotional Life.* New York: Touchstone, 1996.

"Legal Status of Tattooing in the United States." Wikipedia. en.wikipedia.org/wiki/Legal_status_of_tattooing_in_the_United_States. (Accessed January 24, 2019.)

"Let Grow: Future-Proofing Our Kids and Our Country." letgrow.org/. (Accessed January 24, 2019.)

Levine, Madeline. *The Price of Privilege: How Parental Pressure and Material Advantage Are Creating a Generation of Disconnected and Unhappy Kids.* New York: HarperCollins, 2009.

LeVine, Robert and Sarah LeVine. *Do Parents Matter? Why Japanese Babies Sleep Soundly, Mexican Siblings Don't Fight, and American Families Should Just Relax.* New York: Public Affairs. 2016.

Lewin, Tamar. "More Young Women Waiting to Leave Home." *New York Times*, 11 November 2015. www.nytimes.com/2015/11/12/us/more-young-women-waiting-to-leave-home.html. (Accessed December 29, 2018.)

Lieber, Ron. *The Opposite of Spoiled: Raising Kids Who Are Grounded, Generous, and Smart about Money.* New York: HarperCollins, 2015.

Linden, David. *Touch: The Science of Hand, Heart, and Mind.* New York: Viking, 2015.

Lindgren, Astrid. *Pippi Longstocking.* New York: Viking, 1950.

Llinás, Rodolfo R. *I of the Vortex: From Neurons to Self.* Cambridge: MIT Press, 2002.

Maestripieri, Dario, editor. *Primate Psychology.* Cambridge: Harvard University Press, 2003, ProQuest ebrary, Web. 21 September 2015.

Mahler, Margaret S., Fred Pine, and Anni Bergman. *The Psychobiological Birth of the Human Infant.* New York: Basic Books, 1975.

Manfredi, Chiara, Gabriele Caselli, Francesco Rovetto, Daniela Rebecchi, Giovanni M. Ruggiero, Sandra Sassaroli, and Marcantonio M. Spada. "Temperament and Parental Styles as Predictors of Ruminative Brooding and Worry." *Personality and Individual Differences* 50 (2011), 186–191. www.sciencedirect.com/science/article/pii/S0191886910004666. Doi. org/10.1016/j.paid.2010.09.023

Markham, Laura. *Peaceful Parent, Happy Kids: How to Stop Yelling and Start Connecting.* New York: Penguin, 2012.

Marsh, Jason. "Do Mirror Neurons Give Us Empathy?" *Greater Good Magazine*, 29 March 2012. greatergood.berkeley.edu/article/item/do_mirror_neurons_give_empathy. (Accessed January 24, 2019.)

McCloskey, Robert. *Make Way for Ducklings*. New York: Viking Press, 1941.

Meaney, Michael J. "Epigenetics and the Environmental Regulation of the Genome and Its Function." *Evolution, Early Experience, and Human Development*, edited by Darcia Narvaez, Jaak Panksepp, Allan N. Schore, and Tracy R. Gleason. Oxford: Oxford University Press, 2013, 99–131.

Meehan, Courtney M. and Sean Hawks. "Maternal and Allomaternal Responsiveness: The Significance of Cooperative Caregiving in Attachment Theory." *Different Faces of Attachment: Cultural Variations on a Universal Human Need*, edited by Hiltrud Otto and Heidi Keller. Cambridge: Cambridge University Press, 2014, 113–135.

Meltzoff, A.N., and M.K. Moore, "Imitations of Facial and Manual Gestures by human Neonates," in *Science*, 198, 75–78, October 7, 1977. www.ncbi.nlm.nih.gov/pubmed/897687. (Last accessed February 5, 2019.)

Miller, Clair Cain. "A Disadvantaged Start Hurts Boys More Than Girls." *New York Times*, 22 October 2015. www.nytimes.com/2015/10/22/upshot/a-disadvantaged-start-hurts-boys-more-than-girls.html. (Accessed January 24, 2019.)

Minuchin, Salvador. *Families and Family Therapy*. Cambridge: Harvard, 1974.

Minuchin, Salvador and H. Charles Fishman. *Family Therapy Techniques*. Cambridge: Harvard University Press, 2009.

Mischel, Walter. "Processes in Delay of Self-Gratification." *Advances in Experimental Social Psychology, (7)*, edited by L. Berkowitz. New York: Academic Press, 1974, 249–292.

Mischel, Walter. *The Marshmallow Test: Why Self-Control Is the Engine of Success*. Boston: Back Bay Books, 2015.

Moll, Jorge, Ricardo de Oliveira-Sousa, and Roland Zahn. "Neuroscience and Morality: Moral Judgments, Sentiments, and Values." *Personality, Identity, and Character: Explorations in Moral Psychology*, edited by Darcia Narvaez and Daniel K. Lapsley. Cambridge: Cambridge University Press, 106–135.

The Monks of New Skete. *The Art of Raising a Puppy*. Boston: Little Brown, 1991.

Montague, Ashley. *Touching: The Human Significance of the Skin*, 2nd ed. New York: Harper and Row, 1978.

Moore, Adelia. *One Sibling Society: An Observational Study of Three Brothers*. 1984. University of Pittsburgh, Master's thesis.

Moore, Adelia. *Sibling Conflict and Parent Intervention in Middle Childhood: Parents' Perceptions, Beliefs, and Reported Behavior*. 1995. University of Cincinnati, Ph.D. dissertation.

Narvaez, Darcia. "Triune Ethics Theory and Moral Personality." *Personality, Identity, and Character*, edited by Darcia Narvaez and Daniel K. Lapsley. Cambridge: Cambridge University Press, 2009, 136–158.

Narvaez, Darcia, Jaak Panksepp, Allan N. Schore, and Tracy R. Gleason, editors. *Evolution, Early Experience, and Human Development*. New York: Oxford University Press, 2013.

Nelson, Eric. "The Neurobiological Basis of Empathy." *Evolution, Early Experience, and Human Development*, edited by Darcia Narvaez, Jaak Panksepp, Allan N. Schore, and Tracy R. Gleason. New York: Oxford University Press, 2013, 179–198.

Nerve Blog Contributors. "Licking Rat Pups: The Genetics of Nurture." In *The Nerve Blog*. sites.bu.edu/ombs/2010/11/11/licking-rat-pups-the-genetics-of-nurture/.

Neufeld, Gordon and Gabor Maté. *Hold on to Your Kids: Why Parents Need to Matter More than Peers.* New York: Ballantine Books, 2008.

New Oxford American Dictionary for Mac OS. OS X Yosemite, Version 10.10.2.

Nucci, Larry, Yuki Hasebe, and Maria Tereza Lins-Dyer. "Adolescent Psychological Well-Being and Parental Control of the Personal." *Changing Boundaries of Parental Authority in Adolescence,* edited by Judith Smetana. *New Directions for Child Development,* 108. San Francisco: Jossey Bass, 2005, 17–30.

Ochs, Elinor and Carolina Izquierdo. "Responsibility in Childhood: Three Developmental Trajectories." *Ethos 37,* no. 4 (2009): 391–413.

Ochs, Elinor and Tamar Kremer-Sadlik. "How Postindustrial Families Talk." *Annual Review of Anthropology* no. 44 (2015): 87–103.

Ochs, Elinor and Tamar Kremer-Sadlik, editors. *Fast-Forward Family: Home, Work and Relationships in Middle-Class America.* Oakland: University of California Press, 2013.

Ochs, Elinor and Bambi Schieffelin. *Language Socialization Across Cultures.* Cambridge: Cambridge University Press, 1986.

Orenstein, Peggy. *Girls and Sex: Navigating the Complicated New Landscape.* New York: Harper Paperbacks, 2017.

Otto, Hiltrud and Heidi Keller. *Different Faces of Attachment: Cultural Variations on a Universal Human Need.* Cambridge: Cambridge University Press, 2014.

Panksepp, Jaak. *Affective Neuroscience: The Foundations of Human and Animal Emotions.* Oxford: Oxford University Press, 1998.

Panksepp, Jaak. "How Primary-Process Emotional Systems Guide Child Development: Ancestral Regulators of Human Happiness, Thriving, and Suffering." *Evolution, Early Experience, and Human Development,* edited by Darcia Narvaez, Jaak Panksepp, Allan N. Schore, and Tracy R. Gleason. New York: Oxford University Press, 2013, 74–94.

Paugh, Amy and Carolina Izquierdo. "Why Is This a Battle Every Night? Negotiating Food and Eating in American Dinnertime Interaction." *Journal of Linguistic Anthropology 19,* vol. 2, November 17, 2009, 185–204.

Phelan, Thomas, *123 Magic.* Glen Ellyn, Illinois: Parent Magic, 2010.

Plomin, Robert and Denise Daniels. "Why Are Children in the Same Family So Different From One Another?" *Journal of Epidemiology,* no. 40, vol. 3 (June 2011): 563–572.

Pomerleau, Wayne P. " William James." In James Fieser and Bradley Dowden, eds. *Internet Encyclopedia of Philosophy* (2011). www.iep.utm.edu/.

Porges, Stephen W. *The Polyvagal Theory: Neurophysiological Foundations of Emotions, Attachment, Communication, Self-Regulation.* New York: Norton, 2011.

Porges, Stephen W. "The Polyvagal Theory: Phylogenetic Contributions to Social Behavior." *Physiology & Behavior* 79 (2003): 503–513.

Porges, Stephen W. and Sue Carter. "The Neurobiology and Evolution of Mammalian Social Behavior." *Evolution, Early Experience, and Human Development,* edited by Darcia Narvaez, Jaak Panksepp, Allan N. Schore, and Tracy R. Gleason. Oxford: Oxford University Press, 2013, 132–151.

Powell, Bert, Glen Cooper, Kent Hoffman, and Bob Marvin. *The Circle of Security Intervention: Enhancing Attachment in Early Parent-Child Relationships.* New York: Guilford, 2014.

Protchnik, George. "I'm Thinking. Please. Be Quiet." *New York Times*, 24 August 2013. www.nytimes.com/2013/08/25/opinion/sunday/im-thinking-please-be-quiet.html. (Accessed Janiuary 24, 2019.)

Pruett, Kyle D. "Role of the Father." *Pediatrics*, 1998; 102; e1253. www.pediatrics.org/cgi/content/full/102/5/SEI/1253. DOI:101542/peds.102.5.SEI.1253. (Accessed February 5, 2019.)

Raeburn, Paul and Kevin Zollman. *The Game Theorist's Guide to Parenting: How the Science of Strategic Thinking Can Help You Deal with the Toughest Negotiators You Know, Your Kids*. New York: Scientific American/Farrar Straus and Giroux, 2016.

Reiss, David, John E. Richters, Marian Radke-Yarrow, and David Scharff, editors. *Children and Violence*. New York: Guilford, 1993.

Rizzolatti, G., L. Fadiga, L. Fagassi, and V. Gallese. "Resonance Behavior and Mirror Neurons," *Archives Italiennes e Biologie*, 137 (1999): 85–100. www.ncbi.nlm.nih.gov/pubmed/10349488 (Accessed January 24, 2019.)

Rogoff, Barbara. *The Apprenticeship of Thinking: Cognitive Development in Social Context*. Oxford: Oxford University Press, 1990.

Rogoff, Barbara. *The Cultural Nature of Human Development*. Oxford: Oxford University Press, 2003.

Rogoff, B., J. Mistry, A. Goncu, and C. Mosier. "Guided Participation in Cultural Activity by Toddlers and Caregivers." *Monographs of the Society for Research in Child Development*, 58 (1993) (Serial No. 236).

Rohrer, Julia, Boris Egloff, and Stefan Schmukle. "Effects of Birth Order on Personality." *Proceedings of the National Academy of Sciences*, 27 November 2015. doi.org/10.1073/pnas.1506451112. (Accessed February 7, 2019.)

Rothbart, Mary K. *Becoming Who We Are: Temperament and Personality in Development*. New York: Guilford, 2011.

Runkel, Hal Edward. *Scream-Free Parenting: Raising Your Kids by Keeping Your Cool*. Duluth, Ga.: Oakmont Publishing, 2005.

Sapir, Edward. "The Unconscious Patterning of Behavior in Society." *Language, Culture, and Society*, edited by Ben Blount. Cambridge: Winthrop, 1974, 32–46.

Sapolsky, Robert M. *Behave: The Biology of Humans at Our Best and Worst*. New York: Penguin Press, 2017.

Savage Rumbaugh, Sue Stuart G. Shanker, and Talbot J. Taylor. *Apes, Language, and the Human Mind*. New York: Oxford University Press, 1998.

Sax, Leonard. *The Collapse of Parenting*. New York: Basic Books, 2015.

Schieffelin, Bambi. *The Give and Take of Everyday Life: Language Socialization of Kaluli Children*. Cambridge: Cambridge University Press, 1990.

Schore, Alan. *Affect Regulation and the Origin of the Self*. Hillsdale, NJ: Lawrence Erlbaum, 1994.

Scott, Harry. *How to Raise Successful Children: Unleashing Their Hidden Potentials*. Independently published, 2018.

Senior, Jennifer. *All Joy and No Fun: The Paradox of Modern Parenthood*. New York: Ecco, 2014.

Seyfarth, Robert and Dorothy Cheney. *Baboon Metaphysics: The Evolution of a Social Mind*. Chicago: University of Chicago Press, 2007.

Siegel, Daniel J. *The Developing Mind: How Relationships and the Brain Interact to Shape Who We Are*. New York: Guilford, 2012.

Siegel, Daniel J. and Tina Payne Bryson. *No-Drama Discipline: The Whole Brain Way to Calm the Chaos and Nurture Your Child's Developing Mind*. New York: Bantam, 2014.

Siegel, Daniel J. and Mary Hartzell. *Parenting from the Inside Out: How a Deeper Self-Understanding Can Help You Raise Children Who Thrive*. New York: Tarcher, 2003.

Sigel, Irving, Ann V. McGillicuddy-DeLisi, and Jacqueline J. Goodnow. *Parental Belief Systems: The Psychological Consequences for Children*. Hillsdale, NJ: Lawrence Erlbaum Associates, 1992.

Skenazy, Lenore. *Free-Range Kids*. New York: Jossey-Bass, 2010.

Smetana, Judith, Hugh Crean, and Nicole Campione-Barr. "Adolescents' and Parents' Changing Conceptions of Parental Authority." *Changing Boundaries of Parental Authority During Adolescence*, edited by Judith Smetana. *New Directions for Child and Adolescent Development* 108. San Francisco: Jossey-Bass, 2005, 31–46.

Smith, Harriet. *Parenting for Primates*. Cambridge: Harvard University Press, 2005.

Sommer, Dion. *A Childhood Psychology: Young Children in Changing Times*. New York: Palgrave Macmillan, 2012.

Spock, Benjamin. *Baby and Child Care*. New York: Pocket Books, 1968.

Steinberg, Zina. Personal Communication. March 13, 2017.

Stern, Daniel. *The Interpersonal World of the Infant*. New York: Basic Books, 1985.

Steyer, James P. *Talking Back to Facebook: The Common Sense Guide to Raising Kids in the Digital Age*. New York: Scribners, 2012.

Still Face Experiment. Dr. Ed Tronick, 30 November 2009. Zero to Three, University of Massachusetts Boston, 2007. www.youtube.com/watch?v=apzXGEbZht0. (Accessed February 7, 2019.)

Stockton, Nick. "Your Brain Doesn't Contain Memories. It *Is* Memories." *Wired Magazine*, 9 July 2017. www.wired.com/story/your-brain-is-memories/. (Accessed January 24, 2019.)

Sulloway, Frank. *Born to Rebel*. New York: Vintage, 1997.

Sunderland, Margot. *The Science of Parenting: How Today's Brain Research Can Help You Raise Happy, Emotionally Balanced Children*. London: DK, 2006.

Super, Charles M. and Sara Harkness. "The Developmental Niche: A Conceptualization at the Interface of Child and Culture," December 1986. *International Journal of Behavioral Development*, 9, 545–569.

Tabuchi, Hiroko. "Businesses Sweeping Away Gender-Specific Toys and Labels." *New York Times*, 28 October 2015. www.nytimes.com/2015/10/28/business/sweeping-away-gender-specific-toys-and-labels.html. (Accessed January 24, 2019.)

Taffel, Ron with Roberta Israeloff. *When Parents Disagree and What You Can Do About It*. New York: Guilford, 2003.

Taylor, James. *Positive Pushing: How to Raise a Successful and Happy Child*. New York: Hachette Books, 2002.

Thomas, Alexander, Stella Chess, and Herbert Birch. *Temperament and Behavior Disorders in Children*. New York: New York University Press, 1968.

Thompson, Evan. *Mind in Life*. Cambridge: Harvard University Press, 2007.

Tomasello, Michael. *Why We Cooperate*. Cambridge: MIT Press, 2009.

Trivers, Robert L. "Parent-Offspring Conflict." *American Zoologist*, vol. 14, no. 1 (1974): 249–264.

Tronick, Ed. *Neurobehavioral and Social-Emotional Development (Norton Series on Interpersonal Neurobiology)*. New York: W.W. Norton, 2007.

Tronick, Ed, L.B. Adamson, H. Als, and T.B. Brazelton. "Infant Emotions in Normal and

Perturbated Interactions." Paper presented at the biennial meeting of the Society for Research on Child Development, Denver, CO, April 1975.

Tulbert, Eve and Marjorie Harness Goodwin. "Choreographies of Attention: Multimodality in a Routine Family Activity." In *Embodied Interaction in the Material World,* edited by Jürgen Streeck, Charles Goodwin, and Curtis LeBaron. Cambridge: Cambridge University Press, 2011, 79–92.

Turecki, Stanley with Leslie Tonner. *The Difficult Child*. New York: Bantam Books, 2000.

Turkle, Sherry. *Alone Together: Why We Expect More from Technology and Less from Each Other*. New York: Basic Books, 2011.

Twain, Mark. *The Adventures of Huckleberry Finn*. New York: Grosset and Dunlap, 1884.

Vozzola, Elizabeth C. *Moral Development: Theory and Applications*. New York: Routledge, 2014.

Vygotsky, Lev. *Mind in Society*. Cambridge: Harvard University Press, 1978.

Wallin, David. *Attachment in Psychotherapy*. New York: Guilford, 2007.

Weir, Kirsten. "The Lasting Impact of Neglect." *Monitor on Psychology*. American Psychological Association, vol 45, no. 6 (June 2014). www.apa.org/monitor/2014/06/neglect.aspx. (Accessed February 7, 2019.)

Weisner, Thomas. "The American Dependency Conflict: Continuities and Discontinuities in Behavior and Values of Countercultural Parents and Their Children." *Ethos*, vol. 29, no. 3 (2001): 271–295.

Weisner, Thomas. "Culture." *Social Development: Relationships in Infancy, Childhood, and Adolescence*, edited by M.K. Underwood and L.H. Rosen. New York: Guilford: 2011, 372–399.

Weisner, Thomas. "Ecocultural Niches of Middle Childhood." *Development During Middle Childhood: The Years From Six to Twelve*, edited by W. Andrew Collins. Washington, DC: National Academy Press, 1984.

Weisner, Thomas and Carolyn Pope-Edwards. "Introduction to the Special Issue of *Ethos* in Honor of Beatrice Whiting," *Ethos*, vol. 29, no. 3 (2001), 239–246.

Weisner, Thomas and R. Gallimore. "My Brother's Keeper: Child and Sibling Caretaking." *Current Anthropology*, vol. 18, no. 2: 1977,169–90.

Wennerstrom, Ann. *The Music of Everyday Speech: Prosody and Discourse Analysis*. New York: Oxford University Press, 2001.

Wergins, Clemens. "The Case for Free-Range Parenting." *New York Times*, 20 March 2015 www.nytimes.com/2015/03/20/opinion/the-case-for-free-range-parenting.html. (Accessed January 30,2019.)

Wetherell, Margaret. *Affect and Emotion: A New Social Science Understanding*. Los Angeles: Sage, 2012.

Whiting, Beatrice and John W.M. Whiting. *Children of Six Cultures: A Psycho-Cultural Analysis*. Cambridge: Harvard University Press, 1975.

Whiting, Beatrice and Carolyn Pope-Edwards. *Children of Different Worlds: The Formation of Social Behavior*. Cambridge: Harvard University Press, 1988.

Winnicott, D.W. *The Child, the Family, and the Outside World*. Middlesex: Perseus Publishing, 1973.

Winnicott, D.W. "The Theory of the Parent-Infant Relationship." *International Journal of Psycho-Analysis*, 41: 585–595.

Winnicott, D.W. *The Child and the Family: First Relationships*, edited by Janet Hardenberg. London: Tavistock Publications, Ltd., 1957.

Winnicott, D.W. "Contemporary Concepts of Adolescent Development and Their Implications for Higher Education." *Playing and Reality*. London: Tavistock, 1971, 138–151.

Ludwig Wittgenstein. *Zettel*, edited by G.E.M. Anscombe and G.H. von Wright. Berkeley: University of California Press, 1967.

Zeanah, Charles Jr., editor. *Handbook of Infant Mental Health*. New York: Guilford Press, 1993.

Zentner, Marcel and John E. Bates. "Child Temperament: An Integrative Review of Concepts, Research Programs, and Measures." *European Journal of Developmental Science* [EJDS] vol. 2, no. ½ (2008): 7–37.

Index
....

About the Author

Adelia Moore, PhD, is a clinical psychologist in New York City. She specializes in therapy with couples, parents of children of all ages, and families. She also sees young adults still working out relationships with their parents. Moore received her BA in English from Harvard, a master's degree in Child Development from the University of Pittsburgh, and a PhD in Clinical Psychology from the University of Cincinnati. She was an adjunct professor of psychology at Trinity College, Hartford, CT; St. Joseph's University, West Hartford, CT; and New York University. Moore's essays have appeared in *The Christian Science Monitor* and *HuffPost*. She has four grown sons and five grandchildren. She lives in Manhattan and Upstate New York with her husband. You can find her on Facebook, Twitter, and Instagram and at Adeliamoore.com.

9 780984 856077